THE ORIGINS
OF
DEMYTHOLOGIZING

PHILOSOPHY AND HISTORIOGRAPHY IN
THE THEOLOGY OF RUDOLF BULTMANN

STUDIES

IN THE HISTORY OF RELIGIONS

(SUPPLEMENTS TO *NUMEN*)

XXVIII

THE ORIGINS
OF
DEMYTHOLOGIZING

LEIDEN
E. J. BRILL
1974

THE ORIGINS
OF
DEMYTHOLOGIZING

PHILOSOPHY AND HISTORIOGRAPHY IN
THE THEOLOGY OF RUDOLF BULTMANN

BY

ROGER A. JOHNSON

LEIDEN
E. J. BRILL
1974

ISBN 90 04 03903 1

Copyright 1974 by E. J. Brill, Leiden, Netherlands

*All rights reserved. No part of this book may be reproduced or
translated in any form, by print, photoprint, microfilm, microfiche
or any other means without written permission from the publisher*

PRINTED IN THE NETHERLANDS

TABLE OF CONTENTS

PREFACE

I first encountered Rudolf Bultmann's theology as an undergraduate college student. His project of demythologizing appealed to both my budding intellectual interests and a vague but powerful mix of existential concerns. Through his interpretation of human existence, I came to discover new dimensions of myself and my world, and to expect ever new meanings to be generated from the unknown encounters of the future. Much later, I returned to Bultmann's theology as a subject of research. As I began to discover the complexities of his thought—previously unknown to me—as well as the difference between his historical situation and my own, my youthful and enthusiastic espousal of demythologizing receded into the past. Indeed, my own historical inquiry has led me to explicate Bultmann's thought in terms quite different from his own, and I expect that the distance between myself and his original proposal of demythologizing will be apparent in this book. Nevertheless, that sense of distance has not dulled my strong sense of appreciation for a man whose insights have become so much a part of my own life history.

Beyond my sense of gratitude to Rudolf Bultmann, I should also like to thank other persons and institutions who have contributed directly to the completion of this book. Professor Hans Jonas was the first scholar familiar with Bultmann's early intellectual development who encouraged me, at the initial stage of my research, to convert a series of vague hunches into demonstrable propositions. Professors Paul Lehmann, Gordon Kaufman, and Helmut Koester read the manuscript in an early form and many of their corrections and suggestions have been incorporated into the text of this book. Professors Ingrid Stadler and Kent Bendall served as my philosophical tutors for the intricacies of Neo-Kantian epistemology. Wellesley College, through a series of faculty research grants, provided financial support essential to the research and publication of this volume. And the assistance of Miss Kathryn Woodward, a senior student at the College, has been invaluable in proofreading and indexing the book. Finally, I am especially indebted to my parents, Herman and Florence Johnson, who communicated to me early in life a healthy mixture of skeptical and religious sensibilities

—which made Bultmann such a congenial subject—and in later years, provided continuing encouragement and assistance for this project.

While I do not recommend Bultmann's theological program of demythologizing as a viable option for the nineteen-seventies, I do commend his theological style as a persuasive and appropriate model for our own age. Over fifty years ago, in a situation of social turbulence and religious apathy, Bultmann offered the following counsel to his theological peers:

> It is impossible to renew an old cult and myth or artificially create a new one. What can be done, before priestly or prophetic impulses can reorganize, is simply to begin with the present historical situation, and develop it by ruthlessly cutting off what is obsolete and untrue and adding what is most urgent.[1]

Roger A. JOHNSON
Wellesley College
Easter, 1974

---

[1] *The Beginnings of Dialectic Theology*, ed., James Robinson, p. 232.

LIST OF ABBREVIATIONS

AR	Archiv für Religionswissenschaft
ChrW	Christliche Welt
DLZ	Deutsche Literaturzeitung
ExposT	Expository Times
GV	Glauben und Verstehen, volumes I, II, and III
HTR	Harvard Theological Review
IPQ	International Philosophical Quarterly
JR	Journal of Religion
KaM	Kerygma and Myth, volumes I and II
KuM	Kerygma und Mythos, volumes I, II, III, IV, V, and VI, part 1
RGG²	Die Religion in Geschichte und Gegenwart, second
RGG³	and third editions
ThBl	Theologische Blätter
ThLZ	Theologische Literaturzeitung
ThR	Theologische Rundschau
ZKG	Zeitschrift für Kirchengeschichte
ZThK	Zeitschrift für Theologie und Kirche
ZZ	Zwischen den Zeiten

For the sake of chronological clarity and brevity, second citations from periodicals will be identified by year rather than by volume number.

CHAPTER ONE

THE ENIGMA OF DEMYTHOLOGIZING [1]

In 1941 Rudolf Bultmann published his programmatic essay, "New Testament and Mythology."[2] In this essay he proposed a new method for understanding the proclamation of the New Testament in order that men of the contemporary world, in turn, might better understand the preaching of the Church. In Bultmann's judgment, the writings of the New Testament presupposed a mythological view of the world which now presented an unnecessary hurdle to the contemporary hearing and understanding of the Christian Gospel. The New Testament picture of a three-story universe, populated with angels and demons and fraught with miracles and supernatural happenings, was appropriate to the Hellenistic age in which it was written but was necessarily alien to the scientific frame of reference of its modern hearers. Besides, Bultmann also found this mythological form of expression to be in conflict with the real intention of the New Testament itself. According to its mythology, the New Testament appeared to present an objective picture of the world, a cosmology or *Weltanschauung;* in actuality, the New Testament intended to offer man a particular understanding of his own existence. Mythology thus constituted a double problem for understanding. It presented a false barrier to the hearing of faith

---

[1] The English participle "demythologizing" is used as a translation for Bultmann's German noun, "Entmythologisierung." For stylistic reasons, this translation has proven to be preferable to the literal equivalent, "demythologization," and has become standard for the English speaking discussion of Bultmann's proposal.

[2] Originally published in the volume, *Offenbarung und Heilsgeschehen* (München: Lempp, 1941). The second half of the book was republished in 1948 under the title, "Neues Testament und Mythologie," *Kerygma und Mythos,* ed. H. W. Bartsch (6 vols.; Hamburg: Herbert Reich, 1948-1964), I, 15-148. It was translated into English as "New Testament and Mythology," *Kerygma and Myth,* ed. and trans. R. H. Fuller (2 vols.; London: S.P.C.K., 1957-1962), I, 1-44. The first half of the original (1941) volume appeared under the title, "Die Frage der natürlichen Offenbarung," *Glauben und Verstehen* (3 vols.; Tübingen: J. C. B. Mohr, 1933-1962), II, 79-104. This was translated into English as "The Question of Natural Revelation," *Essays: Philosophical and Theological,* trans. J. C. G. Grieg (London: S. C. M. Press, 1955), pp. 90-118. All references to "New Testament and Mythology" are given for *Kerygma und Mythos,* Vol. I, second edition, or to *Kerygma and Myth,* Vol. I, according to table of abbreviations (*KuM,* I; *KaM,* I).

I

for modern man and it betrayed the real intention of the New Testament itself.

In light of this interpretation of the problem, Bultmann proposed his new method of interpretation which he called demythologizing, on the one hand, and existentialist interpretation, on the other. To demythologize meant, in a general way, to strip away from the New Testament its antiquated world view, its objectifying conceptuality, its spatial and cosmological imagery. To engage in existentialist interpretation meant to set free the original understanding of existence offered in the New Testament proclamation from its mythological conceptuality through expression in a form of conceptuality appropriate to it: i.e., the existentialist anthropological categories of Martin Heidegger.

Shortly after the publication of Bultmann's original essay, a heated and prolific discussion of his proposal began which has produced the staggering quantity of literature cited in any bibliography of Bultmann studies. [1] By the nineteen-fifties, it had become a discussion on an international scale, involving participants of many languages, from Protestant and Catholic theological traditions, and from a variety of non-theological disciplines.[2] While the contents of these publications are so diverse as to elude any general description, one question emerged with increasing clarity: namely what does Bultmann mean ? How shall we understand this demythologizing ? Karl Barth brought this central question of the discussion to expression most clearly in the title of his contribution to it: "Rudolf Bultmann: An Attempt to Understand Him." [3] As Barth

---

[1] The core essays of the demythologizing debate have appeared in the six volumes of *Kerygma und Mythos*. For a bibliography on the subject, see Günther Bornkamm, "Die Theologie Rudolf Bultmanns in der neueren Diskussion," *ThR*, XXIX (1963-1964), 33-141. The bibliography on pp. 33-46 was prepared by Egon Brandenburger.

[2] In the nineteen-sixties the discussion of demythologizing developed a lively Italian focus of discussion under the leadership of Enrico Castelli. French, German, and Italian essays and dialogues resulting from international conferences in Italy are published in the three volumes edited by Castelli:

1) *Il problema della demitizzazione* (Padova: Cedam-Casa Editrice Dott. Antonio Milani, 1961);

2) *Demitizzazione e immagine* (Padova: Cedam-Casa Editrice Dott. Antonio Milani, 1962):

3) *Herméneutique et tradition* (Roma; Istituto di Studi Filosofici, 1963).

[3] Karl Barth, "Rudolf Bultmann: An Attempt to Understand Him," *KaM*, II, 83-132.

writes, "I know of no contemporary theologian who has so much to say about understanding, or who has so much cause to complain of being misunderstood." [1]

Diverse reasons have been given in an effort to explain the difficulty in understanding Bultmann's proposal: 1) the polemical tone of the original essay, laden with passion but less determined by careful expression:[2] 2) the atmosphere of heresy-hunting and theological accusation which developed in the German ecclesiastical situation:[3] 3) the offensive character of the *Stichwort*, "Entmythologisierung";[4] 4) the genuine fear of the loss of the substance of faith through demythologizing;[5] 5) the new and different philosophical vocabulary of Martin Heidegger employed by Bultmann. These considerations, while relevant to the early stages of the discussion, would hardly apply to the more recent years, less fraught with passion and more accustomed to the general direction and specific vocabulary of Bultmann's proposal.

As a result, attention turned from these situational elements to the problems of understanding intrinsic to Bultmann's own proposal. In this regard, Karl Barth called attention to Bultmann's idiosyncratic style of thinking, comparing this with the style of New Testament authors.

---

[1] *Ibid.*, pp. 83-84.

[2] Austin Farrer, "An English Appreciation," *KaM*, I, 212-223. "I do not find that it [Bultmann's initial article] makes much attempt at consistent statement or accurate definition, nor do I suppose that it was designed to do so. It was a direct expression of feeling, a covert sermon to the half-believer and an open provocation to the theologian" (*ibid.*, p. 212).

[3] For a description of the controversy between Bultmann and the United Evangelical-Lutheran Church of Germany, together with its impact upon the discussion of demythologizing, see H. W. Bartsch, "The Present State of the Debate," *KaM*, II, 1-10.

[4] "This demythologizing is, of course, no nickname given to it by a third party. It was invented by Bultmann himself; and not only is it a barbarism, but it is unnecessarily provoking. If the wicked (Christian) world fails to understand him, much of the blame is due to his invention of this word, so uninspiring and negative" (Barth, "Rudolf Bultmann: An Attempt . . .," *KaM*, II, 102). (It was, of course, not Bultmann, but Hans Jonas who "invented" the term *Entmythologisierung* and first used it in his 1930 study of Augustine. *Infra.*, Chapter V, section 3.)

[5] "Perhaps we may say that behind all the objections raised against demythologizing there lurks a fear that if it were carried to its logical conclusion it would make it impossible for us to speak of an act of God, or if we did it would only be the symbolical description of a subjective experience" (R. Bultmann, "Bultmann Replies to His Critics," *KaM*, I, 196).

> It has often disturbed me that as a writer Bultmann is not at all
> easy to understand, a fact which has endangered the basis of the
> whole discussion. In this he is like the authors of the New Testament,
> perhaps even worse! What is really at the back of his mind? It is
> so easy to find ourselves at sea as we read him in one passage
> because we have overlooked some hidden dimension, and in another
> passage because we suspect such a dimension where none exists.[1]

In a similar vein, Heinrich Ott also sought to explain the ob-
scurity of demythologizing on the basis of such an *ad hominem*
argument. Throughout the course of his very precise and fruitful
analysis of Bultmann's theology, Ott repeatedly encountered a
certain limit and partiality in Bultmann's execution of what
appeared to be his own ontology. In confrontation with this phenomenon, Ott was compelled to acknowledge that the peculiarly
divided and stunted development of Bultmann's fundamental
conceptuality could not be accounted for on the basis of his philosophical sources and must therefore reflect the "hidden, personal,
existential roots" of his thinking.[2] In his later volume on Heidegger,
Ott went so far as to renounce his earlier efforts to understand
Bultmann by means of an analysis of his fundamental conceptuality.
Instead, he would now be content to simply acknowledge the particularity of Bultmann's existential religious decision, as this, in
turn, gave shape to the whole of his thought.

> Bultmann's position is not reached by such a formal ontological
> criticism, because his position rests finally upon a fundamental
> religious decision which transcends all formal consideration. This
> decision can be defined in terms of an *eschatological-paradoxical*
> dualism, and doubtless has its ground in the dualism of the law
> and the gospel. This decision can only be acknowledged and valued
> in its irreducibility, even if one himself—with Bultmann in the
> same *communio sanctorum*—thinks out of different patterns.[3]

The "hidden, personal, existential roots," which had been a motif
of the Bultmann volume, though as peripheral to the substance of
the analysis, had now become definitive for the comprehension of
Bultmann's thought as a whole. Confronted with the many riddles of

---

[1] Barth, *KaM*, II, 83.
[2] Heinrich Ott, *Geschichte und Heilsgeschichte in der Theologie Rudolf Bultmanns* (Tübingen: J. C. B. Mohr, 1955), p. 181. Cf. *ibid.*, p. 144; p. 172. (The German word *existentielle* will be translated as existential; the German *existential* as existentialist).
[3] Heinrich Ott, *Denken und Sein: der Weg Martin Heideggers und der Weg der Theologie* (Zürich: EVZ-Verlag, 1959), p. 8.

Bultmann's theological conceptuality, which he laid bare with extraordinary clarity, Ott now was moved to abandon the quest to understand Bultmann's proposal in terms of a conceptual eluci- dation of his thought. It appeared as if Bultmann's religious-theo- logical convictions were determinative of the difficulties intrinsic to the understanding of his project of thought.

Still another explanation for the confusion and contradiction present in Bultmann's proposal has been advanced by John Macquarrie. In his second volume on Bultmann, *The Scope of Demythologizing*, Macquarrie set out to examine the "radical inconsistency," "bifurcation," and "arbitrary limit to demyth- ologizing" which he found, initially, to be characteristic of Bult- mann's project. After spending several chapters describing this split in the thought of Bultmann, as noted by himself and others, Macquarrie finally concluded that this apparent inconsistency was, in fact, nothing but a paradox of faith.

> This bifurcation goes back to living Christian experience itself. Neither side can be suppressed without falsification of the whole picture, and if it is the business of theology to give us an account of what Christianity is, then any adequate theology must have room for both sides.[1]

According to Macquarrie's suggestion, it would now appear as if the enigma of demythologizing was to be explained in terms of the peculiar subject matter of theology, which necessarily entailed a "paradoxical" (closely resembling "self-contradictory") mode of thought.

I am not concerned here to assess the relative merits of these explanations for that phenomenon which I call "the enigma of demythologizing." They all point to the problem and suggest something of the persisting confusion in the discussion. However, it is clear that none of these explanations offer a satisfactory resolution to the problem of understanding Bultmann's proposal. They only serve to highlight the presence of the problem.

It is precisely this enigma of demythologizing which is the subject of this study. While there have been abundant studies of Bultmann's controversial proposal in the past, they have made relatively little progress in clarifying the meaning of Bultmann's concept of myth

---

[1] John Macquarrie, *The Scope of Demythologizing* (London: S. C. M. Press Ltd., 1960), p. 228.

or the structure of his theology as a whole. For the most part, these studies have assumed as normative Bultmann's own account of the origins of his proposal: namely, that his concept of myth is a product of his literary-historical studies of New Testament Christianity and reflects the use of the term characteristic of the *Religionsgeschicht-liche Schule* and that the philosophical foundations for his theology have been appropriated from the existentialist ontology (or anthropology) of Martin Heidegger's *Sein und Zeit*. So long as these premises are uncritically accepted as normative for understanding Bultmann's demythologizing proposal, there is little possibility for ever making sense out of that proposal. Demythologizing will remain enigmatic, not because it is intrinsically enigmatic but because it is consistently presented in terms alien to itself. Furthermore, as long as demythologizing remains shrouded in darkness, other theologians will continue to borrow from Bultmann's theology, using concepts like mythology, demythologizing, and existential interpretation, without any clear knowledge of the conceptual content of these technical terms. Now that three decades have passed since Bultmann first articulated his program for demythologizing the New Testament, it seems appropriate to take a second look at this proposal.

For such an inquiry to be fruitful, however, it must be more carefully delimited than previous studies of Bultmann have been. Too often in the past, Bultmann studies have presupposed the adequacy, if not complete accuracy, of Bultmann's own account of the origins of his theological venture and then have plunged ahead to formulate new constructive alternatives to correct and complete Bultmann's original proposal. As a result, Bultmann's theological edifice has been patched, remodeled, painted and refurbished, demolished in parts with new wings added here and there, while the foundations have remain buried and hidden. This inquiry is more archeological and less speculative. It is concerned exclusively with the question of the origins of demythologizing as revealed in Bultmann's early writings of the nineteen-twenties and nineteen-thirties and in the historiographical and philosophical writings of his intellectual antecedents. It does not attempt to formulate a new historiography, a new hermeneutic, or a new metaphysic, as was characteristic of older Bultmann studies, but simply intends to lay bare the structure of Bultmann's concept of myth and the philosophical foundations for his theology by an historical analysis of the origins of his thought. Just as Jesus the proclaimer became the proclaimed one, so has Bultmann's understanding become the subject to be understood.

1. EARLIER STUDIES OF DEMYTHOLOGIZING: H. OTT, S. OGDEN, J. MACQUARRIE AND OTHERS

From the vast quantity of literature generated by Bultmann's proposal, several critics have been selected who address themselves to three issues: 1) Bultmann's definition and use of myth; 2) structural inconsistencies in Bultmann's theology; and 3) ambiguities in the relationship of Bultmann's theology to Heidegger's philosophy.

a. *Bultmann's definition and use of the concept of myth.*

In his original essay on demythologizing, Bultmann dropped in a somewhat casual manner and in a footnote his provocative definition of myth.

> Myth is here used in the sense in which the history of religions school understands it. Mythology is the mode of conceiving in which the unworldly, the divine appears as the worldly, the human; the other side appears as this side.[1]

Since the time of the original essay, Bultmann's critics have wondered if he meant the definition to be taken seriously and literally. Ronald Hepburn, a British language analyst, has argued that Bultmann could not have possibly meant what he said in this original definition. Hepburn develops at least three reasons why this definition could not be sustained within the structure of Bultmann's own argument. First, "by his own test, the definition itself is partly couched in mythological language."[2] Second, the definition "is sufficiently wide to include all pictorial, analogical, and symbolical speech whatever."[3] Taking this definition literally, there would be no possibility for a non-mythological form of theology or preaching, since any form of religious discourse necessarily uses something of "the human or worldly" for the expression of "the divine or unworldly." According to this definition, myth

---

[1] Bultmann, *KuM*, I, 22.

[2] Ronald W. Hepburn, "Demythologizing and the Problem of Validity," *New Essays in Philosophical Theology*, ed. Antony Flew and Alasdair MacIntyre (London: S. C. M. Press, 1955), p. 229.

[3] *Ibid.*

would then be what Hepburn calls a "genus word": analogy, pictorial imagery, or any form of "oblique speech" would then be "species" of this "genus." This, however, is impossible, since Bultmann himself explicitly excludes analogy from the category of myth, and since his whole purpose is to find a non-mythological form for speaking of God. Hepburn thus concludes:

> Bultmann cannot mean this [his original definition]. For if it were true, it would make demythologizing a logically impossible task.[1]

To complicate matters further, Hepburn finds Bultmann introducing still another category definitive of myth: namely, "an interference with the course of nature." This latter qualification, however, specifies myth according to the content of a particular myth, whereas the original definition "concerned itself only with myth as a form of language."[2] In light of all of these logical difficulties, Hepburn dismisses Bultmann's definition of myth with the warning against "crying mystery where there is not always mystery but sometimes only muddle."[3]

H. P. Owen argues in a manner similar to Hepburn: "We are bound to conclude that he [Bultmann] cannot mean by the definition what he appears to mean."[4] Unlike Hepburn, however, Owen goes beyond the logical analysis of the definition itself and finds that it can be vindicated, though only if one imputes to the definition a meaning other than what it literally has. Thus, Owen notes that the definition appears to be epistemological in its itention, which is also the reading of Hepburn: i.e., men know the divine or other-worldly only through the human or the worldly. In contrast with this literal appearance, however, Owen insists that the definition must be understood as ontological in order for it to make any sense: i.e., "Myth is a mode of speech which contradicts what he [Bultmann] considers to be the nature of God's being and act."[5] If one brings to this definition an understanding of Bultmann's ontology, then, according to Owen, the definition is consistent with Bultmann's actual proposal: "Demythologizing would be more

---

[1] *Ibid.*
[2] *Ibid.*
[3] *Ibid.*, p. 242.
[4] H. P. Owen, *Revelation and Existence. A Study in the Theology of Rudolf Bultmann* (Cardiff: University of Wales Press, 1957), p. 5.
[5] *Ibid.*, p. 6.

accurately called deobjectifying." [1] The intention of the definition would then be to eliminate any attribute of God or man which might be construed as "objective" in contrast with "existential."

John Macquarrie, after a detailed survey of other studies of this definition of myth, concludes with the generous understatement: "The definition offered is itself by no means a model of clarity." [2] Or, as he expresses his judgment more accurately later in this volume, "Bultmann's formal definition of myth must be abandoned." [3] Like Owen, Macquarrie then proceeds to construct out of Bultmann's writings a "tolerably coherent concept of myth which is stable for his purposes." [4] In Macquarrie's case, however, the resulting product is a distinct new synthesis of Bultmann with Paul Tillich and others. While interesting, it is of little help in understanding the meaning of Bultmann's original enigmatic definition.

Over against these critics of Bultmann's definition of myth, Schubert Ogden defends the logical consistency of Bultmann's definition: "Macquarrie is mistaken when he claims that Bultmann's concept of myth is 'confused' and that the formal definition of the term can only be 'scrapped' [sic]." [5] Ogden defends this definition only by imputing to the term "world" its technical Bultmannian ontological meaning:

> When Bultmann says that "Mythology is that manner of representation in which the unworldly and divine appears as the worldly and human," the pivotal word "world" is obviously being used with the same restrictive meaning it almost invariably has throughout his writings. That is, it is understood to refer to what he otherwise speaks of as the realm of the "objective" which he sharply distinguishes from the realm of human existence or of men's distinctively personal life. [6]

For an ordinary reader of the text, it is far from "obvious" that the term "world" is the "pivotal" term in this definition. In the German original, "*Weltliches*" is set in apposition with "*Menschliches*" and there is nothing in the German syntax to suggest a

---

[1] *Ibid.*, p. 15.
[2] Macquarrie, p. 199.
[3] *Ibid.*, p. 214.
[4] *Ibid.*
[5] Schubert M. Ogden, *Christ Without Myth. A Study Based on the Theology of Rudolf Bultmann* (New York: Harper and Brothers, 1961), p. 169.
[6] *Ibid.*, p. 168.

distinction between the two, or the primacy of the one over the other. Surely Ogden's reading of the text would require either a clear distinction between *"Weltliches"* and *"Menschliches,"* or at least the use of only *"Weltliches"* to suggest a technical category meaning "the objective" in clear distinction from "the realm of human existence." It is also far from obvious that one may attribute to *"Weltliches,"* alone or in conjunction with *"Menschliches,"* the "restrictive meaning" characteristic of its technical usage in Bultmann's thought. For Bultmann does not offer this definition under his own name, but under the rubric of the meaning of myth in *"religionsgeschichtliche Forschung."* Ogden may be right in imputing to this definition the fundamental ontological distinction between "objective" and "existential," if it is to be made consistent with Bultmann's thought. This is exactly what Owen has done. However, such eisegesis ought to be acknowledged as such and not passed off as an "obvious" reading of this particular text.

Clearly the definition does not mean what it says, as Hepburn and others point out, and it can be construed in a manner consistent with Bultmann's fundamental presuppositions, as Owen and Ogden contend. However, it is somewhat unusual to employ such a double-meaning hermeneutic at the point of the definition of the fundamental concept in a project of thought! Usually, definitions serve as the "clear passages" in terms of which some of the "darker passages" may be understood. Furthermore, it is customary to expect that the basic conceptual tools of theological reflection will enjoy a clarity not expected of the opaque, primary forms of the language of faith itself. In Bultmann's definition of myth, these conditions are clearly not met.[1]

---

[1] The vagueness, ambiguity, and/or logical impossibility of Bultmann's definition of myth has been observed by a wide range of critics:

1) L. Malevez, *The Christian Message and Myth: The Theology of Rudolf Bultmann* (London: S. C. M. Press, 1958), p. 68.
2) Giovanni Miegge, *Gospel and Myth in the Thought of Rudolf Bultmann* (Richmond, Va.: John Knox Press, 1960), p. 91.
3) A. Oepke, "Entmythologisierung des Christentums? Thesen," *KuM*, II, 170.
4) I. Henderson, *Myth in the New Testament* (Chicago: Henry Regnery Company, 1952), p. 54.
5) Regin Prenter, "Myth and Gospel," *Kerygma and History*, ed. and trans. Carl Braaten and Roy H. Harrisville (New York: Abingdon Press, 1962), pp. 125 ff.
6) Ernst Lohmeyer, "The Right Interpretation of the Mythological," *KaM*, I, 125-126.

Beyond the question of the definition of myth, Bultmann's actual use of the term has also appeared to be incapable of any consistent and coherent explanation. Ian Henderson has described Bultmann's apparently random use of myth as follows:

> It seems fair to say that Bultmann groups together a number of not particularly homogeneous elements under the heading of the mythological. The category covers the account of the miracles of Jesus, descriptions of His person as the pre-existent Son of God, of His work as atoning for the sins of mankind, of the Holy Spirit as a quasi-natural force, of grace as a mysterious and similarly quasi-natural power communicated to us through the sacraments. All these elements are enclosed in Bultmann's concept of the mythological but I do not think he objects to them all for the same reason.[1]

H. P. Owen agrees with this criticism of the use of the term, specifying the wide difference between miracles as reputed happenings and the spatial conception of transcendence as a mode of symbolization.[2] John Macquarrie agrees with Owen, though he would utilize Bultmann's concept of legend "to cover the peripheral stories such as miracles . . . which serve to illustrate aspects of the central myth."[3] In this manner, myth would become less of a heterogeneous catchall term. Ogden again differs, contending that "Bultmann's usage is thoroughly consistent and remains completely untouched by the charge of ambiguity."[4] However, Ogden wins this clarity for Bultmann only by demanding of the reader that he "gives due regard to his [Bultmann's] careful explanation of its meanings" and "what he has subsequently written in clarification of it [myth]."[5] Here again is the same quality of enigma: Bultmann's original use

---

7) Friedrich K. Schumann, "Can the Event of Jesus Christ be Demythologized?" *KaM*, I, 190.

8) Wilhelm Knevels, *Die Wirklichkeit Gottes: ein Weg zur Überwindung der Orthodoxie und des Existentialismus* (Stuttgart: Calwer Verlag), 1964, pp. 28-29. Knevels summarizes the impact which the lack of any clear definition of myth has produced upon the total discussion of the problem: "The scientific discussion is lacking in any uniform concept of what myth is. Since every user understands by myth something different from all others, they all speak right by each other. If there were a uniform and generally valid concept of myth, then would the way be clear for a resolution of the decisive problem: namely, myth in the New Testament and in the Christian faith" (*ibid*).

[1] Henderson, p. 46.
[2] Owen, p. 5.
[3] Macquarrie, p. 210.
[4] Ogden, p. 31.
[5] *Ibid.*

of myth discloses in itself no consistent pattern, but the specially attentive reader is able, by following clarifications, explanations, and qualification of later writings, to grasp the unity underlying the actual usage. Henderson also knew this, however. After listing what appears to be a random collection of uses, he goes on to note that they all bear some connection with the natural or the cosmos.[1] The apparently random has its own mode of unity and consistency, if one only knows the right clues to follow.

Still another form of criticism has been directed to Bultmann's use of myth on the grounds of inconsistency. Bultmann speaks often out of a rationalistic world view and anthropology, especially in his concept of the modern *Weltbild*, as a closed cause-effect nexus, and his idea of modern man's self-understanding, as an autonomous self-sufficient unity. Almost every critic of Bultmann has recognized and rejected this rationalistic motif in his discussion of myth: e.g., Karl Barth because it is anti-theological and Karl Jaspers because it is anti-scientific.[2] Several have pointed out the unfortunate consequences of this rationalistic bias for the overall concept of myth. René Marlé finds that this rationalistic view of man and nature gives to Bultmann's discussion of myth an anachronistic quality.[3] In its presupposition of an absolute distinction between the rationality of modern man and primitive man, it reflects the position of Levy-Bruhl, as this has been rejected in contemporary anthropological and historical studies.[4]

Other critics, however, find Bultmann's understanding of myth to be distinguished by its movement beyond the older rationalistic tradition. Gunther Backhaus argues that Bultmann, at this point as at others, has gone beyond the position of David Friedrich Strauss.[5] Günther Bornkamm makes the same point. He cites, with a note of reproof, a recent description of myth formulated by Christian Hartlich and Walter Sachs. He objects to their understanding

---

[1] Henderson, pp. 47 ff.
[2] Barth, *KaM*, II, 117. Karl Jaspers and Rudolf Bultmann, *Myth and Christianity: An Inquiry into the Possibility of Religion without Myth* (New York: The Noonday Press, 1958), pp. 5-6.
[3] René Marlé, *Bultmann et l'interprétation du Nouveau Testament* (Paris [Aubier], Editions Montaigne, 1956), pp. 64-65.
[4] *Ibid.*
[5] Gunther Backhaus, *Kerygma und Mythos bei David Friedrich Strauss und Rudolf Bultmann* (Hamburg: Herbert Reich, 1956), pp. 46-47.

of myth because he sees it as an example of that rationalistic tradition which has been overcome precisely by Bultmann.

> In a dangerous manner is the rationalistic understanding of myth here renewed, which, according to the earlier publication of the cited authors themselves, was rooted in the work of the classical philologist C. G. Heyne and his theological pupils until it was itself overcome in Rudolf Bultmann's understanding of myth.[1]

Which critic is right? Obviously, both sides are right. As Bornkamm himself notes, this rationalistic understanding of myth, constructed by Hartlich and Sachs and overcome by Bultmann, is itself cited by Bultmann as expressive of his own position. Again the enigma. How is it possible to understand myth under the norm of both the rationalistic *Weltbild* and an existentialist anthropology?

Another version of the same problem of consistency has been posed by Regin Prenter. Prenter wonders how it is possible both to demythologize and to interpret mythology. Is not this an either-or? One either eliminates, takes away mythology, as *entmythologisieren* would suggest, or one allows mythology to stand but as interpreted. In any case, Prenter insists that "the concepts of demythologizing and existentialist interpretation are mutually exclusive of each other." [2] Bultmann, of course, has differentiated his own project from the work of liberal theology precisely at this point:

> Whereas the older liberals used criticism to *eliminate* the mythology of the New Testament, our task today is to use criticism to *interpret* it.[3]

One cannot doubt the both-and intention of Bultmann's project, but one could hope for a clarification which would meet Prenter's objection. What does the *"ent"* of *"entmythologisieren"* qualify? Obviously not mythology in its totality and as such, but only mythology in certain respects. But what respects? What precisely is qualified and thus eliminated by the *"ent"* and what remains to be interpreted? Bultmann never develops a terminology sufficiently specific to meet this problem.

In concluding this survey of criticism directed at Bultmann's

---

[1] Bornkamm, p. 59.
[2] Regin Prenter, "Mythus und Evangelium," *KuM*, II, 80.
[3] Bultmann, *KaM*, I, 12.

concept of myth, it may be helpful to quote Bultmann's own assessment of this aspect of the demythologizing debate.

> I do not regard the question concerning the concept of myth to be among the most important questions. Rather, it appears to me as if this discussion leads away from the real subject of concern in the problem of demythologizing. If therefore anyone regards my concept of myth as questionable, and wishes to understand by myth something else, he may do so.[1]

There is little question but that this quotation expresses faithfully Bultmann's real lack of interest in the subject of his concept of myth. Why else would he drop the definition of myth in a footnote in his initial essay on demythologizing? Whenever Bultmann has found himself pressed on the question of the meaning of myth, as in dialogue with Jaspers and with Schumann, he has resolutely abandoned the subject, moving on to the more comprehensive and important hermeneutical question: the question of the right conceptuality for the understanding and proclamation of the Gospel.[2]

It is somewhat ironic, in light of the abundant discussion of Bultmann's concept of myth and the controversy which the project of demythologizing has created, that Bultmann should regard the subject of myth so lightly. He proposes the project of demythologizing in which the decisive concept of myth is judged to be so peripheral as to be of no substantive concern. Little wonder that the whole project has proved to be somewhat enigmatic!

It is no longer possible to accept Bultmann's disclaimer of concern for a critical delineation of the concept of myth.[3] It simply is not possible to retreat from the clear and exposed flank of myth to the more secure, if muddy, sphere of "comprehensive hermeneutical reflection." The key concept for the hermeneutical reflection of

---

[1] Bultmann, *KuM*, II, 180.

[2] Bultmann and Jaspers, *Myth and Christianity* . . ., p. 60. Günther Bornkamm, Rudolf Bultmann, and Friedrich Schumann, *Die christliche Hoffnung und das Problem der Entmythologisierung* (Stuttgart: Evangelisches Verlagswerk, 1954), pp. 48-49.

[3] Günther Bornkamm repeated Bultmann's opinion of 1952 in his survey of Bultmann literature in 1963:

> In fact, in Rudolf Bultmann's own view the issue and concept of demythologizing is, relatively speaking, confined to the surface of the matter. It is not new, and calling attention to it is really a *testimonium paupertatis*. For it has necessarily always been taking place in various ways, although usually without adequate hermeneutical reflection. According to Rudolf Bultmann it has its real theological meaning only within the context of comprehensive hermeneutical reflection (Bornkamm, p. 125).

Bultmann, and decisive also for the writings of his followers, is the technical hermeneutical concept of *"objektivierend."* The concept of "objectifying," however, is in no sense peripheral to the meaning of myth; rather, it is determinative for the conceptual structure of myth. Furthermore, it becomes perfectly clear that one is able to trace out the palimpsest of "objectifying," with its layers of philosophical meaning built one on top of the other, only through an analysis of the history of the development of the concept of myth. For it was precisely at the point of myth, and only here, that Bultmann came to a clear and final understanding of the concept of "objectifying." If, therefore, one would follow Bultmann's injunction, and concern himself with an understanding of the hermeneutical problem, he would not be able to turn away from the concept of myth, but rather would follow it as the golden thread which could unravel the tangled web of hermeneutical discussion.

b. *Structural Inconsistencies in Bultmann's Theology*

As a preface to his own analysis of Bultmann's proposal, Schubert Ogden notes the emergence in the Bultmann discussion of a "common consensus" among critics of the left and of the right concerning the "structural inconsistency of Bultmann's solution."

> Perhaps the "demythologizing debate's" most striking characteristic is the substantial agreement among its various participants that Bultmann's proposal is intrinsically problematic. So much agreement is there, in fact, that we may appropriately speak of an emerging consensus that Bultmann's solution is inherently inadequate. From responsible voices on every side, the claim has come that his theology is structurally inconsistent and therefore open to the most serious criticism.[1]

As evidence for this, he offers a brief resumé of the criticism of Karl Barth and Fritz Buri. He finds that Barth describes this "noteworthy inconsistency" in terms of the discrepancy between Bultmann's kerygmatic and Christocentric intention and his actual existentialist and old liberal interpretation.[2] From the opposite theological stance, Fritz Buri also regards Bultmann's theological proposal as inconsistent. Buri should like Bultmann to follow through his original proposal to demythologize consistently the New Testament by translating without remainder its Kerygma into

---

[1] Ogden, p. 96.
[2] *Ibid.*, pp. 103-105.

existentialist categories. When, instead of doing this, Bultmann persists in telling the story of Jesus Christ and in giving to this story a unique, soteriological role, he is, as Ogden quotes Buri, "falling back into mythology . . . into contradiction with his own presuppositions." [1] Ogden then notes how Buri traces this pattern of contradiction in Bultmann's vacillation between two fundamentally opposed types of understanding: of fallenness (historical-existential vs. mythological-theological), salvation (objective event vs. dehistoricized self-understanding), and Scripture (history vs. proclamation).[2] Instead of persisting resolutely in the project of demythologizing, Bultmann arbitrarily limits this movement of thought by appealing "to an event that is mythological and inexplicable in existential terms."[3]

Ogden's own analysis of the fundamental inconsistency in Bultmann's theology focuses upon the illegitimate nature of the distinction between "a possibility in principle" and "a possibility in fact." Ogden rightly sees that it is precisely by means of this conceptual device that Bultmann attempts to hold together the two sides of his proposal: the demand for an unqualified demythologizing and existentialist interpretation of the Kerygma and the demand for the recognition of the essential role of Jesus Christ as the single locus of salvation or authenticity. As a result of this distinction, Bultmann can define authentic self-understanding as being, on the one hand, actually realized only through the decision of faith in Jesus Christ. The universal possibility is thus made conditional for its becoming a "possibility in fact" upon the historical particularity of the Christ event.[4] In Ogden's judgment, this distinction between "possibility in principle" and "possibility in fact" is either "vacuous," or, if it has positive meaning, it can only serve to undermine Bultmann's constructive proposal for a solution to the contemporary theological problem.[5]

In *The Scope of Demythologizing*, John Macquarrie takes up this same problem of structural inconsistency as the major theme for his consideration of Bultmann's theological proposal. Macquarrie defines the problem in terms of the arbitrary limit which Bultmann

---

[1] *Ibid.*, p. 107.
[2] *Ibid.*, pp. 108-109.
[3] *Ibid.*
[4] *Ibid.*, pp. 111 ff.
[5] *Ibid.*, p. 118; p. 125.

appears to interject, at the last moment, to cut off the consistent execution of his methodological proposal of consistent demythologizing. The "little tableau" with which Macquarrie begins his book best suggests his formulation of the problem:

> Let us picture to ourselves a motorist who has been driving his vehicle at a fairly brisk speed down a long steady incline. At the bottom of the slope the road dips suddenly out of sight. We cannot as yet tell what lies beyond the dip, though it looks as if there may well be a precipitous fall into an abyss of some sort. But the motorist has also noticed the sharp declivity in front of him. Almost at the last moment, as it appears, he has pulled strongly on his wheel, the car has slewed violently round, and instead of going over the dip it now follows a different road in quite a new direction.[1]

In Macquarrie's interpretation of this little tableau, "the road is the way of demythologizing; the sudden change of direction is what we propose to call the limit of demythologizing." [2] This limit appears in Bultmann's interpretation of the Kerygma as "the proclamation of the decisive act of God in Christ."

> When he says this, Bultmann sets a limit to demythologizing. "A decisive act of God" is something radically different from and irreducible to a possibility of human existence, and with the recognition of such an act Bultmann's thought moves in a different direction. This is the paradox with which we are presented in Bultmann.[3]

Here is, then, the same problem with which Barth, Buri, and Ogden have been concerned. Is it possible to hold together in a unified and consistent proposal demythologizing and kerygmatic theology?

> The method of demythologizing calls for the translation of the New Testament teaching into statements concerning human existence, yet at the same time Bultmann insists upon speaking of God's decisive act in Christ. The analysis of human possibilities thus gives place to the proclamation of a divine act .... Can this make sense? Can the two sides of his thinking be properly held together? [4]

The problem of structural inconsistency may be clarified by a critique of Macquarrie's statement of the problem, which is certainly the least helpful. The notion of a limit set en route totally

---

[1] Macquarrie, p. 11.
[2] *Ibid.*
[3] *Ibid.*, p. 13.
[4] *Ibid.*

obscures the stringent theological focus that is present from the very beginning and consistently sustained in the whole of Bultmann's thought. Unlike many of his critics, Bultmann is consistent and clear in his understanding of faith as always and only faith in the revelation of God in Jesus Christ: that means faith in Jesus as the revealer of God, as this is given originally in the Kerygma and now in the present preaching of the Church. Bultmann develops existentialist interpretation and demythologizing for the sake of this proclamation. To turn this upside down, and make the proclamation a limit to the existentialist interpretation, is to fundamentally distort the situation.

What Macquarrie has missed, Ogden has seen far more clearly: namely, the coinherence in Bultmann's thought of the absolute autonomy of the substance of faith with the absolute autonomy of the conceptuality of profane reason. This is the locus of the riddle. How—and why—does Bultmann attempt to hold together faith and reason, theology and philosophy in this peculiar pattern? On the one hand, the language of existential confession of faith and kerygmatic narration; on the other hand, the philosophical conceptuality appropriate to the structure of human existence and of the world: these are the two—or are there four?—poles of Bultmann's theology which appear to clash in the so-called structural inconsistency. It may still be true that Bultmann's thought is far more systematic and unified than his critics have allowed, granted his fundamental premises. This, however, is precisely the problem: to lay bare those premises on the basis of which the genuine consistency of the so-called structural inconsistency is disclosed. Needless to say, as long as one looks for such foundations in the philosophy of Martin Heidegger, as Barth, Buri, Ogden, and Macquarrie have done, he can only be confounded by the inconsistency. For this reason, I now turn to the critique of Bultmann's use of Heidegger, a critique which has made this old path of inquiry such an implausible one.

c. *Ambiguities in the relationship of Bultmann's theology to Heidegger's philosophy*

Bultmann's self-declared dependence upon Heidegger's philosophy had been one of the most stable principles of interpretation of his theology. From 1925, when Bultmann first began employing existentialist categories (two years before the publication of *Sein und Zeit*), through the formative essays of the late twenties and early thirties (in which Bultmann worked out the fundamental systematic-theological and historical-exegetical appropriation of Heidegger's philosophy) up to his most recent writings on myth and hermeneutics, Bultmann has consistently acknowledged his indebtedness, at the point of his fundamental philosophical conceptuality, to Martin Heidegger. In light of such a long testimonial, it has been no accident that Bultmann's interpreters have proceeded under the same assumption.[1]

The decisive breakthrough in this self-evident principle of interpretation occured in 1955 with the publication of Heinrich Ott's study of Bultmann, *Geschichte und Heilsgeschichte in der Theologie Rudolf Bultmanns*. To be sure, there had been occasional doubts raised, prior to this time, regarding the adequacy of Bultmann's philosophical self-interpretation: e.g., by Karl Jaspers.[2] However, it was only in Ott's work that there began the systematic exploration of the connection between Bultmann's anthropological theology and Heidegger's ontological philosophy.

Ott develops his analysis of Bultmann's theology around four major themes: 1) the double concept of history; 2) the hermeneutical problem; 3) the concept of time; 4) the concept of self-understanding. At each of these issues, Ott reaches a conclusion which follows a similar pattern and which may be summarized under the following five points.

1. Ott recognizes and appreciates the highly original nature of Bultmann's work, drawing upon Heidegger's ontology to formulate new resolutions for old theological problems. Whether this appears in the overcoming of the old positivistic view of history or the orthodox doctrine of inspiration, Ott sees Bultmann moving "in the direction of an original historical interpretation of biblical reality."[3]

2. At the same time, Ott acknowledges that in each case Bultmann fails to bring to its fulfillment the direction of thought with which he began: e.g., in considering the double concept of history

---

[1] For English language theology, it was perhaps John Macquarrie's book, *An Existentialist Theology* (London: S.C.M. Press, 1955), which was most influential in establishing the premise that Heidegger was in fact the fundamental philosophical source for Bultmann's theology. By consistently juxtaposing the thought of Heidegger and Bultmann, Macquarrie showed in a persuasive manner "the connection between the two" (*ibid.*, Preface, p. xi).

[2] Jaspers, "Myth and Religion," *Myth and Christianity*, p. 8.

[3] Ott, *Geschichte und Heilsgeschichte* . . ., p. 43.

he concludes that "Bultmann remains bound to the positivistic understanding of reality and therefore does not bring his own thought to its end."[1] Ott is thus consistently puzzled by the limited and partial execution of Heidegger's ontology in Bultmann's theology.

3. What does appear in each of these cases is the fundamental dualism which Ott characteristically expresses in terms of the two spheres of being: the existential and the objective. Thus, in discussing the double concept of history, Ott finds that "either the deity of Christ is interpreted cosmologically or objectively or it is interpreted soteriologically in an existential manner. *Tertium non datur.*"[2] This is "the ultimate and most simple ontological foundation" of Bultmann's concept of history.[3]

In considering the hermeneutical issue, Ott finds a similar limit in Bultmann's appropriation of Heidegger's thought—and in the same dualistic motif—as fundamental to his theology. The reality of faith always finally escapes hermeneutical explication since faith is ultimately of the order of existence while hermeneutics is of the order of reflection.

> The Christian self-understanding, faith, remains in its specific existentialist structure unclarified, an enigmatic leap, for which the name of Jesus Christ serves a a cipher. .... Hermeneutical reflection

---

[1] *Ibid.*

[2] *Ibid.*, p. 50.

[3] *Ibid.* Ott begins his discussion of the double concept of history by noting the fundamental ontological cleavage between nature and history. However, within history itself, there is a similar distinction between *Historie*, as this is "methodologically and objectively apprehended," and *Geschichte*, as "the real essence of history" (*ibid.*, pp. 9 ff.). Bornkamm rightly notes Ott's failure to adequately grasp Bultmann's conceptuality at this point (Bornkamm, p. 94). In my judgment, this dichotomy is formulated more accurately in terms of the distinction of *Historie* (history objectively determined according to appropriate cause-effect connections) and *Geschichtlichkeit* (the realization of the reality of *Dasein* in decision). It was not Bultmann, but his followers, who became concerned with the *Geschichte* of Jesus. Bultmann himself rejects *Geschichte* in all its forms as inappropriate for the understanding of the New Testament. He instead is concerned with the *historische* Jesus and the *Geschichtlichkeit* of faith as mediated by the eschatological, *mythologische* Kerygma. The dichotomy in Bultmann is not between a meaningful past and a merely factual past; rather, the dichotomy is between all that is objective, including the meaningful (idealistic or *Heilsgeschichte*) past, and the present reality of the particular lived existence of *Dasein*.

It is for this reason that I do not tend in any detail to the dichotomy of *Historie-Geschichte*, as Ott develops this, but to the more fundamental and appropriate distinction between the "existential" and the "objective."

and existentialist thinking remain fundamentally restricted to the preliminaries of historical being.[1]

In the case of the concept of time, Ott finds the same dualistic principle at work. Time is time of the now, the present, the moment, or time is time of the past, of duration, of continuity. The first is existential, the second is objective.[2]

> The Now corresponds to *Geschichtlichkeit*, the reality constituted in decision; the time of continuity corresponds to the being which is "disposable," insofar as it may be appropriated without existential decision.[3]

The principle of the *"tertium non datur"* is also decisive here. Between past objectified time and present existential time there is no possible grounds for synthesis.[4]

Finally, in the discussion of self-understanding, Ott finds the dualism expressed in terms of the categories of authentic and inauthentic. Self-understanding is authentic when it is existential, not objective, not oriented toward the worldly or that which is

---

[1] *Ibid.*, p. 108. At the hermeneutical level, Ott stipulated the dualism in terms of the unbreachable gulf that separated hermeneutical, existentialist, and theological reflection from the existential reality of *Dasein* in decision (*ibid.*, p. 105). Ott does not make it clear that this is but a variant of the "existential"—"objective" dualism. For this, he should have had to have known Bultmann's later discussion of the objectifying character of all hermeneutical and theological reflection, which provides the decisive mark of distinction between faith and theology. Bultmann explicated this clearly, however, only in response to Ott's own theological work, especially Ott's appropriation of Heidegger's "primal thinking." (For a summary of Bultmann's statement in reply to Ott, see: James Robinson, "The German Discussion of the Later Heidegger," *The Later Heidegger and Theology*, ed. James M. Robinson and John B. Cobb, Jr. [New York: Harper & Row, 1963], p. 48.) In light of this discussion, it is now clear that objectifying refers to any rational form of conceptuality, for any and every rational construct stands in clear opposition with the immediately given reality of individual existence. This includes the "objectifying" reason of science, mythology, and also, existentialist philosophy or theology. The latter happens to be a mode of objectifying more appropriate to the existential reality of faith, but is no less distinct from it. In light of these later writings of Bultmann, as well as his very early writings, it is now clear that the distinction between existence and rational reflection is equal to the fundamental and comprehensive distinction between "existential" and "objective." (Cf. Schubert M. Ogden, "The Understanding of Theology in Ott and Bultmann," *ibid.*, pp. 157-173, especially pp. 154 ff.; Schubert M. Ogden, "Theology and Objectivity," *JR*, XLV (1965), 175-195, especially 179-182.

[2] *Ibid.*, p. 127.
[3] *Ibid.*, p. 128.
[4] *Ibid.*, pp. 137-138.

"disposable"; self-understanding is inauthentic insofar as it is objectifying, that is insofar as it is continuous with a particular interpretation of reality.[1] In conjunction with this, Ott notes that Bultmann has here hypostatized an objective mode of knowing into an objective sphere of being.[2]

4. In relating this fundamental ontological dualism to the philosophical conceptuality of Martin Heidegger, Ott is repeatedly struck by the incongruity of the two. Thus, in relation to Bultmann's conversion of objectifying thinking into an always present mode of knowing and possibility of being, Ott writes:

> Heidegger does not appear to be familiar with the extension of objectivity into the sphere of the ontic and the status of a fundamental principle. The comprehension of reality as it is set over against the knower is understood by him as a passing phenomenon, present only in our "Age of the *Weltbild*." [3]

In a similar manner, Heidegger does not know the transposition of the existential categories of authentic and inauthentic into the sphere of the ontic and as defined by objectivity.

> The opposition of authentic and inauthentic is fundamental ... in Heidegger's apprehension of *Dasein*. However, with Heidegger the existentialist category of inauthentic is not closely bound up with objectivity, as is the case with Bultmann. ... In any case, Bultmann cannot appeal to Heidegger for his fusion in principle of inauthentic with "having at one's own disposal" and authentic with "not having at one's disposal." [4]

Ott summarizes the general line of distinction between Heidegger and Bultmann as follows:

> One may characterize the distinction in the thinking of both men as follows: Bultmann is concerned with *Dasein* (as self-understanding) for the sake of *Dasein*; Heidegger is concerned with *Dasein* as a preliminary level for the sake of *Sein*. Has Bultmann not seen this? Has he also fallen victim to the widespread anthropological misunderstanding of the philosophy of Heidegger? [5]

Ott's fundamental conclusion regarding the relationship of Bultmann to Heidegger, which he first put forth in his 1955 study of Bultmann, has since then been confirmed by a variety of Bult-

[1] *Ibid.*, pp. 170-171.
[2] *Ibid.*
[3] *Ibid.*, pp. 171-172.
[4] *Ibid.*, p. 172.
[5] *Ibid.*, p. 173.

mann studies.[1] Indeed, there has developed a broad consensus concerning the partiality and anthropologically limited appropriation of Heidegger in Bultmann's theology. Thus, Ott was able to express this same point in much stronger language in his 1959 study of Heidegger, *Denken und Sein*:

> Only individual aspects of Heidegger's thought have played a significant role in the work of his theological pupils, F. Gogarten and R. Bultmann. With Bultmann, it was the existentialist analytic of *Dasein*, with its concepts of existentiality, existence, being-at-hand, authenticity and inauthenticity, and temporality as the fundamental condition of *Dasein*; in *Sein und Zeit*, however, this existentialist analytic belonged to the elaboration of the question of being. It is a fact that Bultmann has taken and considered as isolated in itself the existentialist analytic ... which in Heidegger was subordinate, as a methodologically necessary level, to the more comprehensive question concerning being. Concerning the question of being in Heidegger's sense, Bultmann offers no hint of interest in his theological work. Because of this, the later work of Heidegger, in which the existentialist analytic scarcely appears ... has no further significance for Bultmann's theology.[2]

---

[1] Pierre Barthel has summarized the situation succinctly when he writes. "Everywhere one finds Bultmann's reading of Heidegger being corrected from its anthropological focus to an ontological one" (Barthel, p. 106). W. Bernet has extended Ott's original critique, offering a detailed study of Bultmann's transposition of Heidegger's formal ontological categories of authentic and inauthentic into material ontic possibilities of *Dasein* (Bernet, *Verkündigung und Wirklichkeit* [Tübingen: J. C. B. Mohr, 1961]). H. Franz has worked out a careful specification of Bultmann's borrowings from Heidegger around six themes:
1) The historicity of *Dasein*;
2) The concepts of authentic and inauthentic;
3) The centrality of decision;
4) The overcoming of the subject-object schema;
5) The understanding of being as event or encounter;
6) The orientation of *Dasein* to the future (Franz, "Das Denken Heideggers und die Theologie," *ZThK*, LVIII (1961), 81-118. A. Malet has posed an unpersuasive, *ad hominem* argument in reply to Ott's critique. Malet regards the whole of the reinterpretation of Bultmann's relationship to Heidegger to be a result of the most unfortunate influence of Karl Barth's understanding of the relation of theology and philosophy, as this has been disseminated by the work of his pupils, H. Ott, K. Ittel, and others (André Malet, *Mythos et Logos: la pensée de Rudolf Bultmann* [Genève: Libraire Protestante, 1962], p. 302). Barth and Ott are completely incorrect in accusing Bultmann of having failed to understand Heidegger: "Bultmann has understood Heidegger's thought perfectly" (*ibid*). As support for this contention, Malet draws upon the testimony of Heidegger himself, since "Heidegger conceives of the relationship between theology and philosophy exactly as does Bultmann" (*ibid.*, p. 295).

[2] Heinrich Ott, *Denken und Sein* . . ., p. 21.

It would thus appear as if Bultmann had employed Heidegger's conceptuality only within very strict anthropological limits: for the articulation of the being of man in his historicity. If this is the case, then it should be necessary to give an account of this Heideggerean anthropology within a more comprehensive ontology: namely, the dualistic structure of all reality which Ott repeatedly discovers in his analysis of the fundamental motifs of Bultmann's thought. It would thus appear—and here I go beyond Ott—as if Heidegger's conceptuality served as the explication for only "one side" of Bultmann's dualistic ontology: namely, the explication of being in the mode of existence. As Ott has shown, it is precisely Bultmann's radical extension of the objective, as both a noetic and ontic principle, that has no corresponding formulation in Heidegger. It would therefore appear necessary to develop a conceptuality which was sufficiently comprehensive to include Heidegger's philosophy, or rather Heidegger's anthropology, together with the objectified understanding of being that functions as its necessary correlate in Bultmann's thought.

5. While this is the problem which is the clear legacy of Ott's work, it is just as clear that Ott himself has not extended his own analysis to provide such a clear and comprehensive conceptuality. Quite the contrary. Ott began his work with the premise that Heidegger's ontology provided the fundamental conceptuality for Bultmann's theology. When he discovered the limited and partial use of Heidegger in a more comprehensive dualistic framework at each of the themes he developed, he concluded that he was confronting a phenomenon of a psychological-religious order, not susceptible to conceptual analysis. The following conclusion to his discussion of the concept of time is typical:

> What comes to expression here is ultimately something very personal, a fundamental existential experience of Christianity in a definite form, a specific, original orientation of faith: this is the root of the doublesided understanding of time. It does not lie in the sphere of our inquiry, perhaps not in the sphere of any inquiry, to press the analysis of the thought of a given thinker to its deepest existential roots.[1]

In concluding the discussion of self-understanding, Ott again poses the riddle of Bultmann's sharp divergence from Heidegger, here

---

[1] Ott, *Geschichte und Heilsgeschichte* . . ., p. 144. Cf. Bornkamm's criticism of Ott's psychologizing of Bultmann: Bornkamm, p. 95.

suggesting that Bultmann's peculiar use of authentic and inauthentic bears the imprint of his encounter with the New Testament.[1] His later identification of this dualistic perspective with the law-Gospel dualism of Luther has been previously noted.[2] In each of these cases Ott's quest for an adequate philosophical conceptuality, having met with failure at the point of his original premise in Heidegger, has been diverted to a phenomenon of a purely existential order.

One obviously needs not be bound by Ott's premature abandonment of his own quest. One can only appreciate the clarity and objectivity of his analysis, which demolished his own original premise in the course of its execution, and thereby left the way open for new patterns of inquiry into the fundamental conceptuality of Bultmann's theology.

Beyond the clarification of the relationship of Bultmann's theology to Heidegger's philosophy, together with the delineation of the dualistic structure of Bultmann's thought, Ott has raised a further issue of particular relevance to this inquiry. This is what Ott describes as Bultmann's "individualistic tendency." While many critics have observed this characteristic of Bultmann's theology, and its constricting influence upon his interpretation of the New Testament Kerygma, Ott has been one of the first to establish methodologically the evidence for its role in Bultmann's thought, together with an analysis of the relationship of this motif to the fundamental ontological concepts of Bultmann's thought. It is a motif of particular interest because, like the dualism of existential and objective, it is a primary determinant of Bultmann's thought while remaining somewhat shrouded in darkness.

Ott acknowledges that the first difficulty in any consideration of Bultmann's individualism is rooted in the vagueness of the idea in Bultmann's own writings. Indeed, Ott does not even give to Bultmann's individualistic anthropology the status of an idea: it is rather "the atmosphere which pervades the whole of this thought," "a fundamental disposition which cannot be apprehended conceptually," a "tendency" or an "attitude."[3] Ott states repeatedly that Bultmann never explicitly develops a concept of individualism.[4]

---

[1] Ott, *Geschichte und Heilsgeschichte* . . ., p. 172.
[2] Ott, *Denken und Sein* . . ., p. 8.
[3] Ott, *Geschichte und Heilsgeschichte* . . ., p. 192; p. 188.
[4] *Ibid.*, p. 182; p. 188; p. 192.

Because of this vague, non-conceptual status of individualism in Bultmann's thought, Ott begins by presenting the evidence for this motif, through an exegesis of selected Bultmann texts, and an analysis of theological themes and methodological characteristics. In this respect, he notes the following as evidence for the individualistic bias of Bultmann's theology:

1) The interpretation of the message of Jesus "which is not directed to a people as a whole, as were the prophets of the Old Testament, but to the individual";
2) The understanding of the nature of the Church, which in the style of the Gospel of John means "the community of gathered individuals who become his disciples through their decision of faith";
3) The basic categories of self-understanding, authenticity, and inauthenticity, which may properly be used only in relation to the individual;
4) The understanding of the nature of theological reflection, "not as a living dialogue with the ecclesiastical theological tradition, but only as a single man";
5) The reality of God's saving deed, which comes to fulfillment only in the new self-understanding of the individual believer who has come to faith.[1]

Having established the significant role of this motif in a wide spectrum of examples, Ott then proceeds to relate the individualistic focus of Bultmann's thought to his fundamental ontology. This task is considerably more difficult, since Ott is dealing with a vague, amorphous disposition, on the one hand, and a body of clearly stipulated ideas, on the other. In this relation, Ott is limited to the negative route of proving the inconsistency of Bultmann's fundamental conceptuality with any non-individualistic anthropology: that is, Ott establishes that it is not possible to develop a theological understanding of man as a member of an organic community, in the style of the Old Testament covenant tradition, on the basis of Bultmann's fundamental ontological categories. He easily shows how the punctilinear understanding of time and the role of self-understanding necessarily excludes an explication of existence in faith in terms of an organic community.[2] It is only by this negative and highly indirect route that Ott establishes the connection between Bultmann's fundamental conceptuality and the individualistic bias of his anthropology.

---

[1] Ibid., pp. 182-188.
[2] Ibid., pp. 188-191.

The limitations of Ott's analysis of Bultmann's individualism are striking. The location of the discussion, which appears as a post-script to the analysis of the fundamental ontological categories, already suggests something of its weakness. Ott has rightly recognized the role of Bultmann's individualistic orientation as "pervasive for the whole of his thought" but, in relegating it to a virtual appendage to his work, he cannot disclose the actual significance of this motif in Bultmann's thought. Furthermore, Ott offers very little clarity as to the exact meaning of "individualism" in Bultmann's thought, on the grounds that Bultmann himself has not offered a clear formulation of the idea. This view of the matter can only be due to a neglect of relevant Bultmann texts, in which the idea of individuality is thematically presented.[1] The one motif which Ott says is not applicable to Bultmann's understanding of individualism is "the isolation of the ego"; yet, Bultmann uses precisely that phrase to describe the unique contribution of Christtianity to the understanding of individuality.[2]

Not only is the meaning of individuality vague, but its place in Bultmann's thought is equally unclear. While Ott begins by acknowledging that it is a fundamental and pervasive tendency, he ends by noting that Bultmann has not said the last word yet on the subject of individuality and community.[3] He even quotes a long description of the corporate understanding of the life of the Church which Bultmann attributes to the primitive Christian community.[4] In light of this quotation, Ott concludes that one may speak of a Bultmannian individualism only with the greatest "caution and restraint." [5] The implication is that individuality is a single idea of Bultmann's which may be revised at some future writing. In such a

---

[1] Rudolf Bultmann, "Religion und Kultur," *ChrW*, XXVII (1920), cols. 417-421; 435-439; 450-453.

[2] Ott, *Geschichte und Heilsgeschichte* . . ., p. 186. "Historical individualism consists in the knowledge and perception of this basic isolation of the ego . . . This individualism was brought with Christianity into the West, transmitted in part through the Old Testament and in part through the New Testament" (Rudolf Bultmann, "Christianity as a Religion of East and West," *Essays: Philosophical and Theological*, p. 225). The fact that Bultmann uses this phrase in relation to man's standing in the world while Ott uses it in relation to the neighbor suggests Bultmann's dialectical use of the phrase, but does not justify Ott's unqualified exclusion of such a decisive motif for the meaning of individualism in Bultmann (*ibid.*, pp. 226-227).

[3] Ott, p. 192.

[4] *Ibid.*, p. 193.

[5] *Ibid.*

conclusion, it is clear that Ott has not yet discovered the structural role of individuality in Bultmann's thought. As with his discussion of dualism, so here Ott understands Bultmann's individualism in terms of "the hidden, personal, existential roots" of his thinking.[1] As a result, the relationship of this individualism to the fundamental conceptuality of Bultmann remains obscure and tenuous.

Ott has thus brought to a clear focus both the individualistic bias of Bultmann's anthropology and the dualistic structure of Bultmann's ontology. In neither case, however, has he grounded these two fundamental motifs of Bultmann's thought in a comprehensive philosophical conceptuality, nor has he shown the organic connection between the two. Yet, it is precisely Ott's analysis which has set free these fundamental issues in Bultmann's thought, and thus disclosed the essential criteria for further analysis. To understand Bultmann is to understand the philosophical origins and conceptual formulation of his inner-worldly, ontological dualism of existence and objectivity as this ontology is absolutely bound up with an anthropology of individuality. Any comprehension of Bultmann which is not able to give an account of this nexus as an organic whole has failed to meet the decisive issues in the enigma of his thought.

Heidegger's ontology will obviously not meet specifications such as these. Nor need one presume, with Ott, that Bultmann's conceptuality is best understood as a "partial, thwarted, limited" appropriation of Heidegger, deflected from its goal by some mysterious existential quirk of Bultmann's religious and psychological temperament. Rather, one may presume that Bultmann's execution is consistent with his intention, and that his intention, in turn, is consistent with his philosophical origins and open to conceptual analysis. Bultmann's partial use of Heidegger need not be attributed to Bultmann's "anthropological misunderstanding" of Heidegger. We may say, rather, that Bultmann uses precisely those aspects of Heidegger's thought which fit within the limits of his own fundamental philosophical perspective. Need we presume that Bultmann misunderstands Karl Barth's theology because he basically appropriates the radical eschatological understanding of revelation and consistently rejects Barth's Christology? Is it not more plausible, simple, and in accord with the textual evidence, to

---

[1] *Ibid.*, p. 181.

say instead that Bultmann finds in the dialectical theology of early Barth an understanding of revelation congruent with his own thought, just as he finds in early Heidegger a body of existentialist categories suited to his own anthropology? We do not need to make of Bultmann either a poor philosopher or a befuddled theologian simply because he selectively appropriates a limited body of motifs from others into the thought project which is genuinely his own. Too often we have been so struck by Bultmann's creative eclectic borrowings that we have lost sight of his own indigenous, unchanging perspective into which and through which all his borrowings must pass. Ott has discovered in a preliminary manner something of the shape of this edifice, and it is the task of this study to advance further along these lines.[1]

2. DEMYTHOLOGIZING DEMYSTIFIED

Prevalent interpretations of demythologizing, while recognizing the logical contradictions in the concept of myth, structural inconsistencies in theology, and ambiguities in the use of Heidegger, have not resolved the problems which they have so clearly identified. To strip away the enigma shrouding Bultmann's proposal of demythologizing it is necessary to abandon the presuppositions which informed earlier studies of Bultmann and initiate a whole new pattern of inquiry. Because the argument developed in this book is a complex web of interlocking parts, it may be helpful to the reader to summarize the argument as a whole. For only by first under-

---

[1] This discussion of Ott has not touched upon his analysis of Bultmann's use of the concept of myth. Ott understands Bultmann's concept of myth, like the concept of history, in terms of its dualistic ontological foundations: 1) Myth is thus a definite way of conceiving of reality; and 2) myth is an expression of a particular self-understanding (*ibid.*, p. 24). Ott thus argues that Bultmann's concept of myth is more consistent than his critics—F. Schumann, A. Oepke, and R. Prenter—would allow; granted, that is, its dualistic foundations (*ibid.*, p. 25). Ott defines demythologizing as follows: "Demythologizing resolves the inner tension of the mythical totality, as it separates the conflicting modes of being from each other: i.e., the mode of being of the conceptualized world and the mode of being of existentialist self-interpretation" (*ibid.*, p. 26). Or again: "Demythologizing separates out the primary *Geschichtlichkeit* from the objectifying thinking" (*ibid.*, p. 27). Ott then proceeds to interpret the dualism of "the worldly" and "the unworldly" in terms of the more comprehensive dualism of the existential and the objective (*ibid.*, p. 34). His work thus provides the foundation for a host of later studies, previously cited in this chapter, which have recognized this dualism as the only way open to the unravelling of the enigma of demythologizing.

standing the argument in its totality will the reader be able to follow the connections which link one step to another.

Three propositions are crucial for this reinterpretation of demythologizing.

a. *The historical origins and structure of the concept of myth*

Bultmann's concept of myth is an eclectic construct consisting of three elements logically and historically independent of each other:

    1) The *Religionsgeschichtliche* formulation of myth;
    2) The Enlightenment formulation of myth;
    3) The existentialist formulation of myth.

According to the first, myth is understood as a particular soteriological, cultic narrative, prevalent in the Hellenistic world, originating in Iran. Specifically, myth is used to indicate the pre-Christian story of the Heavenly Redeemer or Primal Man, together with the motifs and ideas associated with this. According to the second formulation, myth specifies a particular kind of thinking (pre-rational) characteristic of a primitive period of history and manifest in a pre-scientific view of the world. According to the third, myth intends to offer a very particular understanding of human existence ("*entweltlicht*") but does this in a mode of thought alien to itself ("*objectivierend*").

In terms of a chronological pattern, these three formulations of myth are related as follows. The *Religionsgeschichtliche* formulation of myth is the only one which Bultmann uses in the early twenties (1920-1926), and it remains predominant in his discussion of myth through the early thirties (1933). Bultmann receives this understanding of myth from R. Reitzenstein and W. Bousset. He uses it in both historical-exegetical and systematic theological writings of the twenties. Remnants of this formulation of myth continue to find expression in Bultmann's use of the term after 1941. However, the basic formulation of myth characteristic of this tradition recedes into the background after 1934. The discussion of the *Religionsgeschichtliche* formulation of myth provides the subject matter of Chapter III.

The Enlightenment formulation of myth is never used by Bultmann until 1930. Prior to this, he rejects this understanding of myth in an unqualified, undialectical manner. From 1930 on, this formulation of myth continues to appear in his writings until it acquires the strong, though subordinate, position which it enjoys in his discussion of 1941. After 1941, Bultmann continues to speak of myth in terms of this Enlightenment use of the term. This formulation of myth was first developed in 1681 by Bernard Fontenelle, mediated to German biblical criticism through the classical studies of C.G. Heyne, first appropriated in biblical studies by J. G. Eichorn in his *Einleitung ins Alte Testament* of 1787 and, in countless variations, became the predominate form of the concept of myth in nineteenth-century biblical studies. The discussion of this formulation of myth constitutes the subject matter of Chapter IV.

The existentialist formulation of myth appears in two distinct moments in the development of Bultmann's thought. In the period 1925-1933, when Bultmann was most creatively developing his theological and exegetical appropriation of Heidegger's existentialist categories, references to myth as an expression of self-understanding began to appear. However, the technical, existentialist, hermeneutical concept of myth as "objectifying" is not present in this period, nor is there any systematic connection established between Bultmann's *Religionsgeschichtliche* understanding of myth and his Heideggerean anthropological categories. This occurs only in the second phase of development, after 1934, when Hans Jonas joined together Heidegger's ontology with an Hegelian dialectic. The hermeneutical concept of "objectifying" was born of this union of Hegel and Heidegger, first developed by Jonas in his study of Gnosticism and later appriopriated by Bultmann for demythologizing the New Testament. The elucidation of this idealist-existentialist formulation of myth is the subject matter of Chapter V.

b. *The philosophical-theological origins of demythologizing*

Bultmann's theology as a whole, including demythologizing, is rooted in the fusion of a particular philosophical conceptuality with a distinct theological intentionality. The fundamental philosophical conceptuality is derived from Marburg Neo-Kantianism, especially its epistemology, and even more particularly, its radical transmutation of the object given for thought into the objectified construct of thought. The fundamental theological intentionality is rooted in the tradition of Lutheran theology, especially its anthropology, and even more particularly, its understanding of the being of man in terms of the radical dichotomy of "faith" and "works." The mean-

ing of Bultmann's concept of myth, and his project of demythologizing in general, may be understood in a coherent, consistent, and
comprehensive manner only as grounded in this particular philosophical-theological matrix.

Several elements in this proposition require preliminary clarification.

By Neo-Kantianism, I refer to a philosophical movement which
flourished in Germany at the end of the nineteenth and beginning
of the twentieth centuries. While fundamentally Kantian in its
methodology and epistemological focus, it was genuinely new in its
adaptation of Kant's philosophy to the problems arising out of new
forms of scientific inquiry and knowledge. I specify Marburg Neo-
Kantianism, however, and have no concern with Neo-Kantianism
as a general philosophical movement. For only in Marburg did Neo-
Kantian philosophy take as its epistemological point of departure
the new mathematics and mathematical physics. The Neo-Kantianism of Heinrich Rickert, for example, found its point of departure
in the historical and social sciences, and hence developed along
sharply different lines. Bultmann's fundamental dualism of existential and objectified reality is thoroughly consistent with the Marburg interpretation of Kant, but bears no peculiar affinity to other
forms of Neo-Kantianism.

By Marburg Neo-Kantianism, I mean specifically three thinkers:
Paul Natorp, Hermann Cohen, and Wilhelm Herrmann. Herrmann
was Bultmann's beloved theological mentor and Marburg theologian; Natorp and Cohen were the philosophical founders of the
school. I am concerned with Bultmann's relationship with these
three figures insofar as they share in common a particular epistemological position.

Chapter II begins with an exposition of Bultmann's appropriation
of Marburg Neo-Kantian philosophy. This chapter comes first in the
statement of the argument since it discloses the conceptual foundations for Bultmann's entire discussion of myth. Apart from the
unifying philosophical conceptuality provided by this initial
chapter, it would be difficult, if not impossible, to discern the connection between the three distinct formulations of myth developed
in the succeeding chapters. In light of Chapter II, however, each of
the three following chapters comes to express a movement of
thought comprehensible in terms of this fundamental understanding
of reality. The focus of this chapter falls upon an analysis of Bult-

mann's essay of 1920, "Religion und Kultur." This essay is examined in the context of his related writings of this period and in light
of the larger tradition of Marburg Neo-Kantian philosophy.

While Neo-Kantianism provides the conceptual foundations for
Bultmann's theology, it should be folly to suggest that his thought
could be adequately understood as if it were driven or determined
in its intention by any philosophical conceptuality. Ott discovered
the impossibility of reducing Bultmann's thought to the philosophy
of Heidegger; I should not want to repeat this error by substituting
Marburg Neo-Kantianism for Heidegger, however more appropriate
the former may be than the latter. Therefore I also speak of the
theological intention which informs—in the sense of motivating and
giving shape to—Bultmann's thought. At this point, it is necessary
to speak of Bultmann's continuity with an understanding of human
existence rooted in a particular version of the Lutheran dichotomy
of "faith" and "works."

Considerable caution is required in any statement of Bultmann's continuity with Lutheran theology. I therefore stress the
distinction between a theological *intentionality* and a philosophical
conceptuality. It is hermeneutical folly to attempt to specify the
structure of Bultmann's thought by reference to the sixteenth-
century theological concepts of Luther. In the case of Bultmann,
as with any other thinker, it is necessary to understand the fundamental conceptuality of his thought in terms of a precise and coherent body of concepts available to him in his own historical situation. Vague references to a religious-existential continuity with
Luther and the Reformation may not become a substitute for a
rigorous understanding of Bultmann's thought in his own historical
context and in clear, univocal concepts. Therefore, I identify
Bultmann's continuity with Lutheranism at the level of intentionality, and not conceptuality; for when this fundamental
Lutheran apprehension of existence comes to expression in Bultmann's thought, it does so only in the specific conceptuality and
context of thought provided by Neo-Kantianism.

Furthermore, I do not speak of Bultmann's continuity with
Luther, but rather of Bultmann's Lutheran theological tradition.
To the best of my knowledge, Bultmann did not pursue an independ-
ent study of Luther or the thought of the Reformation, and the
Luther he knows is always mediated to him through the specific
traditions of late nineteenth-century Lutheranism. To specify this

further, I speak of Bultmann's continuity with Lutheranism as limited to a particular anthropology; one is not likely to find a Lutheran theology of the Church, sacraments, or Christology in Bultmann. Even at the point of anthropology, however, the limits of this continuity need to be recognized. In Bultmann's version of Lutheran anthropology, the twentieth-century insecurity of the ego before a threatening world has replaced the sixteenth-century insecurity of the conscience before a judging God. In its existential intentionality, as well as in its formal conceptuality, Bultmann's modern theology is qualitatively distinct from its Reformation ancestry. Hence, all references to the Lutheran theological intentionality of Bultmann must be understood as bearing within them these qualifications.

Nevertheless, with these qualifications in mind, it is proper, and necessary, to speak of a particular Lutheran *dynamis* in Bultmann's theology. This theological intention finds expression in a decisive, clear, and systematic form for the first time in Bultmann's early existentialist writings of 1925-1933. The problem of human existence is here grasped as the condition of insecurity: man's responsibility and care for his own being in the face of a future not at his disposal. In this situation there are two concrete existential options present to man: he may try to secure his threatened existence by means of his own achievements through placing the known, visible, tangible world at his disposal; or, he may accept his insecurity through faith in the God of the future whom he knows in the revelation of Jesus Christ. It is precisely these two fundamental antithetical existential attitudes which Bultmann finds expressed in the Lutheran dichotomy of justification by faith and justification by works.

This proposition specifies not only Marburg Neo-Kantianism and Lutheran anthropology, but a particular fusion of the two. In Bultmann's theology, one never encounters the one apart from the other, but always as present in and through the other. Bultmann's form of Neo-Kantianism is idiosyncratic, decisively modified by his theological position. And the reverse of this is also true. Bultmann's Lutheranism is inseparably bound up with the presuppositions of his Neo-Kantian philosophy. The fundamental category through which Bultmann develops his Lutheran anthropology is the so-called existentialist hermeneutical concept of objectifying. Objectifying, however, is in its origins a Neo-Kantian epistemological category—indeed, the Neo-Kantian epistemological category —which has been here adapted by Bultmann for the purposes of his theological-existential intention. Its meaning, however, even at an existential level, always presupposes the epistemological dualism of its Neo-Kantian roots. This is why the theological category of "works" can come to express, not the false understanding of man's standing before God as conscience, but the false understanding of man's standing before the threatening world as reason. In Bultmann, one does not meet Lutheranism apart from Neo-Kantianism, or Neo-Kantianism apart from Lutheranism.

While Bultmann's Neo-Kantian categories are clarified in Chapter II, his theological intentionality appears first in section one of Chapter V. This is the chapter devoted to the existentialist formulation of myth. Bultmann's theological concern is set in this chapter in order to make it clear that Bultmann's earliest appropriations from Heidegger—as expressed in his writings of 1925-1933— —are already informed by his particular Lutheran concern. One never meets, at any point of Bultmann's thought, Heidegger as Heidegger, but always and only Heidegger's anthropological categories set within the context of a more comprehensive Neo-Kantian conceptuality and placed in the service of a Lutheran anthropology of faith and works.

c. *The historical development of the concept of myth*

The *telos* of the historical development in Bultmann's use of myth is the full and systematic expression of that Lutheran Neo-Kantianism which is the philosophical-theological foundation of his thought: a total and unified epistemological-existential understanding of man's being in the world and before God.

The first proposition stated the historical hypothesis of the argument: namely, Bultmann's use of myth changed significantly from the nineteen-twenties to the period after 1941. After 1934, Bultmann rejected a unified apprehension of myth, as a soteriological narrative given in the context of the cult and in the form of a cosmic drama, for a double-sided understanding of myth, as a prescientific world view, on the one hand, and as a particular understanding of existence, on the other hand. This is the conceptual shape of the historical transition from a *Religionsgeschichtliche* understanding of myth in the nineteen-twenties to the existentialist-Enlightenment interpretation of myth predominant after 1941.

The second proposition identified the systematic structure of Bultmann's theology in terms of a fusion of Neo-Kantian epistemology with Lutheran soteriology.

The third proposition sets forth the connection between the historical hypothesis and the systematic hypothesis: namely, the changes and historical development in Bultmann's use of myth, which may be traced through his writings from 1920 to 1941, disclose a pattern of adaptation through which the concept of myth comes to express in an ever more adequate manner that Lutheran Neo-Kantianism fundamental to Bultmann's thought. The *Religionsgeschichtliche* formulation of myth thus is a genuinely "borrowed" element in Bultmann's thought: that is, it is appropriated by Bultmann as an historiographical tool, for the purpose of New Testament historical-literary research, and without any organic relation to the roots of his own thought. It is therefore no accident that the only creative and significant use of this formulation of myth appears in Bultmann's New Testament studies. His one effort in 1920 to develop the theological significance of this formulation of myth, while of great interest retrospectively, never acquired a systematic unified form, and Bultmann did not make such a venture again. On the other hand, through the combination of the existentialist and Enlightenment formulations of myth Bultmann created a full and systematic expression for that understanding of the world, man, and God which appeared in his early Neo-Kantian writings. Bultmann's fundamental philosophical-theological position is thus a constant throughout his career, while the concept of myth goes through a series of changes in order that the early, borrowed formulation might be replaced by a later formulation of myth more expressive of his own thought. The process of development was a successful one; by 1941, the concept of myth had become a norm for systematic theology giving clear and forceful expression to Bultmann's Lutheran Neo-Kantian origins.

The argument is stated here without regard to the complexities which will appear in the course of its execution. Bultmann, as everyone knows, is a highly eclectic thinker, who has creatively appropriated motifs from a variety of sources, including especially Karl Barth's eschatological understanding of revelation, Martin Heidegger's existentialist anthropological categories, and Hans Jonas' adaptation of nineteenth-century historical idealism to an existentialist anthropology. These other voices will be heard as they appear in the course of a more detailed discussion. Nevertheless, Bultmann interpretation has long been confused because one or another of these eclectic motifs has been taken as the center of his thought. It is therefore essential to state very clearly the foundation indigenous to Bultmann's own thought in order that these other motifs might be properly assessed, as appropriated within and through the center of his own philosophical-theological position.

CHAPTER TWO

THE PHILOSOPHICAL ORIGINS OF DEMYTHOLOGIZING:
MARBURG NEO-KANTIANISM

In the history of modern philosophy, Neo-Kantianism does not occupy a particularly significant role.[1] It most often appears as a transitional movement between nineteenth-century Kantian philosophy and the phenomenology of Husserl and Heidegger.[2] As an historical phenomenon, Neo-Kantianism is sufficiently vague so that there is no clear agreement concerning the precise meaning of the term. M. Bochenski, for example, uses the term 'Neo-Kantian' to designate at least seven distinct schools of thought, including the materialist Hermann Helmholtz and the Neo-Hegelian Johannes Volkelt.[3] In its more technical, and frequent, usage however, the term is reserved for application to the two schools of Neo-Kantianism in Germany at the turn of the century: the Marburg School and the Baden School.[4] The distinction between these two forms of Neo-Kantian philosophy is fundamental. While the Marburg School takes as its point of departure the exact sciences, more specifically pure mathematics and mathematical physics, the Baden School developed out of a concern with the social and historical siences.[5]

---

[1] For brief but helpful introductions to the central tenets of Neo-Kantian philosophy in the history of philosophy, see:
a)   W. Tudor Jones, *Contemporary Thought of Germany* (2 Vols.; London: Williams & Northgate Ltd., 1930), II, 30-75;
b)   John Theodore Merz, *A History of European Thought in the Nineteenth Century* (4 Vols.; Edinburgh: William Blanshard & Son, 1914);
c)   August Messer, *Die Philosophie der Gegenwart* (Leipzig: Quelle & Meyer, 1920), pp. 100 ff.
[2] The significance of the writings of Paul Natorp for Husserl and Heidegger has been recognized, but, as yet, has not been systematically explored: J. Klein, "Paul Natorp," *RGG*[3], IV, col. 1322; Fritz Kaufmann, "Cassirer, Neo-Kantianism, and Phenomenology," *The Philosophy of Ernst Cassirer*, ed. Paul Schillp (Evanston, Ill.: The Library of Living Philosophers, Inc., 1949), pp. 801-802.
[3] M. Bochenski, *Contemporary European Philosophy* (Berkeley: University of California Press, 1956), pp. 93ff.
[4] Richard Falckenberg, *A History of Modern Philosophy* (New York: Henry Holt & Co., 1893), pp. 617ff.; Messer, p. 16.
[5] Bochenski, p. 95; Messer, p. 16. "We must understand that the founders of the Marburg School were interested primarily in scientific knowledge, and that they saw in scientific cognition the prototype of all cognition worthy

For the purposes of this study, the term 'Neo-Kantianism' shall refer only to the Marburg School.

Even here, however, there is some confusion as to the proper use of the term. A. Messer describes the Marburg School as beginning with F. H. Lange and running through Paul Natorp and Hermann Cohen to Ernst Cassirer.[1] More frequently, however, Natorp and Cohen are regarded as the founders of the Marburg School, with Cassirer understood as an independent thinker whose epistemology is rooted in the thought of Natorp and Cohen.[2] For our purposes, the use of Marburg Neo-Kantianism is restricted to three figures:

> Hermann Cohen who taught philosophy at Marburg from 1876-1912;
> Wilhelm Herrmann who taught theology at Marburg from 1879-1922;
> Paul Natorp who taught philosophy at Marburg from 1885-1922.

Natorp and Cohen are the primary philosophical spokesmen of the movement; Herrmann, as a theologian, appropriates their basic epistemology and philosophy of culture and religion, as this provides the context for his constructive theological work.

Considered from a theological perspective, there are significant differences between Herrmann as a Christian theologian, Cohen as a practicing Jew, and Natorp as a self-avowed atheistic humanist.[3]

---

of the name. Scientific cognition, moreover, they identified in all essentials with mathematics and mathematical physics. Epistemology, therefore, became for them an analysis of 'the logical foundation of the exact sciences'; and this limitation of the scope of their analysis became decisive for their whole point of view" (William H. Werkmeister, "Cassirer's Advance beyond Neo-Kantianism," *The Philosophy of Ernst Cassirer*, ed. Paul Schillp [Evanston, Ill.: The Library of Living Philosophers, Inc., 1949], p. 761).

[1] A. Messer, p. 102.

[2] For a discussion of the points of continuity and difference between Cassirer and Natorp and Cohen, see Werkmeister, pp. 773 ff. Cassirer is consistent with Natorp in his fundamental understanding of reason as objectification. However, "in the course of his many-sided investigations, Cassirer became convinced that the traditional epistemology in its usual limitation to 'scientific' cognition does not provide a basis for the *Geisteswissenschaften* or cultural sciences" (*ibid.*, p. 792). As a result, Cassirer attempted to develop a diversity of forms of cultural objectification in which the determining principle was not simply that of logic or causality. "Cassirer finds that the causal mode of integration is only one of many which are equally possible and equally actual. Objectification is carried on, and the particular is fused into context, by means quite different from that employing logical concepts and laws of logical relations. Art, mythology, and religion exemplify these other types of integration" (*ibid.*, p. 794).

[3] For a study of the relationship between Cohen and Judaism, see Trude Weiss-Rosmarin, *Religion of Reason: Hermann Cohen's System of Religious Philosophy* (New York: Block Publishing Co., 1936). For a bibliography

There is also a sharp line of distinction, especially at the point of the philosophy of religion, that should have to be drawn between the writings prior to and after World War I in both Cohen and Natorp.[1] While it is necessary to recognize this sharp turn in Marburg Neo-Kantianism at the end of the war, in order to understand Bultmann's relationship to this movement, it is not necessary or possible to enter into a detailed discussion of the changes in the positions of Natorp and Cohen. Nor is it possible to enter into a discussion of those differences which divide them from each other and from Herrmann. Rather, our attention is focused on the fundamental epistemology which they share in common. It is, therefore, quite specifically the concept of reason of Marburg Neo-Kantianism that is of concern in this study, together with the understanding of the object and the subject of the epistemological relationship.

With few exceptions, modern theology and philosophy have ignored the legacy of Neo-Kantianism. The dearth of philosophical discussion of this tradition represents a great loss for theology. For the philosophical roots of mid-twentieth century theology are firmly

---

of Cohen's writings on Judaism, see Jacob Klatzkin, *Hermann Cohen* (Berlin: Jüdischer Verlag, 1919), pp. 95-100. Paul Natorp understands the divisive effects of religion on society to be rooted in the claim of religion to speak for a transcendent God; it is this claim which a critical philosophy of religion must root out. "In the place of the transcendent God steps man—humanity itself" (Paul Natorp, *Religion Innerhalb der Grenzen der Humanität* [Leipzig: J. C. B. Mohr, 1894], p. 71).

[1] For a study of the several stages of Paul Natorp's philosophy of religion, see Karl Vornhausen, "Der Religionsphilosophie Paul Natorps," *ZThK*, VI (1925), 403-417. Natorp's early religious views were bound up with questions of social ethics and pedagogy and appeared in his volume, *Religion innerhalb der Grenzen der Humanität*, discussed later in this chapter. Vornhausen notes, however, that for the late Natorp, religion acquires much greater autonomy, ceasing to be simply a social vehicle for the actualization of practical reason (Vornhausen, p. 412). Religion becomes necessary to reason as it stipulates the "tension between thinking and believing" (*ibid.*). Religion is rightly understood as the "essence of the German soul as this is expressed in Eckhart, Luther, Leibniz, and Kant" (*ibid.*).

For Natorp's own account of this fundamental shift in his own thinking, see his recapitulation of the history of his thought: "Paul Natorp," *Philosophie der Gegenwart in Selbstdarstellungen*, ed. Raymond Schmidt (Leipzig: Felix Meiner, 1921), I, 151-176. Natorp there describes the impact of the war as "requiring a wholly new focus, a new direction of thought" (*ibid.*, p. 159). The decisive text for the development of Natorp's new philosophy as a coincidence of opposites is his *Practische Philosophie* (1925).

Cohen moves from a strict Kantian rationalism to a religious personalism in his *Religion der Vernunft* (1919). For a discussion of the nature of the shift in Cohen's thought, see Kaufmann, pp. 801-802.

embedded in Marburg Neo-Kantianism. I refer here not only to Bultmann's theology, but also to Karl Barth and the religious philosophy of Martin Buber. In addition, the reformulation of Neo-Kantian philosophy after 1912—when Cohen left Marburg and Natorp began to articulate a more speculative, paradoxical mode of thought—also plays a significant role in the development of modern theology. For a reader familiar with the "later Heidegger," it is impossible to read the "later Natorp" without the strange sensation of *déjà vue*. A striking continuity of vocabulary, themes, and perspective flows from Natorp into Heidegger's later discussion of language and ontology. It is surely not accidental that Hans-Georg Gadamer has written the introductory essay to the posthumously published volume by Natorp, *Philosophische Systematik* (1958). Gadamer recalls with affection and respect his former teacher, and rightly sees his continuing philosophical significance as the point of transition between a critical nineteenth-century Neo-Kantianism and the speculative idealism and Neo-Platonism of the mid-twentieth century.[1]

Furthermore, the anthropological question—which is strictly of secondary concern in this study—should have to become a central theme in any thorough study of the origins of the existentialist anthropology in the German philosophy and theology of the nineteen-twenties. What are the anthropological lines of continuity between Natorp, Gogarten, Bultmann, and Heidegger? From the time of *Allgemeine Psychologie*, Natorp is increasingly preoccupied with the anthropological question, and the task of developing for this question, for the first time, a systematic philosophical conceptuality appropriate to the subject of consciousness and qualitatively distinct from any and every objectified content of consciousness.[2] The correspondence between Natorp and Gogarten during these years is available, and Bultmann, by 1920, is already acknowledging his own debt to Gogarten.[3] However, a systematic historical study

---

[1] Hans-Georg Gadamer, "Die philosophische Bedeutung Paul Natorps," *Philosophische Systematik* by Paul Natorp, ed. Hans Natorp (Hamburg: Felix Meiner, 1958), p. xvi.

[2] Paul Natorp, *Allgemeine Psychologie nach kritischer Methode* (Tübingen: J. C. B. Mohr, 1912), pp. 29 ff. "It is axiomatic that we may not objectify the 'I.' The 'I' and its relation to the object should in no sense be made itself into a *Gegenstand*" (*ibid.*).

[3] For the correspondence of Natorp and Gogarten, see Heinrich Knittermeyer, "Zur Entstehungsgeschichte der *Philosophische Systematik*," *Philosophische Systematik* by Natorp, pp. xxxii-xl.

of the creative interaction of philosophy and theology during these formative years is lacking. This much is clear, however: the older view of Heidegger's radicalism must be rectified in light of a reappraisal of Natorp's writings.

However, all scholarship proceeds under the liberating demand of finitude. Our concern now is not with a full restatement of Neo-Kantianism and its significance for understanding the immediate past and present of theology. Our concern here is only with the riddle posed by Bultmann's thought, and with the task of discerning in his Neo-Kantian sources an understanding of reason which allows one to understand the epistemological presuppositions of his thought.

1. Neo-Kantian Epistemology: H. Cohen and P. Natorp

As their name suggests, the Neo-Kantians were philosophers who took the critical philosophy of Immanuel Kant as their own point of departure. Natorp and Cohen were not, however, nor did they ever intend to be, mere mimics of Kant, and they rejected any responsibility for revising an orthodox Kantianism.[1] They explicitly intended to advance from the position of Kant, specifically to bring Kant's epistemology up to date with the developments of modern science in their own age. Indeed, it was precisely in this adaptation of Kantian epistemology that the novelty of their thought appeared. The science which they knew as innovation was the mathematical physics developing near the end of the nineteenth century. What was distinctive about this new physics was its relative independence, at a fundamental conceptual level, of any empirical movement of thought. Science here did not take the form of an organization and interpretation of empirically given data on the basis of which hypotheses were formulated and tested. Rather, science took

---

[1]When critics of Neo-Kantianism argued that Natorp's position had little in common with Kant, Natorp replied that "it had never been the intention of the Marburg School to revive orthodox Kantianism; that, on the contrary, the step back to Kant had been taken only in order to gain a more profound understanding of the genuine insights of the Sage of Koenigsberg, and to advance from his position in a direction more in conformity with the developments of modern science; that, finally, the spirit of Kant, rather than any one of his propositions, was to be preserved. A poor student of Kant is he who understands the meaning of 'critical philosophy' in any other way" (Paul Natorp as paraphrased by Werkmeister, p. 759). In a similar context, Cohen expressed the matter even more succinctly: "We do not quarrel concerning the name [Kant]; it is the *Sache* that is of concern here" (Cohen, *Logik der reinen Erkenntniss* (Berlin: Bruno Cassirer, 1902), p. 117.

the form of a logical or mathematical unfolding of thought in which the validity of a given concept was established strictly according to its logical and/or mathematical relationship with a larger body of concepts. It is this particular scientific development which provided the model for Neo-Kantian philosophy and determined the fundamental direction of their thought.

In examining Neo-Kantian epistemology, I shall focus upon a specification of the meaning of "object." By "object" I mean the object of the subject-object structure of knowledge. According to the Kantians, how shall the nature of the object of thought be understood?

Kant himself had been wonderfully complex and ambiguous at this point. However, his decisive contribution consisted in his apprehension of the object as a product of the synthesizing activity of the intellect. The mind apprehends a given object only as the intellect integrates sensation received according to spatio-temporal forms of intuition by means of the categories of thought. Any given phenomenon thus becomes a clear and definite object only in and through the act of thought itself.

The Neo-Kantians begin with this legacy of Kant: the nature of the object of thought must be understood by reference to the act of thought itself. In their judgment, this meant that it was not proper to speak of "*Objekt*" as if it preceded thought in any form whatsoever, or as if it were a thing independent of thought itself. Cohen thus regarded it as necessary to subordinate radically the very concept of "*Objekt*" in epistemological reflection. For to speak in the language of the "*Objekt*," unless carefully qualified, was necessarily to lapse into the perspective of a naïve subjectivism or objectivism which the critical philosophy of Kant had overcome.[1] Cohen thus sees the semantic revolution of the German Enlightenment to be itself expressive of the fundamental new understanding of the nature of the object of thought and essential to continuing epistemological reflection.

> The word which presents the new meaning of the "*Objekt*" is "*der Gegenstand*." The distortions, which had been present in "*Objekt*," are now removed. Any subjectifying activity is rejected. The object is set on its own feet and held over against the understanding as "*Gegenstand*." [2]

---

[1] Cohen, p. 274
[2] *Ibid.*

While Kant had moved in the right direction in specifying the nature of the object as *"der Gegenstand"* of thought, he had, according to the Neo-Kantians, not been consistent and thorough in executing his own critical movement of thought. He had thus allowed elements extrinsic to the act of thought to enter into the determination of the nature of the object of thought. For the Neo-Kantians, this was Kant's fundamental failure and it appeared at two decisive points: 1) Kant's theory of sensibility, especially the role of sensation (*Empfindung*) as the 'given' for thought and necessary to knowledge; 2) Kant's notion of the *Ding-an-sich* or "transcendental object."[1] In both of these instances, the Neo-Kantians found Kant to be defective in carrying through his own methodological revolution. To understand the epistemological schema fundamental to Bultmann's theology, one must first come to terms with the Neo-Kantian revision of Kant at these two points.

Concerning their understanding of the point of departure of thought, the Neo-Kantians were clear, consistent, and unanimous in their rejection of Kant. As Cohen writes,

> Here is the fundamental weakness of Kant: that thinking has its beginning in something outside of itself. We begin with thinking itself. Thought does not need to have its origins outside of itself.[2]

For Cohen, this "something outside of itself" refers specifically to the manifold of sensory intuition which Kant regards as "the presupposition for the unity of the synthesis of thought."[3] That a unified object of thought should arise out of such a plurality is inconceivable to Cohen, and he regards this "weakness" of Kant to be symptomatic of the continuing influence on Kant of the "sensualist and scientific empiricism" of his English predecessors.[4]

Cohen thus rejects unqualifiedly any notion of a manifold of sensa given independently of thought itself and understood to be *"gegeben"* for thought. On the contrary, "thought may regard as *'gegeben'* only that sort of thing which it may discover itself."[5] As an example of this right understanding of the *"gegeben"* of

---

[1] For a discussion of Kant's use of these terms in the *Critique of Pure Reason*, see Norman Kemp Smith, *A Commentary to Kant's "Critique of Pure Reason"* (New York: Humanities Press, 1962), pp. 79-85; 204-208.

[2] Cohen, p. 11.

[3] *Ibid.*, p. 24.

[4] *Ibid.*

[5] *Ibid.*, p. 68.

thought, Cohen refers to a writing of Euclid in which the concepts of
point, line, and space are treated as *"gegeben."* [1] Since these may be
discovered by thought, they are rightly regarded as that which is
given for thought. As for sensation, Cohen's last word is as follows:
"Empfindung" finally can be nothing else but a question mark." [2]

Two factors inform this Neo-Kantian departure from Kant in
understanding the nature of the "given" for thought. The first
involves their new interpretation of space and time. For Kant,
space and time were forms of intuition and as such were distinguished from the categories of thought. It was therefore possible for
Kant to speak of sensory intuition as having a definite content—as
being in immediate relation to the object—even as considered apart
from the categories of thought. To be sure, such sensory intuition
apart from the categories of thought was "blind," but it was not
"empty," without definite content.[3] The Neo-Kantians, however,
rejected the distinction between forms of intuition and categories of
thought. As a result, space and time became categories of thought
so that it was obviously no longer possible to speak of a discreet
content of sensory intuition apart from thought itself. Sensation,
considered as the content of sensory intuition, could only be
understood as an "undetermined x," "a fleeting impression,"
"a mere blob," "a question mark," "the chaotic unstructured flow . . .
that constitutes the mother's lap of consciousness." [4]

The second factor which enters into the Neo-Kantian revision of
the Kantian *"gegeben"* appears in their distinction between a psychological consciousness and a logical consciousness. Cohen and
Natorp were quite clearly responding in their epistemology not
only to the new mathematical science of their age, but also to the
new psychology. Indeed, what Hume was to Kant, the new psychology was to the Neo-Kantians. If it did not arouse them from a
deep slumber, it did alert them to the confusion inherent in any
effort to include in an understanding of reason any data other than
that intrinsic to reason itself. G. Lotze had attempted to include
psychic data as an element intrinsic to the act of knowledge, and

---

[1] *Ibid.*

[2] *Ibid.*, p. 389.

[3] As illustrative of this point, Smith cites the dictum of Kant, "Thoughts
without content are empty; intuitions without concept are blind" (Smith,
p. 80).

[4] Natorp, *Religion innerhalb* . . ., p. 45.

thus join the results of the new psychology with epistemology. Johannes Volkelt, a Neo-Hegelian contemporary of Natorp and Cohen, had proposed a double foundation for knowledge: the immediacy of the phenomena of consciousness and the transcendental laws of thought.[1] The Neo-Kantians rejected these, and similar epistemological ventures, which failed to sustain the fundamental distinction between a logical structure of *Denken* and a psychological description of *Vorstellung*. Thought is grounded only in itself, and is not to be confused through any accidental connection with the individual psychological consciousness of the thinker.

Cohen and Natorp agree in distinguishing between this psychological consciousness of the individual and the logical consciousness of pure thought according to the concepts of *Bewusstheit* and *Bewusstsein*. *Bewusstheit* means that immediate consciousness which includes sensations, as well as instincts, and which man shares in common with the animals.[2] *Bewusstsein* means the consciousness which is the subject and ground of knowledge. It is equivalent with the "scientific *Bewusstsein*" or, more simply, "*Geist*."[3] Cohen regards Kant's view of sensation as a pre-critical motif of his thought, in that it fails to distinguish between the content of *Bewusstheit* and *Bewusstsein*. "Whoever takes *Empfindung* as independent data for thought confuses *Bewusstheit* with *Bewusstsein*."[4]

The Neo-Kantians thus corrected Kant's understanding of the nature of the object of knowledge by eliminating any data given for thought independently of thought itself. However, Cohen was clear that this epistemological defect of Kant was itself rooted in the "pre-critical ontology" which Kant had in his own work. This ontology found its decisive expression, of course, in Kant's notion of the thing-in-itself, or transcendental object, as the ultimate and non-empirical unifying ground of our knowledge of the object. Unlike other interpreters of Kant, Cohen was not willing to dismiss the *Ding-an-sich* as an early and peripheral motif: "it appears everywhere, from beginning to end, and it cannot be placed in brackets."[5] This "old ontology" permeates Kant's view of sensa-

---

[1] Johannes Volkelt, "Mein philosophischer Entwicklungsgang," *Philosophie der Gegenwart in Selbstdarstellungen*, ed. Raymond Schmidt (Leipzig: Felix Meiner, 1923), pp. 232ff.

[2] Cohen, p. 365.

[3] *Ibid*.

[4] *Ibid*., p. 392.

[5] *Ibid*., p. 363. Cf. Smith, p. 232.

tion because, in some sense, Kant suggests the object transcending thought is the determinant of the materials of sensation. Hence, sensory intuition was a necessary condition for any cognitive judgment concerning an existent object. Therefore, for the Neo-Kantians to correct the epistemology it was also necessary to correct Kant's ontology; the notion of the *Ding-an-sich* had to be eliminated, and Being (*Sein*) had to be understood as grounded in thought itself.

At this point also, the Neo-Kantians were clear, consistent, and unanimous in their revision of Kant. The notion of *Objekt*, which had been rejected as the initially given referent of thought, now reappears as the stated goal of end of thought. In its new status, the object, as the product of thought, replaces the Kantian "thing." Natorp describes this particular Neo-Kantian extension of the Kantian understanding of object as follows:

> An object, whether it be of knowledge or of the will, exists for our consciousness only through a positing or being formed by consciousness. Objects are not "given"; consciousness forms them, out of given materials to be sure, but according to its own laws of form. In this respect is all objectifying the creative deed of consciousness.[1]

The object, rejected as given for thought, now reappears as the product of thought. The semantic legacy of this Neo-Kantian extension of Kant's epistemological revolution appears in the double fate of the term "*Objekt*": on the one hand, as already observed in Cohen, the noun form of "*Objekt*" recedes into the background and is replaced by "*der Gegenstand*"; on the other hand, the verbal form ("*objektivieren*"), together with the verbal form of the adjective ("*objektivierend*") and noun ("*Objektivierung*"), become increasingly prominent. Thinking is objectifying; it is that activity which has as its goal and product the "construction," "positing," or "projecting" of objects. Even when the noun form of "*Objekt*" is used in Neo-Kantianism, it must be understood within this verbal epistemological and ontological perspective. For it is finally this verbal formulation of objectifying that comes to replace the "old ontology" of Kant's "thing." Werkmeister has summarized this Neo-Kantian movement of thought as follows:

> So interpreted the "object" of cognition becomes an anticipation, a "projection," and ceases to be an unapproachable "thing-in-

---

[1] Natorp, *Religion innerhalb* . . ., p. 39.

itself," a something which literally and in the absolute sense transcends all cognition. There is no longer any need for the assumption that objects exist in and by themselves. All we need accept now is the possibility of an orderly progress of cognition, the possibility of establishing an all-comprehensive context according to law, the method of securing scientific cognition. The "object" becomes the ultimate goal of that process, the ultimate determination of the "x" in our original question.[1]

Two observations may be helpful in considering this Neo-Kantian ontology. First, it must be recognized that for Natorp and Cohen in their early writings, Being is systematically and seriously grounded in the objectifying movement of reason. This point needs to be made only because a theological reader is likely to approach this Neo-Kantian discussion with Bultmann's deontologized form of objectifying reason in mind. However, Cohen and Natorp use the full resources of the language of Being to describe the fullness of reality which is the product of objectifying reason. As Cohen writes, "Only thinking may produce that which may be regarded as Being (*Sein*)." [2] Or again, "In a nutshell, the *Gegenstand* comprehends within itself the world. One need no longer appeal to nature, as Kant had done." [3] There is thus a correlation between the contents constituted in consciousness and the objects of the real world. "In place of the old ontology, in which the thing serves as the foundation for the actuality of *Sein*, steps forth here *Bewusstsein*. For the possibilities of *Sein* correspond to the possibilities of *Bewusstsein*." [4] In a somewhat more lyrical fashion, Natorp expresses the relationship between objectifying reason and the fullness of that reality which man knows as his world:

> In the beginning was the act, the creative act of the formation of the object, in which alone man built up himself, his human nature, and as he objectified himself in this, the stamp of his spirit was fundamentally and in a completely unified manner impressed upon his world. Rather, a whole world of such worlds, all of which he may call his own. The creative ground of such a deed as the formation of the objects is the law: that fundamental law which one still designates as *Logos, Ratio, Vernunft.*[5]

---

[1] Werkmeister, p. 765.
[2] Cohen, p. 67.
[3] *Ibid.*, p. 275.
[4] *Ibid.*, p. 363.
[5] Paul Natorp as quoted by Messer, p. 106.

A second observation relevant to this Neo-Kantian ontology is suggested in the Natorp quote cited above: namely, the subject of reason or consciousness must be understood in terms of the strictly logical form of Neo-Kantian idealism. By logic is not meant a logic, or any logic, but the logic of pure knowledge, a logic which is articulated in the form of universal and necessary concepts. Thus, one may not construe the terms "objectify," "posit," or "project" along the lines of a subjectivistic epistemology. Everything that belongs to the merely individual, the psyche, or the accidental has been eliminated from the understanding of *Bewusstsein*. Cohen speaks with scorn of this subjectifying view of knowledge, which he identifies with Medieval scholasticism, and which invests all substance in an absolute subject and regards the object as its "mere plaything." [1] It is thus not man in his individuality who is understood to be the subject of knowledge within the Neo-Kantian schema, but *Geist*, understood as a transcendental, purely logical point of consciousness. Bochenski describes this Neo-Kantian position as follows:

> The idealism of Neo-Kantianism is transcendental, not subjective. The knowing subject is not that consciousness which constitutes the object of psychological inquiry. All that belongs to the body, to the particularity of the self is excluded. What remains is consciousness pure and simple, which has no more reality than a mathematical point. [2]

While the knowing subject of Neo-Kantianism is not to be identified with man as an individual subject, neither is this consciousness to be confused with an Hegelian form of idealism. The Neo-Kantian *Geist* is more akin to mathematical *Vernunft* than it is to a dialectical movement in history. It is, as Werkmeister proposes, a "logical ideal": "the all-comprehensive context of experience in and through which each 'posited' element leads to all other elements of that context." [3]

In this logical form of Neo-Kantian idealism, the principle of law has replaced sensory data as evidence for the objective validity of any cognitive judgment. Kant's insistence that knowledge include evidence of the senses has been systematically rejected by the Neo-Kantians. A cognitive judgment is true for them only by the evi-

---

[1] Cohen, p. 273.
[2] Bochenski, p. 92
[3] Werkmeister, p. 763.

dence of its integration into a lawful, unified, total structure of thought. The role of mathematics and mathematical physics as an epistemological model is most clear at this point. Basic mathematical concepts are posited, and are justified only in accordance with their connection with the structure of laws of mathematical reasoning. For Cohen, however, there is no qualitative distinction between the objectivity of the mathematical concept and the objectivity of the constructs of pure physics. [1] In both cases, the objectivity of each is determined in accordance with the laws of thought; the laws are not abstracted from any "given" objects.[2]

I may summarize in a single sentence the Neo-Kantian theory of knowledge: to know is to objectify in accordance with the principle of law. In this account of knowledge, the Neo-Kantians have moved beyond Kant in understanding reason as both beginning and ending with itself: thinking begins from its own concepts (not a plurality of data) and ends with the object as the product of thought. I may also summarize what has happened in this Neo-Kantian extension of Kant's epistemology in a formula: namely, the object given for thought has become the objectified construct of thought.

It is my contention that Bultmann's theology as a whole, and his project of demythologizing in particular, presupposes in its fundamental conceptual structure this very particular Neo-Kantian epistemology.

2. Neo-Kantian Epistemology in Bultmann's Theology

One of Bultmann's earliest theological essays is entitled "Religion und Kultur," originally published in three installments in *Christliche Welt* in 1920.[3] Bultmann's Neo-Kantian roots appear most clearly in

---

[1] Cohen, p. 111.

[2] Werkmeister makes this same point in describing the continuity in Neo-Kantianism between mathematics and physics: "The only difference between physics and mathematics is that the axiomatic assertions of mathematics are replaced in physics by hypothetical 'posits' of such a type that their interrelations constitute the most complete system, the most comprehensive context, of the phenomena of experience. In neither case are the laws derived from existing 'objects' by a process of abstraction, but the objects are constituted and determined through the laws of integration" (Werkmeister, p. 777).

[3] Rudolf Bultmann, "Religion und Kultur," *ChrW*, XXVII (1920), cols. 417-421; 435-439; 450-453. All citations in this text are to this original edition. The essay has been reprinted in *Anfänge der dialektischen Theologie*, Jürgen Moltmann ed. (Munich: Chr. Kaiser Verlag, 1963), II, 11-29. An English translation is available in *The Beginnings of Dialectic Theology*,

this early essay, uncluttered by later philosophical and theological influences. Obviously, the validity of the Neo-Kantian interpretation of demythologizing depends not on this essay alone, but on the continuity of Bultmann's later writings with this early essay. For the purpose of this chapter, however, the focus of analysis is provided by "Religion und Kultur."

In an incidental but revealing manner, Bultmann suggests his affinity with the philosophy of Natorp and Cohen by his repeated references throughout this essay to mathematics and mathematical physics. It is Pythagoras whom Bultmann selects as an example of the autonomy of reason from the individuality of its author.[1] He also specifies "the development of a mathematical natural science" as one of the formative events in the modern "emancipation of culture from religion." [2] He understands mathematics itself as "first becoming meaningful in conjunction with the body of theoretical science." [3] While these references to mathematics and the mathematical sciences only serve illustrative purposes in Bultmann's essay, they do provide a clue to the understanding of original principles of his thought which may not be ignored. They remind us of a dimension of Bultmann's intellectual heritage which has fallen out of sight in his later writings but which continues to provide an indirect foundation for his theology of comparable importance with existentialism: namely, mathematics and the mathematical sciences. For it is this particular instance of human knowledge which provides Bultmann, as well as others of the Marburg School, with the basic model for understanding the nature of all other forms of knowledge, human conduct, and the very structure of reality itself.

As described in section one, the distinctive character of Neo-Kantian epistemology appeared in the two fundamental concepts of "object" and "law." The "object" of the subject-object schema was transposed from the status of "object given for thought" to "objectified construct of thought." On the basis of the point of departure in mathematics, this epistemological transposition was a natural one. The mathematical object does not exist as an entity transcending thought nor is it given for thought in a form other than

---

James Robinson, ed. (Richmond, Virginia: John Knox Press, 1968), 205-220. English translations in the text are my own.

[1] *Ibid.*, col. 421.
[2] *Ibid.*, col. 419.
[3] *Ibid.*, col. 450.

thought: e.g., sensation. Rather, the object is the construct of the activity of reason itself. Furthermore, it is also clear in mathematics that there is only one criterion determinative for the validity of any given mathematical construct, and that is its correspondence with the laws of mathematical thinking. For this reason knowledge was defined as objectification in accordance with the principle of law.

Bultmann's use of the categories of "object" and of "law" are consistent with this fundamental Neo-Kantian premise. He also understands the object of reason as that which is "built" or "created" by the "activity" of reason.[1] In a similar manner, he can speak of "the self-unfolding of reason" in its various objective forms.[2] However, Bultmann's continuity with the Neo-Kantian understanding of object is probably manifest most clearly and simply at a purely semantic level. In discussing the object of the subject-object schema, Bultmann occasionally uses the noun form of *Objekt* and its derived adjective, *objektiv*; more frequently, however, he transposes this into the verbal form of *objektivieren* together with its derived adjective, *objektivierend*, and its noun, *Objektivierung*.[3] This semantic peculiarity is present, not only in this 1920 essay, but throughout the body of his writings. It expresses most clearly the epistemological revolution at the foundation of Neo-Kantian philosophy: namely, the transposition of the object given for thought into the objectified construct of thought.

Like the concept of objectifying, so the concept of law is basic to Bultmann's understanding of the nature of knowledge and all cultural forms. He can speak of the *Gesetz* of mathematical thinking, the *Gesetz* of the good will, the *Gesetz* of artistic forms, or the *Gesetz* of scientific thinking.[4] In such a variety of applications, it is clear that Bultmann does not use the concept of law in terms of any concrete system of laws. Rather, law is used here in the purely formal sense of the fundamental principle which determines the structure of relationships in a given mode of thought or activity. It is in this sense that law provides the foundation for each of the forms of culture, and thus is the basis for their autonomy.[5] Or, it is in this sense that Bultmann frequently uses *Gesetz* as the principle of

---

[1] *Ibid.*, col. 420.
[2] *Ibid.*, cols. 421, 451.
[3] *Ibid.*, cols. 421, 419, 420.
[4] *Ibid.*, col. 420.
[5] *Ibid.*, cols. 436, 438.

connection or relation (*gesetzmässige Verknüpfung; gesetzlicher Zusammenhang*). [1]

For the same reason, Bultmann speaks of law as providing the norm in terms of which any particular cultural phenomenon is assessed.[2] Quite obviously the particular laws which ground, connect, and provide the norm for any one sphere of reason differ from every other: the laws of scientific thought are not the same as the laws of artistic creations. Bultmann's emphasis, however, is not upon the diverse sets of laws, but rather upon the quality of law-fulness which is common to every mode of cultural activity. For this reason, he speaks of the *Gesetzmässigkeit* of nature, of the will, of *Erfahrung*, and in a general way, of any rational sphere.[3] To understand this all-encompassing and strictly formal use of the concept of law, it may be helpful to remember Natorp's description of law as "the creative ground of the formation of all objects" and as virtually identical with *"Logos, Ratio, Vernunft."*[4]

Knowledge is thus defined by Bultmann, with the Neo-Kantian tradition in general, as objectification in accordance with the principle of law. On the basis of such a fundamental definition, it is not difficult to see how he could extrapolate this epistemological position into the form of a history of reason. Indeed, the basis for such an historical schema is already developed by Bultmann in this 1920 essay. He quite clearly distinguishes here between the period of the primitive and religious epochs as set over against the period of Greek culture and the modern world.[5] Culture is present in both of these qualitatively differentiated ages of human history. That can only mean, though Bultmann does not explicate this here, that objectification must be present in both of these ages, for the objectifying of the human spirit is the essence of all culture. It is therefore necessary to distinguish these two periods of objectification according to the principle determinative for each. In the primitive-religious period, all cultural objectifying is dependent upon religion and determined according to the purposes of religion,

---

[1] *Ibid.*, cols. 42, 438.
[2] *Ibid.*, col. 421.
[3] *Ibid.*, cols. 435, 450,
[4] Above, p. 48. Like Natorp, Bultmann can use *"vernunftsmässig,"* as equivalent with *"gesetzmässig"* ("Religion und Kultur," col. 421).
[5] *Ibid.*

especially the cult.[1] The objectifying activity of the spirit has not
yet become independent and self-grounded but is mixed with "religious phantasy" and determined by personal-emotional factors alien
to its own systematic, scientific intention.[2] It is only in the Greco-
modern periods that this objectifying activity has won its autonomy
and is now grounded only in its own *Gesetzlichkeit*.[3] It is thus the
introduction of the principle of law that constitutes the decisive
point of transition in the history of objectifying.

In this essay of 1920 Bultmann does not bring together in a
systematic manner his Neo-Kantian epistemology with an Enlightenment philosophy of history. When he does do this, some ten
years later, it will be the concept of mythology that provides the
bridge between the two. Then, under the discussion of mythology,
Bultmann will explicitly set forth this historical distinction between
objectification and law which is implicit in this essay. Objectification
will then become the more comprehensive category, from an historical perspective, embracing both the primitive-religious and Greco-
modern ages of history. The objectifying thought of the Greco-
modern period will then be described as scientific and defined in
terms of a self-grounded sphere of reality unified by the law of
causality. The objectifying thought of the primitive-religious age,
in turn, will be described as mythological and defined according to
its violation of the appropriate principle of law: i.e., the apprehension of the world as a closed cause-effect nexus.[4]

While Bultmann's extension of Neo-Kantian epistemology in this
historical schema is more characteristic of his own thought than of
his philosophical mentors, there are other extensions of this epistemology in which Bultmann simply follows along the lines already
established for him. First among these is the extrapolation of the
understanding of knowledge acquired in the analysis of mathematical, scientific reasoning to become the fundamental form of

---

[1] "The systematic-scientific motive first steps forth in the service of the
cult" (*ibid.*, col. 417).

[2] *Ibid.*

[3] *Ibid.*, cols. 436, 420.

[4] One point of confusion frequently present in the discussion of Bultmann's
proposal may already be clarified on the basis of this epistemology. This
involves the dual relationship of science and mythology. On the one hand,
science is continous with mythology in that both are species of the common
genus, objectifying modes of thought. On the other hand, science is the
opposite of mythology in that it is a mode of objectifying determined by law.

knowledge for all spheres of inquiry. All forms of knowledge, the *Geisteswissenschaften* as well as mathematics, are understood as forms of objectification according to law. As Werkmeister describes Natorp's postion,

> Natorp is committed to the idea that the prototype of all knowledge is found in the mathematical sciences. The cultural sciences find no consideration in the *Logische Grundlagen* or in Natorp's other epistemological writings. The epistemological problems of these sciences are not recognized as such.[1]

Cohen is also committed to the unification of all forms of knowledge in terms of a common epistemological structure. He thus understands chronology to be the link which binds history with mathematics.

> History must be recognized as analogous with mathematics. It is the form of inquiry into the nature of reality. Its sources are the writings in which the representations of the authors are presented with the claim to be real. This claim may not be ignored, but must be tested. Chronology establishes the methodological foundation for this testing. ... Thus, reality for history is analogous to what reality is for the mathematical sciences of nature, and so through chronology, history is bound together with mathematics.[2]

Bultmann's discussion of history in this 1920 essay is consistent with this methodological commitment. History is understood to be constituted through the objectifications of reason in accordance with the laws of historical development just as mathematics is built up through the formation of concepts in accordance with mathematical laws. Throughout Bultmann's discussion of history, it is clear that the categories of objectification and lawful connection are definitive for his understanding of historical knowledge and reality.[3] It does not finally matter whether the law of history be conceived of in terms of causality or teleology; what is significant is that history is objectification of reason determined by some principle of law.[4] Religion, in turn, may not be construed as historical because religion may not be described either according to the mode of being of objectification or according to the principle of determination of law.

Bultmann's own idea of history, and the dualistic method of

---

[1] Werkmeister, p. 792.
[2] Cohen, pp. 426-427.
[3] Bultmann, "Religion und Kultur," col. 438.
[4] *Ibid.*

historiography which he eventually evolves, must be always understood against the background of the Neo-Kantian integration of history into a unified structure of knowledge.[1] Historiography is here determined by the mathematical sciences, not only in its formal method, but also in terms of its content. For the possibilities of historical reality are determined always in accordance with the fundamental conditions of reality as such. Like thought, *Erfahrung* is a unity, but a unity whose structure of possibilities is always determined by the mathematical natural sciences.[2] The historian, in testing the representations of past authors, is therefore bound to determine whether a reputed happening is consistent with the structure of reality as known in the natural sciences. Historiography is thus subordinated to the mathematical sciences both at the points of method and content. For both of these reasons, I have stressed throughout this discussion the importance of the mathematically determined sciences for understanding the philosophical foundations for Bultmann's idea of history.

In light of these philosophical roots, I would reject as inadequate any attempt to account for Bultmann's idea of history on the grounds of the biographical fact that Bultmann is himself a practicing historian. Or, to take up another familiar argument, it is simply not correct to suggest that Bultmann's view of history is a remnant of a positivistic tradition in his thought.[3] The Neo-Kantians are systematically non-empirical in their orientation, and Bultmann's historiography is no exception to this rule. Bultmann's own work as an historian suggests that the "firm results" of reason are indeed highly invulnerable to the difficulties of a merely empirical order.[4] It is therefore a rationalist, not an empiricist, understanding of history that comes to expression under these categories of objectification and law. Furthermore, it is also clear that when Bultmann speaks of history as objectification in accordance with law, he is not speaking of a limited, factual *Historie*. He means *Geschichte* as a

---

[1] For a particularly striking statement of this dualistic historiography, see Rudolf Bultmann, "The Problem of Demythologizing," trans. S. Ogden, *JR*, XLII (1962), 96-102.

[2] Natorp, *Religion innerhalb* . . ., p. 41.

[3] Cf. Heinrich Ott, *Geschichte und Heilsgeschichte* . . ., p. 43.

[4] For example, Bultmann continued to hold to the theory of the pre-Christian origins of the Heavenly Redeemer myth even after the textual evidence for it had been thoroughly disproven. See Chapter III, section 4.

whole, as *Geistesgeschichte*.[1] It makes little difference whether this history is organized according to a mechanistic law of causality or a more idealistic law of teleology, which apprehends the whole of history as moving toward a meaningful human goal, or, for that matter, a Christocentric, theological formulation of any such structured total history in the form of a *Heilsgeschichte*. Any such formulation of history falls under the rubric of objectification according to law, and hence is necessarily alien to religion. The one exception to this, of course, is *innere Geschichte*, or in its later form, *Geschichtlichkeit*. This history of the individual self, however, is constituted neither in the form of objectification nor according to the principle of lawful connection, but in the free decision of the moment.[2]

Our emphasis thus far has fallen upon the extension of one model of knowledge into another sphere of knowing: i.e., history. Working within the Neo-Kantian schema, however, it has not been possible to confine the discussion to the question of knowledge, but it has repeatedly spilled over to include the nature of historical reality. From the perspective of logical idealism, the nature of thought is determinative for the nature of the reality constituted in that sphere of thought. Because of this, the reality of history is understood to be a series of objectifications developed out of each other in accordance with their lawful connection. For what does history consist of? "Ideas, institutions, works of art": all of these are ob-

---

[1] Bultmann, "Religion und Kultur," col. 420.

[2] The nature of *Geschichte*, as determined by the categories of objectification and law, and as in opposition with the nature of man as individual or existential, appears in the two following citations:

In criticizing the liberal identification of revelation with an idealistic, teleological historical process, Bultmann writes, "Man, insofar as he participates in this *Geschichte*, is seen in the same way, of *Objekt*, from the outside, so to speak, not under categories which have been won out of himself" ("Die liberale Theologie und die jüngste theologische Bewegung," *GV*, I, 5).

In criticizing an idealist view of history, Bultmann writes, "He [man] is still only a special case of man in general and every individual is apprehended as the expression of a lawful structure of development. That means the subordination of the existential subject of history . . . at least if the existence of man rests not in the general, in reason, but in individuals, in the concrete moment of the here and now" ("Das Problem einer theologischen Exegese des Neuen Testaments", *ZZ*, III (1925), p. 337).

The last citation, which appears in an essay of 1925 as Bultmann begins to introduce existentialist categories into his Neo-Kantian perspective, discloses something of the continuity of the concepts of individual with existential (*Individuum, existentielle*).

jectifications of the human spirit.[1] Again, of course, there is the one
exception of the individual life which comes to expression in auto-
biography and biography.[2] But, with this exception, the substance
of history falls in the category of "the real which is apprehended as
a rationally conceived connection of laws." [3] This is the reality of
Erfahrung which Bultmann sets over against the reality given and
constituted in *Erlebnis*.[4] Heinrich Ott was thus perfectly correct
when he noted that Bultmann understood objectifying, not only as a
universal and timeless epistemological principle, but also as an
ontological principle definitive for a definite sphere of beings.[5] At
this point also, Bultmann is consistent with Cohen and Natorp.

Beyond the diverse disciplines of knowledge and their corresponding spheres of reality, the concepts of objectification and law
have also become determinative for the Neo-Kantian interpretation
of all other cultural forms: i.e., the sphere of practical reason or
morality and the sphere of esthetic reason or art. For theology, it is
the Neo-Kantian revision of Kant's understanding of morality that
is of greatest import. In Kant's own writings, the sphere of practical
reason enjoyed a relative autonomy in relation to pure reason.
While it was not possible to speak of God, freedom, or immortality
as objects of knowledge within the critique of pure reason, it was
necessary to speak of these same subjects within the sphere of
moral experience under the rubric of the critique of practical reason.
As a result of this distinction, Albrecht Ritschl and other nineteenth-century theologians could develop an anti-metaphysical
theology faithful to Kant's first critique and a theological account
of man's moral experience faithful to the second critique. Theology
thus found a secure notch for faith, far from the onslaught of criti-

---

[1] Bultmann, "Religion und Kultur," col. 420.
[2] *Ibid.*
[3] *Ibid.*, col. 451.
[4] *Ibid.*
[5] Ott, *Geschichte und Heilsgeschichte . . .*, pp. 171-172. Bultmann describes
the reality made available through objectifying thinking as follows: "The
reality about which we usually speak is the world-image which has dominated
our thinking since the Renaissance and Enlightenment, under the influence
of the world-view of Greek science. We accept something as real when we can
comprehend it in the total unity of this world, whether this relationship is
conceived of in terms of the law of causality or teleological destiny, whether
its elements and powers are conceived of as material or spiritual. For the
contrast of materialistic and idealistic ideology is, in terms of the issue here
at stake, irrelevant" ("Welchen Sinn hat es, von Gott zu reden? *GV*, I, 31).

cal reason and science, in the depths and mystery of man's experience as a moral creature.

After the Neo-Kantian reinterpretation of Kant, however, this interpretation of faith within the sphere of morality was no longer a possibility. The experience of man taken as a whole, in its noetic, moral, and esthetic forms, was now regarded as an essential unity. Therefore, the language of God, freedom, and immortality was just as inappropriate in the sphere of morality as it had been for Kant in the sphere of knowledge.

For the history of theology, this Neo-Kantian reinterpretation of reason was of great influence It necessarily drove theology out of a dependent relationship upon morality and culture and into a more autonomous understanding of its own foundations in revelation. This is a theme that is decisive for the early, as well as the later, theological writings of Bultmann. Too frequently, however, it has been attributed solely to the influence of Karl Barth, whereas in actuality, Bultmann had already come to realize the necessity for such a non-moral, autonomous interpretation of faith, through the Neo-Kantian theology of Wilhelm Herrmann.[1] Herrmann develops the sharp delimitation of the sphere of religion from the spheres of both science and moral experience as the major theme of his book, *Die Religion im Verhältniss zum Welterkennen und zur Sittlichkeit* (1879). Both the continuity with the earlier Kantian-oriented theology, and the distinctive extension of this in Neo-Kantianism is apparent in the two following citations:

> The fundamental idea which I set forth here, that the object of Christian faith does not fall within the sphere of world knowledge I have already developed in my essay, "Die Metaphysik in der Theologie." I have there attempted to show that the purpose of the Christian community is not known more deeply, but loses its

---

[1] Bultmann has himself made this same point in his 1922 review of Karl Barth's *Römerbrief*. He there describes the agreement between himself and Barth as sharing a common understanding of religion as grounded in revelation and sharing a common rejection of any moralistic, psychological, or cultural grounding of religion. However, concerning Barth's polemic against any immanental understanding of religion, Bultmann writes that Barth "is not original here" ("Karl Barth's Römerbrief in zweiter Auflage," *ChrW*, XXXVI (1922), col. 322). "In fact, Barth must be understood in the total context of the modern polemic against historicizing and psychologizing" (*ibid.*). Herrmann's polemic against these immanental interpretations of religion was no less radical than Barth's" (*ibid.*, col. 321). "In this affirmation of the uniqueness and absoluteness of religion, Barth and Herrmann are one" (*ibid.*, col. 322).

original meaning, if one attempts to make it into an object of world
knowledge by mixing it with metaphysics.

It has been affirmed that the moral consciousness of the individual
should be the source of religious knowledge, and the practical power
of this should be the ground of religious certitude of the reality of
the object of faith. Both of these are false. However, if one calls
for help to metaphysics against this error, so one only repeats in
another direction this fundamental error of Kant to ground
Christianity in that alien to it. The source of our religious knowledge
is for us neither our morality nor any kind of metaphysic, but
revelation. So we call a happening in which we have known the
demonstration of the divine will directed to our blessedness.
If revelation were not presented as the deed of God for us, so could
it also not communicate to us the knowledge of God. For God is
conceived in no other way than as the all powerful will of our
blessedness. His revelation is therefore only possible through an
event in which his will meets us in this definite direction. The
gospel is not for us in the first instance communication of supernatural truth, an extension of our spiritual horizon, but the coming
forth of God into the narrow sphere of man, as Melanchthon expressed
it, *"testimonium benevolentiae dei erga nos."* [1]

Herrmann is not unusual in his critique of Kant's interpretation
of morality and religion. All the Neo-Kantians agree that Kant was
incorrect in linking morality with the individual and that Kant was
incorrect in linking religion with morality. Morality, unlike religion
and the individual, is to be understood as a particular form of objectification in accordance with the laws of the transcendent
"Sollen"; the proper context for morality was the state, or body
politic, not the individual.

The Neo-Kantians had a passion for the unity of reason, albeit a
highly formal and abstract reason, as sovereign over the total
structure of man's experience: noetic, moral, and esthetic. Natorp's
discussion of the nature of the object of the moral will, and its

---

[1] Wilhelm Herrmann: *Die Religion im Verhältnis zum Welterkennen und
zur Sittlichkeit* (Halle: Max Niemeyer, 1879), Preface, p. iii, pp. 364-365.
Herrmann makes this same point in another context. After describing how
Kant contributed to the emancipation of religion by severing its connection
from science, he goes on to note that "he failed to present religion in its
independent and underivable essence" (Wilhelm Herrmann, *Systematic
Theology*, trans. N. Mickelm and K. Saunders [London: George Allen and
Unwil Ltd., 1927], p. 27). "No less clear is the distinction between morality
and religion. In morality man must not obey an alien will, but his own
sense of absolute obligation, which is the moral end of all volition. Morality
always means independence, whereas in religion man feels himself in the
power of a Being to whom he surrenders himself" (*ibid.*, p. 31).

relation to the fundamental unified structure of *Erfahrung*, is illustrative here. Natorp begins by acknowledging the traditional Kantian distinction between the nature of the object of knowledge, as this is established in the time-space continuum of *Erfahrung*, and the nature of the object of the moral will, as this is determined solely by reference to the transcendent *"Sollen."* [1] Having acknowledged this, Natorp then proceeds to show how the distinction is finally overcome in the realization of the act of the will. For "if the object of the will is to be realized, it must conform to the fundamental laws of possible experience (*Erfahrung*)." [2] The same, of course, is true for the realization of the object of creative phantasy in the sphere of art. The result is that the unified structure of *Erfahrung* provides the actual context for the realization of all acts of knowing, willing, and feeling. All of these acts both occur in a common context and share a common structure. The moral deed or the work of art is as clearly an objectification of reason as is the activity of scientific knowledge; knowledge, goodness and beauty are all determined by transcendent *a priori* norms. Neither the moral act nor the creative deed is to be understood as the product of the psychic disposition of the individual, but rather each of these is understood according to the structure of law appropriate to it.

Furthermore, all of these productions of reason were developed only through their essential relationship to the state. Natorp expresses the matter in this fashion:

> All objective forms of the contents of consciousness, in science, morality, and art, are postulated through society and, at each of its levels, establishes itself only through its relationship to society. [3]

Cohen describes the relation between morality and the state as follows:

> The institution of law, which points to the achievement of international law in a coming Union of States, connects the individual with humanity. Ethically the state is thus the medium through which the individual realizes himself, as a member of a suprapersonal community. [4]

---

[1] Natorp, *Religion innerhalb . . .*, p. 41.
[2] *Ibid.*
[3] *Ibid.*, p. 43.
[4] Hermann Cohen, *Religion der Vernunft* as translated by Mordecai M. Kaplan in *The Purpose and Meaning of Jewish Existence* (Philadelphia: The Jewish Publication Society of America, 1964), p. 67.

Because of this position, the Neo-Kantians had an affinity with a variety of social movements in Germany which they saw as appropriate to the realization of the "good will": Marxism, the folk school movement, and German nationalism. The interpreters of Cohen are still embarrassed by his commitment to implement the Torah, as the concrete expression of the rational will, through the educational means of the German state, and thus his rejection of any form of separatist, especially Zionist, movement.[1]

Bultmann's interpretation of morality and its relation to religion is thoroughly consistent with this Neo-Kantian position. Neither the individual nor God may be construed as the ground of moral self-understanding, but reason with its transcendent norms as mediated through the laws of the state and the educational system of the community.[2] Bultmann thus uses consistently the central concepts of objectification and law to describe the character of morality, as already noted. Indeed, it was precisely in the course of his discussion of morality that Bultmann articulated most clearly that principle which Ott and others have called the *"tertium non datur."*

> The pious man may wish to attribute the rational law of his conscience to God. That, however, does not change the fact that, in the sphere of his reason, God does not speak to him.[3]

It is clear enough: where reason is, there God cannot be. *Tertium non datur.*

The connection between this Neo-Kantian view of morality and Bultmann's exegesis of the New Testament also appears in this essay. The radical eschatological interpretation of the New Testament, with the systematic negation of its significance for the sphere of ethics, is obviously consistent with the fundamental exclusion of morality from the sphere of religion.[4] Bultmann further develops this New Testament point in another essay of 1920 entitled, "Ethische und mystische Religion im Urchristentum."[5]

---

[1] *Ibid.,* pp. 53ff. In this volume, Kaplan offers both a discussion of Cohen and a translation and condensation of *Religion der Vernunft.* The latter appears in pages 61-254.

[2] Bultmann, "Religion und Kultur," col. 420.

[3] Bultmann, "Religion und Kultur," col. 420.

[4] Bultmann, "Religion und Kultur," col. 421.

[5] Rudolf Bultmann, "Ethische und mystische Religion im Urchristentum," *ChrW*, XXXIV (1920), cols. 725-731; 738-743.

Bultmann here formulates a sharp critique of liberal theology for its false focus upon the figure of the historical Jesus. Of all the errors involved in this liberal 'life of Jesus' theology, most of which are of a literary-historical character, the "most serious is the confusion of a religiously colored moralism with an ethical religion." [1] For "the image of Jesus which liberal theology has set forth is simply one more expression of a religious moralism." [2]

Bultmann then proceeds to distinguish between religious moralism and an ethical religion of grace. The distinction itself is familiar enough in the history of theology. However, Bultmann does not establish this point on theological grounds: i.e., the distinction of the law from the Gospel. Rather, the foundation for his argument is the philosophically grounded distinction of morality, as an autonomous expression of the rational will, from religion as an equally autonomous phenomenon of *Erlebnis*. As a result, his critique of liberal theology spills over to include a critique of the religion of Jesus, which had become the model of liberal theology.

Bultmann describes the religion of Jesus as a naïve mixture of "worldly hopes, moral ideals, and pious devotion, in no sense a specifically religious value." [3]

> Jesus' belief in God appears in many of his expressions to be a childlike belief in providence and a naïve optimism, as is present in the Psalms and Wisdom literature of Israel as well as in the naïve beliefs of people in many times and cultures. In other expressions his representation of God takes the mythical form of eschatology. One can hardly describe either of these representations as authentically religious. [4]

Fundamentally, Jesus has not yet "de-moralized" religion; that is, he has not yet separated out the idea of God from the idea of the good. Rather, his idea of God is thoroughly determined by the idea of the good. [5]

> [With Jesus] God's will is the demand for the good. ... That is not an authentic religious idea of God; as is always characteristic of naïve thinking, the good appears under the mythical representation of the demanding and punishing, forgiving and rewarding God. [6]

---

[1] *Ibid.*, col. 741.
[2] *Ibid.*, col. 742.
[3] *Ibid.*, col. 741.
[4] *Ibid.*
[5] *Ibid.*
[6] *Ibid.*

In contrast with this naïve and mixed representation of God, which is characteristic of the religion of Jesus and unacceptable to critical modern thinking, Bultmann proposes Rudolf Otto's category of the "wholly other" as a more adequate guide to an authentic religious understanding of God.

> The world of the good is not the "wholly other," but is the creation of our own moral reason. The "wholly other" of which ethical religion speaks is not the demand of the good, but of God, who meets man in his experiences (*Erlebnissen*) in the obedience of the good. Such a man knows, when he feels himself to be a sinner, that it is not the law of the good, his own moral conscience, that judges him in his depths, but he is impure before the "wholly other." And he also knows, if he feels himself graced, that there does not arise in him the majesty of moral thinking, but in the peace of the "wholly other" he knows purity. . . .[1]

It is clear from his appropriation of Otto that there does remain for Bultmann a connection between morality and religion. However, the connection is like the connection between all of culture and religion: in the course of coming under the demands of the moral ideal of the good, something happens to man, inner experiences, which form the grounds of his individuality. Hermann Cohen in his philosophy of religion developed this bond between morality and religion through the category of "sin." Moral conduct fell under the direction of the rational will, as this, in turn, was formed through the education of the state. Sin, however, is the absolutely individual feeling that accompanies moral failure. As such, sin falls pre-eminently within the sphere of religion.

> Religion uses sin to lead the individual to the discovery of his own self and his individuality. Now he ceases to be merely a member of the plurality or universality of men, and acquires an altogether new meaning of his own. This God, whom the individual discovers through his sin, is the God of religion, in contradistinction with the universal God of humanity, the God of ethics. It is the task of the God of religion to accomplish what others have failed to accomplish: the deliverance of the individual from sin, but in such a way that ethical autonomy should not be impaired.[2]

Bultmann develops a similar pattern of connection between the rational will of moral conduct and the interior history which the self experiences as it submits to the moral demand.

---

[1] *Ibid.*, col. 742

[2] Hermann Cohen, *Religion der Vernunft aus Quellen des Judentums* (Leipzig: Gustav Foch, 1919), p. 219.

> When man submits to the demand of the good, he experiences an inner history (*eine innere Geschichte erlebt*) in which he grasps a reality which is not that of moral ideals but a reality of life. ... When man stands in obedience to the good, he experiences through this a destiny which leads him through depths and heights, experiences which in religious language are called sin and grace.[1]

The relationship of religion and morality is thus like that of the relation of religion and culture in general. Religion does not contribute to the formation of moral conduct, but the demand of morality is a condition for the emergence of religion. For morality, like history, is constituted in the form of objectifications according to the principle of law.

Bultmann thus gives to Neo-Kantian epistemology a fundamental role in his own theology. For Bultmann, as for other Neo-Kantians, the object given for thought has become the objectified construct of thought determined by an appropriate principle of law. Mathematics provides the model for all of cultural creativity, and history is understood as consistent with the noetic model of the mathematical sciences. In contrast with Kant, Bultmann and other Neo-Kantians extend the sphere of Reason to encompass morality and art. But with this all-encompassing vision of Reason and its objectifications, what then is the role of religion? What sphere does it occupy in human life? To answer this question is to introduce a wholly new perspective; for to speak of religion is to speak strictly and exclusively of the individual and his experience.

3. NEO-KANTIAN PHILOSOPHY OF RELIGION: P. NATORP, H. COHEN, AND BULTMANN

In turning from Neo-Kantian epistemology and philosophy of culture to its anthropology and philosophy of religion, we cross over a great divide. The change of mood, sources, vocabulary, and even style of language is so sharp that it might appear as if we had lost touch with our original sources. Gone is the cold, formal, rationalistic and monolithic structure of epistemology and culture. The mood is now one of warmth and affection of men of deep feelings. Gone is the figure of Kant as the founder of critical philosophy as the foundation for knowledge; the heroes of the past to which Natorp, Cohen, and Bultmann look are Schleiermacher and Goethe. Gone is the vocabulary of law, of object, of unity, of form, of continuity,

---

[1] Bultmann, "Ethische und mystisch...," Col. 741.

development and connection. The concepts that matter now are immediacy, experience (not *Erfahrung* but *Erlebnis*), the pure presence of the subject, feeling (*Gefühle*) not as the structured feelings
of esthetic reason but as the pure objectless feeling of Schleiermacher's *Reden*, the moment, and above all else, the individual.
Gone is the model of mathematics and the mathematical sciences;
the subject of concern now is religion and its experiences. Every
Neo-Kantian has a philosophy of religion, regardless of theological
beliefs, and before the war as well as after the war, for every Neo-
Kantian must somewhere give expression to this other side of his
nature. Where else can one legitimately express this within a Neo-
Kantian perspective except in a philosophy of religion? Paul Natorp
suggests something of the spirit of Neo-Kantian religiosity, and the
reason for the natural link between their piety and anthropology, in
the following comment from his own philosophy of religion:

> The claims of individuality remain unsatisfied in relation to the
> abstract and impersonal laws of reason; after all, we are individuals,
> feeling men, not merely rational creatures who are subjects of knowl-
> edge and will. We are the heirs of Goethe as well as of Kant.[1]

The Neo-Kantian concern with the individual as a distinct focus
of philosophical attention followed naturally from the radical
exclusion of the individual from any participation in the spheres of
knowledge, morality, and art. It thus became axiomatic to establish
the fundamental differentiation between the categories of *"Individuum"* and *"Gegenstand."* As Cohen expressed the matter in his
Logik,

> The problem of life requires a new kind of *Gegenstand*, a new category
> which appears to create a *Widerspruch*, a *Gegensatz* against the
> structure of the whole system. This new category is to be designated
> as the category of the individual (*Individuum*).[2]

---

[1] Natorp, *Religion innerhalb* . . ., p. 59.
[2] The degree of tension between the categories of *"Individuum"* and
"Gegenstand-Gesetzlichkeit" varied according to the particular author and the
time of writing. Thus, Cohen can write that "the individual appears to
contradict every system, every connection, and every relation" (Cohen, p.
300). The emphasis here clearly falls upon the word appears (*"scheint"*).
By means of the categories of good and evil, considered as the end of human
development, Cohen discerns the moral categories appropriate to the integration of the individual with humanity. The absolute isolation of the
individual from all relations thus appears to be "an error" and "an abstraction" (*ibid.*, pp. 301-304). There is, thus, a wide divergence between Cohen's
overcoming of this tension in the unified moral structure of humanity and

The appearance of the subject matter of the individual not only required a new category, which appeared to overcome the *Gegenstand* appropriate to the sphere of nature, but also a new mode of understanding.

> What is fundamental to the understanding of the individual is the isolation of the individual from any system of connections in which the *Gegenstand* might be considered.[1]

There is thus established through the whole of Neo-Kantianism a fundamental tension between the category of the *Individuum*, on the one hand, and the categories of *Gegenstand* and *Gesetzlichkeit*, on the other hand. It is therefore not possible to move directly and continuously from epistemology to anthropology. Rather, "the consideration of the individual sets before philosophy a fundamentally new task, which requires a new method and a new perspective."[2]

Natorp works out this same fundamental distinction between the individual and the objectified contents of consciousness in the early pages of his *Allgemeine Psychologie*.

> It is axiomatic that we must not objectify the "I." The "I" and its relation to the object, should in no sense be made into a *Gegenstand*.[3]

Natorp moves beyond Cohen, however, in developing a philosophical perspective and method appropriate to the question of the "I." While he regards Pythagoras as the discoverer of subjectivity, he finds that the question of the meaning of subjectivity has been consistently pushed aside, in favor of the more pressing task of objectivity, in the history of philosophy. The result is that we are still lacking, long after the "turn" of Pythagoras, a philosophical statement as to "what subjectivity itself should authentically be."[4]

> So was subjectivity discovered, but not really apprehended, not raised to the level of an independent theme of inquiry.[5]

Bultmann's absolutizing of this tension in the dichotomy of the individual and his objectified world. What is common to the whole of the Neo-Kantian tradition, however, is the recognition that the categories of the individual and the object constitute two qualitatively distinct modes of being and require two equally distinct modes of philosophical understanding.

[1] *Ibid.*, p. 301.
[2] *Ibid.*
[3] Natorp, *Allgemeine Psychologie* . . ., p. 29.
[4] *Ibid.*, p. 10.
[5] *Ibid.*

Modern psychology also has not resolved, nor can it resolve, the question of the meaning of the "I," since psychology concerns itself with the objectified contents of *Bewusstheit*.[1] Natorp insists upon the differentiation of the "I" from the objectified contents of *Bewusstheit* as examined by psychology, as well as from the objectified contents of *Bewusstsein*. It is therefore necessary for a critical philosophy to raise the question of the philosophical meaning of the "I," and it is to this task which Natorp directs himself in his *Allgemeine Psychologie*.

In his essay on religion and culture, Bultmann is quite clearly using the category of *Individuum* or the "inner living I" with the specific meaning of the Neo-Kantian tradition of Natorp and Cohen. The individual is thus defined through a relationship of absolute differentiation from the objectified contents of consciousness. Thus, when Bultmann wishes to define the difference between religion and culture, he need only specify the distinctive form of culture as *"objektive Gestaltung"* and the distinctive form of religion as the *"Individuum."* [2] The *Individuum* may not be confused with any kind of *Objektivierung*, but neither may the *Individuum* be understood by reference to any structure of *Gesetzlichkeit*.[3] Bultmann extends this pattern of absolute differentiation in a somewhat more extensive manner than Cohen or Natorp, but the foundation for his extension is clearly given in this larger tradition. Thus, for example, *Individuum* finds fulfillment only through passivity, in the feeling of dependence, whereas *Geist* finds fulfillment through the active, building, creating orientation to reality.[4] *Geist* or *Vernunft* is constituted in an order of necessity; the individual realizes his own being only in the order of freedom, in voluntary self-abandon.[5] Reason manifests itself in forms that endure through time—ideas, institutions, works of art, and the like; the individual is manifest only in the immediacy of the moment.[6] Reason moves towards externality; it unfolds itself in the objectifications of the visible world. Individuality moves toward internality; the individual is realized only through the interior tension of his own being.[7]

---

[1] *Ibid.*, p. 13.
[2] Bultmann, "Religion und Kultur," col. 421.
[3] *Ibid.*, col. 438.
[4] *Ibid.*, col. 421.
[5] *Ibid.*, col. 438.
[6] *Ibid.*, col. 421.
[7] *Ibid.*, col. 451.

Bultmann is thus consistent with the Neo-Kantian tradition in establishing the meaning of *"Individuum"* through its antithetical relationship with the objectified contents of consciousness. For Bultmann, as for Natorp, the individual is the interior, subject side of consciousness, present only in the mode of *Gefühle* or *Erlebnis*. In no sense, may the reality of the individual be construed along the lines of an objectifying perspective. Or, as Natorp writes, if the primordial subjectivity of man's being must continue to be presented in this alien mode, the element of distortion and deception intrinsic to such an objectifying mode of self-understanding must be recognized.

> We do not demand of ourselves or of others that one gives up this objectification of the "I" (*Objektivierung des Ich*); only one must know that it is no longer the "I" that one has before his eyes, but its image, reflection, representation in another form, a content or object, a conscious *Etwas*. ... As a result, when I recognize myself as an object, when I stand outside of myself to perceive myself, I can do this only in an inauthentic mode, only as I apprehend a fiction.[1]

To apprehend man in his individuality, it is therefore necessary to alter the perspective of inquiry in a manner appropriate to the subject matter. For Natorp, it is a critical philosophy which is preeminently qualified to allow the subject to appear as pure subject precisely because it has first apprehended the object as pure object.[2] The locus for the uncovering of man's being as individual, however, does not fall within the limits of culture and its three rational forms of knowing, willing, and feeling. To discern the presence of the subject as individual in his individuality, one must turn to religion, since it is precisely in this mode of experience that man's being as individual is realized.

Thus, the concepts of individual and religion come to mutually define each other within the Neo-Kantian philosophical perspective. As Bultmann writes, it is the individual that provides the criterion for the distinction of the essence of culture from the essence of religion.[3] Or, to state the matter in its corresponding form, individuality finds its fulfillment only in that transcendence of nature and culture which is the distinct sphere of religion.[4] In Natorp, this

---

[1] Natorp, *Allgemeine Psychologie* . . ., p. 30.
[2] *Ibid.*, p. 8.
[3] Bultmann, "Religion und Kultur," col. 421.
[4] *Ibid.*, col. 436.

systematic definition of religion in terms of the limits of individuality leads to his rejection of transcendence, or any referent beyond the immediacy of the feeling of the individual.[1] In Bultmann, there is a continuing reference to that transcendent power which is apprehended in experience, freeing the self to be itself while giving itself up in abandon.[2] In either case, however, the conventional sociological, theological, and historical dimensions of religion have been ignored or explicitly dismissed as a remnant of pre-critical thinking. Religion is wholly and exclusively defined according to its anthropological focus: it is only that which happens to and concerns the individual.

In a similar manner, the individual is not understood as a totality including somatic, social, and psychic dimensions. The body enters into the meaning of individuality only through the presence of the chaotic drives of nature. Society, which trains the self in terms of character, moral habits, and stable feelings, is important for the upbuilding of the autonomy of the rational will, but this is not to be confused with the concept of individuality, realized only in the moment and defined in terms of that which is absolutely unique, not that which is shared in common.[3] The individual is thus understood as a purely interior phenomenon, divorced from any significant expression in the body or society. With religion, individuality participates in the transcendence, depths, and dynamics of being.[4] For this reason, individuality and religion may be understood only in relation to each other: the power of religion is the ground for the realization of individuality; individuality is the goal or end of religion.

While the limits and goal of religion may be stipulated in terms of the category of *Individuum*, the nature of religion as a distinct human phenomenon appears through a consideration of *Gefühle* or *Erlebnis*.[5] Like *Individuum*, *Gefühle* acquires its distinctive Neo-

---

[1] Natorp, *Religion innerhalb* . . ., p. 71.
[2] Bultmann, "Religion und Kultur," col. 451.
[3] *Ibid.*, col. 452.
[4] *Ibid.*
[5] The Neo-Kantians obviously borrow their category of *Gefühle* from Schleiermacher. They all acknowledge their debt to Schleiermacher, and regard him as the foundation for any further work in the philosophy of religion just as Kant is the foundation for all further work in epistemology. However, they also agree in their criticism of Schleiermacher. The Schleiermacher of *Reden* understood correctly the nature of religion as an individual reality. This is why Bultmann (in this essay), Natorp, Cohen, and Herrmann

Kantian meaning as a polar concept: that is, as it is set in opposition with the activity of *objektivieren* as this is manifest in the *Gesetz-lichkeit* appropriate to each of the three forms of reason. For just as the object has become pure object, with no determination from the individual subject's psychic data of sensation, so has the subject of *Gefühle* become pure subject, distinguished by the absence of any object. *Gefühle* thus acquires its technical meaning as a mode of consciousness which is objectless. As Natorp writes,

> What should be the proper object of *Gefühle*, its special manner of form different from all others? Or, if it has no such manifestation as an object, what defines it as a proper sphere of consciousness? Is there also an objectless consciousness? In a certain sense, yes. For if all consciousness is, on the one hand, essentially a relation-ship to an object, so there is, on the other hand, also a relationship to a subject, whose consciousness it is. In feeling, it is not the content which is brought forth in consciousness but the inward side of the subject which matters.[1]

The distinction between *Gefühle* and the objectified contents of consciousness is thus of a qualitative, not a quantitative order. The three fundamental forms of reason, manifest in the spheres of knowl-edge, morality, and art, are clearly distinct from each other but may—indeed, must—be coordinated with each other. This is not true for *Gefühle*:

> It [*Gefühle*] does not allow itself to be coordinated with knowledge, will, and creative phantasy. It does not designate a particular province (*abgesonderte Provinz*), but rather the entire foundation of

---

quote extensively from *Über die Religion. Reden an die Gebildeten unter ihren Verächtern,* but not from *Der christliche Glaube* except for the purpose of criticism. Herrmann's critique of Schleiermacher's later philosophy of religion expresses the Neo-Kantian position:

> Before Schleiermacher formed the untenable theory of the essence of religion, which aimed at demonstrating it to be a constituent part of every consciousness, he had in his earlier work, his *Über die Religion. Reden* . . ., developed quite a different conception, which in spite of its violent polemics against Kant, betrays the characteristic quality of Kantian thought. He does not treat religion as a demonstrable element in all human consciousness, but as an historical phenomenon which is to be seen in actual existence only in individuals (Herrmann, *Systematic Theology,* p. 30).

For a statement of Natorp's indebtedness to Schleiermacher, see *Religion innerhalb* . . ., p. 37. For Natorp's critique of the later Schleiermacher's failure to respect the limits of religion see: *ibid.,* pp. 55ff.

[1] Natorp, *Religion innerhalb* . . ., p. 45.

all spiritual life, not a proper sphere, but a level, specifically the deepest level, above which all the special contents of consciousness are built, all objectifying, whether it is of that which is or of that which ought to be.[1]

Natorp thus clearly distinguishes between *Gefühle* and knowledge, morality, and art according to "level," not "form." It is therefore axiomatic in the Neo-Kantian tradition that religion, which must be understood in its limits and nature strictly according to an examination of the laws of consciousness, is absolutely to be distinguished from any sphere of consciousness or being constituted through the objectifying activity of reason.[2]

Bultmann draws up this same qualitative distinction in his 1920 essay, only using the category of *Erlebnis* rather than *Gefühle*. It is clear from his one reference to *Gefühle* that he regards the term as inappropriate to express what he intends: i.e., it may be interpreted as a special form of consciousness, like esthetic feeling, rather than as the ground of consciousness.[3] He finds sufficient difficulty in winning an accurate understanding for the theological meaning of *Erlebnis* because of this same confusion. Thus, in a 1922 review of the second edition of Karl Barth's *Römerbrief*, Bultmann has to chide Barth for his incorrect interpretation of Herrmann's concept of *Erlebnis*.[4] Barth treats *Erlebnis* as if it were some kind of psychic process, some objectified content of consciousness. Herrmann never understood *Erlebnis* as a *"Bewusstseinvorgang,"* but always as a totality concept, meaning "the total determination of our consciousness," and it is this characteristic which Barth has failed to grasp.[5] Bultmann makes this same point thirty-eight years later when he describes Karl Barth's attack on *Erlebnis* as suffering from a "psychological misunderstanding of the life of the soul." [6] It is precisely the totality character of *Erlebnis*, together with its qualitative differentiation from any objectified contents of consciousness, which Natorp has described under his category of *Gefühle* and which Barth had failed to recognize in Herrmann.

---

[1] *Ibid.*
[2] Natorp defines the philosophy of religion as "an examination of the formulation of religion according to the laws of consciousness" (Natorp, *Religion innerhalb* . . ., p. 115).
[3] Bultmann, "Religion und Kultur," col. 435.
[4] Bultmann, "Karl Barth's Römerbrief . . .," *ChrW* (1922), col. 320.
[5] *Ibid.*, cols. 358-359.
[6] Rudolf Bultmann, *Jesus Christ and Mythology* (New York: Charles Scribner's, 1958), p. 70.

Having briefly sketched Bultmann's continuity with Neo-Kantianism, at the points of his understanding of the individual and of religion, I will now bring together in a systematic manner the two sides of Bultmann's Neo-Kantian legacy: namely, the Neo-Kantian epistemology and philosophy of culture, on the one hand, and the Neo-Kantian anthropology and philosophy of religion, on the other hand. The pattern of thought to be described is peculiar to Bultmann and not characteristic of his philosophical predecessors. Nevertheless, it will be obvious that Bultmann is simply developing in a partcular version that fundamental philosophical conceptuality already examined in Natorp and Cohen. While developing this pattern on the basis of Bultmann's essays of 1920, I understand the fundamental conceptual structure to be the continuing philosophical foundation for Bultmann's theology as a whole. For the sake of clarity, I shall develop this pattern in terms of three perspectives of interpretation.

The fundamental concepts in this position are *Vernunft* and *Individuum*, *Objektivierung* and *Erlebnis*, together with their derived forms. In both of these pairs of concepts, the relationship between the two is defined strictly in terms of mutual exclusiveness and discontinuity. The individual is systematically excluded from any participation in the spheres of reason.[1] The categories of law and objectification, definitive for the understanding of reason, are systematically excluded from any application to the individual. In contrast with every *Objektivierung*, the *Individuum* is pure subject; in contrast with every principle of law, the individual is absolutely unique and may not be subsumed under any system of relations.[2]

What is true for the relation of *Individuum* and *Vernunft* is also true for the relation of *Gefühle* and/or *Erlebnis* and *objektivieren* and/or *Objektivierung*. As Natorp writes,

> To objectify means to form, to limit, to hold fast. Feeling is much more that which is itself a limitless and formless heaving and stirring, which precedes all formation of objects and is at their foundation. In consciousness the subject is a firm and fixed item, but in feeling, nothing is firm and fixed, but all is in the flow of becoming, all is united with an uninterrupted continuum.[3]

---

[1] Bultmann, "Religion und Kultur," col. 421.
[2] *Ibid.*, col. 438.
[3] Natorp, *Religion innerhalb* . . ., p. 45.

In Bultmann's language, the same dichotomy appears between *Erlebnis* and the *Objektivierung* which appears as the by-product, qualitatively distinguished from *Erlebnis* itself.[1] Religion is "nothing but *Erleben selbst*," and so may not be confused with history, education, morality, the state, or any other expression of man's being which is realized through *objektivieren* and *Gesetzlichkeit*.[2]

In Bultmann's writings, this pattern of antithetical concepts comes to constitute the dualistic structure which pervades the whole of his theology. It is necessary to recognize, however, that this is a very particular dualism, and may not be confused with a myriad of other philosophical and theological dualisms. This is not a dualism of God and the world, the body and soul, inner and outer, finite and infinite, law and Gospel. All of these dimensions come to participate in this schema but none are constitutive of it. Nor is it a dualism which may be confined to epistemology, historiography, or anthropology, since it is always finally ontological. It is epistemological in its foundation, but it is extended throughout the full range of man's being in the world and before God. No dimension of human existence escapes the structure of this dualistic perspective.

At the level of anthropology, this dualism appears in the form of a double human subject. Man is the bearer of reason, the point of break-through of *Geist*, and as such, the creator of the world of objective forms which he knows.[3] Man is also the individual, the subject of his own being, who experiences himself in the mode of subject in the immediacy of the moment.[4] As the subject of objectifying reason, man is universal, one with all men. He counts as reality (*Wirklichkeit*) only that given in the mode of universality and necessity.[5] As the subject of *Erlebnis*, man is absolutely unique, like no other man in history. As such, he is certain of the *Wirklichkeit* of his own life only in *Erleben*.[6]

This same dualism appears in man's twofold relation to his world. On the one hand, he experiences his world in the mode of sovereignty, knowing the world as the objectified construct of reason in which he participates. On the other hand, he experiences

---

[1] Bultmann, "Religion und Kultur," col. 436.
[2] *Ibid.*, cols. 436-438.
[3] *Ibid.*, col. 421.
[4] *Ibid.*, col. 452.
[5] *Ibid.*, col. 421.
[6] *Ibid.*, col. 452.

his world as a threat, as he meets the irrational events of history
which befall him and which compel him to come to terms with his
own destiny as something radically transcendent of his own rationality.[1] In *Erfahrung*, the world is experienced as infinitely rational:
that is, fundamentally determined by lawful orderings and infinitely
open to that movement of reason which would further unfold this
rational structure. In *Erlebnis*, the world appears as enigmatic,
mysterious, irrational, not at man's disposal or available to his
knowledge.

The ultimate religious or ontological symbol of this dualism in
Bultmann's essay of 1920 is the mutually exclusive relationship of
God and *Geist*. *Geist* is that immanental but self-transcending ground
of reason, which is also the ground of the objectified worlds of
knowledge, morality, and art. God is defined as *"die Macht"* which
is *"jenseits"* in relation to nature and culture, *"jenseits"* in relation
to the present expected and the actual events of history encountered.[2] What is fundamental here, as at every other point, is the
relationship of mutual exclusiveness which inheres between God and
Geist.

It is thus obvious that Bultmann's dualism may not be reduced
to an ontic dualism: i.e., a dualism of man and his alien world, or of
God and the world. This dualism is fundamentally epistemological,
with ontological implications for the understanding of any given
ontic phenomenon: man, world, or God. It is a dualism which may
be extended into historiography: history requires objectifying
reason which necessarily demythologizes the past as it integrates all
objectifications into a unified causal nexus; history requires
existentialist interpretation which inquires into the meaning of a
given text for the individual subject.[3] It is a dualism which may be
transposed into the double history of *Geist*: *Geist*, in the mode of
objectifying reason, appears initially in Greece, becomes dormant,
and is reborn in the Enlightenment and mathematical science of
modernity; *Geist*, in the mode of *Existenzverständnis*, appears in the
decisive mode of individuality in the Hellenistic world and, after the
long detour of medieval dogmatic objectification, reappears in the
existentialist philosophy and theology of the modern world. Being
occurs in the form of *Individuum* and in the mode of *Erlebnis*; being

---

[1] *Ibid.*, col. 451; *Infra.*, section four of this chapter.
[2] Bultmann, "Religion und Kultur," col. 451.
[3] Bultmann, "On the Problem of Demythologizing," *JR* (1962), pp. 98-99.

occurs in the three forms of *Vernunft* and in the mode of *Objekti-vierung. Tertium non datur.*

While it is necessary to develop the relationship of these polar concepts in the form of conceptual antitheses, it is also necessary to change our perspective and examine their meaning from the point of view of the existing individual. What then appears is a pattern of subordination and dynamic movement toward a subject-centered unity which includes and overcomes the dualism. Bultmann is thus clear that, from the point of view of the experiencing subject, the dualism is never one of parity. In anthropology, *"Individuum"* is not the equal opposite of *"Vernunftwesen."* Rather, the opposite of *"Vernunftwesen"* is *"Naturwesen."*[1] The being of man as subject is constituted through the tension between the equal opposites, *"Vernunftwesen"* and *"Naturwesen."* The livelier this tension is, the "richer" is the "inner living 'I.' "[2] From the perspective of the actualization of individuality, *Vernunftwesen* appears as a necessary but subordinate element which is overcome even as it is taken up in the living unity of the individual. Bultmann relates *Religion* and *Kultur* also in this structure of subordination. The opposite of *Kultur* is *Natur*, while *Religion* is defined as *"jenseits"* precisely through its relation to *Natur* and *Kultur*.[3] Seen from the perspective of the dynamics of self-realization, the dualism is clearly one of subordination, a lop-sided, unequal dualism. As Bultmann writes in the closing line of his essay, *"Höher als Schaffen steht das Erleben."* [4]

The dynamics of subordination also point toward an integration which necessarily qualifies the dualism. Indeed, the concept of individuality always entails for Bultmann self-unity, not as a given condition, but as a goal to be realized. The "inner living individual" is thus born in the overcoming (though not in the sense of annihilating) of the tension of nature and culture.[5] Beyond this identification of individuality with the actualization of interior self-unity, Bultmann also understands the meaning of individuality to include the intuition of the subject's unity with his own history and universe. Indeed, individuality finds its fulfillment only in religion

---

[1] *Ibid.*, col. 451.
[2] *Ibid.*
[3] *Ibid.*
[4] *Ibid.*, col. 453.
[5] *Ibid.*, col. 451.

precisely because it is only in religion that such an historical-cosmic apprehension of unity is made manifest.

Thus, for Bultmann, the decisive religious question is this: how does a man understand the course of events in which he is set? Does he recognize in this history a destiny which he claims as his own and in which he apprehends an "*einheitliche sinnvolle Macht*?"[1] Or, to express this same point in the language of Schleiermacher, religion means simply an "intuition of the universe" in which reality is apprehended, not according to a rational system of lawful connection, but rather "beyond worldly *Erfahrung* is won a point from which everything real appears as a meaningful unity (*sinnvolle Einheit*)." [2] The unity of the self as subject, with itself and with its own history and cosmos, in a mode appropriate to itself: this is the theme of religion and the fulfillment of individuality. Any description of the dualism inherent in Bultmann's conceptuality may not ignore this dynamic, dialectical interior movement toward unity. The unity of the subject, in its totality of subject-oriented relationships, is a goal to be realized within *Erlebnis* just as the unity of the object, established through its integration in a total system of law-determined relationships, is a goal to be won through the logical unfolding of reason.

However, this qualification also needs to be qualified; for Bultmann's dualism is never genuinely overcome. For this to happen, it would be necessary that the scope of individuality, in the existential act of self-realization, should not be circumscribed by the confines of reason. The dimensions of being which had been originally assigned to reason would then be won back again for man's own existence. Man should find then the realization of that being which is his own precisely in his embodied deeds with others in the structured possibilities of society, and within a continuum of history. But, alas, this never happens. The meaning of individuality, and the possibilities of existence which it encompasses, never spill over to include those expressions of human existence originally claimed as the province of reason. Thus, while it is true that individuality transcends reason in the act of self-realization, it is also true that the concrete possibilities of this self-realization are themselves already determined by the *a priori* limits of reason itself.

It is therefore essential to recognize that reason is not simply one

---

[1] *Ibid.*
[2] *Ibid.*

element in this dualistic schema of Bultmann's, but the foundation
for the whole edifice. In the tradition of critical philosophy, the
object of thought and the nature of thought itself are determined
first; the interpretation of individuality and of religion accounts for
the "left-overs" which could not find expression within the limits
of reason. Natorp and Bultmann are clear and consistent in respect-
ing the critical determination of the laws of consciousness as decisive for the limits and possibilities of religion and man's being as
individuality.[1]

Because of this priority of reason over anthropology, this chapter
has focused upon Neo-Kantian epistemology. Bultmann's anthropology changes. The problematic of the inner tensions of nature
becomes converted to the insecurity of historical existence. Similarly, the philosophy of religion changes: the immediacy intended in
the passive *Erlebnis* becomes replaced by the immediacy of the
more active *Entscheidung*. There is, therefore, no reason to become
unduly preoccupied with these transitory anthropological and
religious concepts of Bultmann's Neo-Kantian writings. What is of
concern, however, is the Neo-Kantian epistemology, as this provides
the fundamental structure and limit for any particular anthropological or religious motifs. For new wine will not change old wineskins.
Unless this epistemological premise is made explicit, confronted, and
challenged, theology shall continue to find itself confined within the
box of nineteenth-century anthropological dualism and distortion.

The critical question for further inquiry into demythologizing is
therefore this: has Bultmann overcome the limits of his Neo-
Kantian epistemological point of departure, or has he simply
explicated the dualism intrinsic to Neo-Kantianism as a systematic
norm for theological expression in the project of demythologizing?

4. Lutheran Neo-Kantianism: W. Herrmann and Bultmann

Throughout this chapter, Bultmann's use of Neo-Kantian
philosophical categories has been considered as consistent with the
writings of Natorp, Herrmann, and Cohen. While acknowledging
the divergence of Bultmann from his Neo-Kantian heritage, I have

---

[1] Natorp appropriately insists that the limitation which reason establishes
for religion is intended for the sake of religion. "Through this limitation is it
[religion] not broken down, but held together. If it goes beyond all limits, it
loses in purity and intense energy what it gains in an extension that is more
apparent than real" (Natorp, *Religion innerhalb* . . ., p. 63).

not attempted to specify or interpret this divergence. I turn to this task in this concluding section.

The difference between Bultmann's version of Neo-Kantianism and the philosophy of Natorp and Cohen may be stated briefly: Bultmann has inverted the ontology of the classical Marburg Neo-Kantian position. In the writings of Cohen and Natorp, the concept of objectifying appears as a creative, dynamic term laden with the substance of being. *Sein* is grounded in *Vernunft*, and the fullness of that reality of man and his world appears through the creative act of reason itself.[1] In Bultmann this ontological pattern is reversed. Objectification, in all its spheres, is stripped of any positive ontological significance and is left standing as an empty shell, bereft of Being. To be sure, these spheres of objectification continue to merit for Bultmann the attribute of *Wirklichkeit*. However, the *Wirklichkeit* which is attributed to the sphere of *Vernunft* or *Geist* is set over against the *Wirklichkeit* of "the *Ich* . . . one's own life which becomes certain only in *Erleben*" and the *Wirklichkeit* which faith apprehends in *Erleben* and which is *"die Macht"* which enables men to become men.[2] In this opposition, there is little question as to which *Wirklichkeit* is the "really real" *Wirklichkeit*: i.e., that which is of concern to the being of man. The *Wirklichkeit* of *Gesetzlichkeit* is appropriately qualified as *"blosse"* when contrasted with *"die Macht"* to which one submits in his inner life.[3] In a similar manner, both *Naturwesen* and *"Subject der geistigen Kultur"* are qualified by a *"blosses"* when contrasted with the *Wirklichkeit* of the *"Ich."*[4] For Bultmann, the total epistemological structure— the rational *Subjekt* and its *Objektivierung*—merits the attribute of *Wirklichkeit* only with the qualification of *"blosse."* This *Wirklichkeit* may include both the spheres of *Natur* and *Kultur*, and may correspond with *"den Hauptinhalt des Lebens unseres Bewusstseins"* but men would look in vain to this *Wirklichkeit* for that fullness of being which they seek.[5]

Bultmann thus preserves for reason and its objectifications the claim of reality, but nothing beyond that. His vocabulary here is thoroughly consistent in expressing his systematic deontologizing

---

[1] Above, p. 48.
[2] Bultmann, "Religion und Kultur," col. 452.
[3] *Ibid.*, col. 451.
[4] *Ibid.*, col. 452.
[5] *Ibid.*

of reason. He never uses an active verb of being in conjunction with reason, objectifying, or law. *Schaffen* or *bilden*, which he does use of reason, are always qualified by the object *"Gestaltung,"* never *Sein* or an equivalent. On the other hand, he invests all the richness of the language of being at his disposal at the point of the individual and his fulfillment in religion: *verwirklichtwerden, Vollzug, Geschehen, Leben, Verwirklichend.*[1] Here there is no qualification of *Gestaltung*, no pejorative ascription of "merely," no differentiation from the really real. It is therefore not surprising that, by the end of the essay, objectifying reason and its cultural construct have become not only ontologically neutral, but even a threat to being, the potential enemy to the realization of individuality. While religion is that which makes the *"Ich" "reich"* and *"lebendig"* through *"Erlebnis,"* rational culture, in its absolutized form, is that which makes the *"Ich" "entleert, . . . inhaltnis, erlebnisarm."* [2] Objectifying reason in its unqualified sovereignty is thus exposed as—not the bearer of Being—but the threat to Being: an enemy that would, if it could, undermine, impoverish, and destroy the lives of concrete men in the name of an abstract ideal of humanity, reason, or culture.[3]

Bultmann has thus sundered in a radical way the connection between reason and Being. In no sense could this ontological denigration of reason be attributed to his Neo-Kantian professors. Rather, we must come to terms with this turn in Bultmann's appropriation of Neo-Kantianism by reference to the very particular shape of his own thought. Two factors are relevant here: first, the social-existential and intellectual trauma which occurred in Germany in response to World War I; second, the Lutheran anthropology of Wilhelm Herrmann.

World War I had an overpowering impact upon German intellectuals. The comprehensive and rigid rational schema for interpreting man's social and cultural existence, of which Marburg Neo-Kantianism was a particularly vivid expression, was obviously unable to comprehend the irrationality and chaos unleashed by the war. As a result, there occurred in both theology and philosophy a widespread disavowal of pre-war modes of thought, together with a devaluation of the social-cultural bonds which unite men in their common life. Somehow, the point of connection between men and

---

[1] *Ibid.*, cols. 436, 438, 451.
[2] *Ibid.*, col. 453.
[3] *Ibid.*

their rationalized culture and society seemed to be lost. There was, therefore, a determined effort to turn away from old patterns of thought. Similarly, there was a new turning toward the irrational and the individual, in both theology and philosophy, as these appeared to offer a new point of connection between men and those forms of meaning in which they live.

Bultmann expresses something of his own existential and intellectual response to the war in a 1917 sermon entitled "The Hidden and Revealed God." [1] As a result of the experiences of the war, he finds himself standing before a new reality, a new abyss and depth of life; "the veil that hid the reality of life from us" had been stripped away and the irrational dimensions of self and society were exposed.[2]

> We no longer understand ourselves and become strangers to ourselves. For we gaze into the abyss of our nature, and our self appears as a play of strange powers. We gaze into the abyss of life, and its opposing powers are incomprehensible to us. We look down into a depth of which we never dreamed.[3]

It is with a sense of shock and wonder that Bultmann asks: "What is it that is still our self, our nature?" [4] There have been unleashed "such dark forces of the human heart," "forces in the heart of man of which we never dreamed." [5]

This encounter with the irrational was not limited to the depths within man. The face of his world had also changed. It was no longer a world of objective forms, constituted and ordered by reason; it was now also the world of the enigmatic, the mysterious, the uncanny, the world of abysmal darkness.[6] The realization of individuality was thus as closely bound up with the encounter with the irrational in the world without as in the world within. In the language of Bultmann's 1920 essay, there is not only the inner tension of nature and reason, but also the confrontation with destiny, "the events in which a man is placed." [7] In his 1917 sermon,

---

[1] Rudolf Bultmann, "The Hidden and Revealed God," *Existence and Faith*, pp. 23-34.
[2] *Ibid.*, p. 31.
[3] *Ibid.*, p. 25.
[4] *Ibid.*, p. 24.
[5] *Ibid.*, p. 32, p. 31.
[6] *Ibid.*, pp. 30-32.
[7] Bultmann, "Religion und Kultur," col. 451.

Bultmann expresses the meaning of destiny in terms of man's reconciliation with the enigmatic forces that are present in his world.

> For what does "experience" mean? It means constantly to enrich oneself anew, to allow oneself to be given something anew. It means to perceive that miraculous forces hold sway in the world, which we cannot reckon with, cannot enlist as mere factors in our work. It means to know that over and above our knowledge, our work, yes, and even our moral duty, there is something else—a fullness of life that streams in upon us completely as a gift, completely as grace. Experience means to receive a destiny into oneself.[1]

To have a destiny is thus to find that unity of individuality which transcends and heals "the split . . . which runs through our lives here and now," [2] it is to enter into that paradoxical and dynamic process of becoming which takes up the conflict between the rational and the irrational in a felt unity of life.[3]

The experience of the war thus brought into sharp focus the fundamental inadequacy of the original Neo-Kantian interpretation of man and his world. The real forces of life appeared to be cut asunder from the objectifications of reason, as well as from those social-cultural bonds which had sustained life. Bultmann was not alone in his quest for a new form of thought, a new understanding of man and his world which takes up "the split that runs through our life here and now," transcends it, and allows for its healing. Paul Natorp, in an autobiographical essay written in 1921, describes the depths of his own reaction to the war. He describes his pre-war philosophy as one which attempted to build, on the basis of the unity of reason, the unity of humanity: to unify the various sciences at a methodological level, and to unify the individual with the community.[4] All of this is past now. As a result of the war, he has to "take up a wholly new focus," "develop a radically new direction of thought." [5] Like Bultmann, his own endeavor is concerned with overcoming the gulf between the rational and the irrational, and with articulating a new understanding of the individual, especially in relation to religion.[6] Unlike Bultmann, however, he sees the

---

[1] Bultmann, "The Hidden and Revealed God," p. 27.
[2] *Ibid.*, p. 25.
[3] *Ibid.*
[4] Paul Natorp, "Paul Natorp," *Philosophie der Gegenwart in Selbstdarstellung*, ed. Raymond Schmidt (Leipzig: Felix Meiner, 1921), I, 152 ff.
[5] *Ibid.*, p. 159.
[6] Natorp understands religion as the realization of the individual self in

necessity for beginning this venture at the fundamental point of his own philosophy: i.e., the concept of reason and its objectifications. He thus focuses his own post-war efforts on the task of a reinterpretation of reason, drawing upon the Eastern religious understanding of the unity of opposites. He expresses this in his idea of "the primordial *Logos*," the *Logos* that precedes Being, the *Logos* that is the *Sinn* of *Sein*, the *Logos* that is the unity of being and non-being.[1]

> This *Logos* is the rationality of the irrational, which only the partial rationality denies, the true reason affirms. Indeed, the integrity of the true *Logos* shows itself in the denial of this contradiction.[2]

The success of Natorp's reinterpretation of the pre-war Neo-Kantian understanding of the nature of reason and being remains somewhat dubious. He himself acknowledges that few seemed to understand the nature of his present work, and perhaps even fewer have understood it since his time.[3] What is worthy of note, however, is the fact that the impact of the war led Natorp, and Cohen along with him, to a critique and reinterpretation of their earlier epistemology.[4] Bultmann, by way of contrast, shared a similar response to the war, expressed a similar concern with the dimension of the irrational and the meaning of religion and individuality, but was not led to revise in the slightest the fundamental pre-war Neo-Kantian epistemology. Nor, I might add, did his later contact with Heidegger change these basic epistemological and ontological presuppositions, even though Heidegger understood his

its present reality within a tradition of German mysticism and idealism. "It is not sufficient for us that Christ has once appeared; we must all become Christs. So it does not help us that an Eckhart, a Luther has lived, a Kant and Fichte, a Rembrandt, Goethe, Beethoven. All historical remembering is as worthless ballast, if it does not enter into our true living again, repeat itself in our souls, become deeper and deeper" (Paul Natorp as quoted by Vornhausen. "Der Religionsphilosophie Paul Natorps," *ZThK* (1925), p. 413.
[1] Natorp, "Paul Natorp," p. 172.
[2] *Ibid.*
[3] *Ibid.*, pp. 153ff. Cf. J. Klein, "Paul Natorp," *RGG*³, IV, col. 1322.
[4] For a systematic statement of Natorp's new philosophy of the unity of opposites, see his *Practische Philosophie* (1925). For a statement of Cohen's transition from his early rationalism to a religious individualism, see his *Religion der Vernunft* ... (1919). For a discussion of the nature of this shift in Cohen's thought, see Kaufmann, pp. 801-802; also, J. Klein: "Above all, it was the question of the individual that was central in Cohen's later years in the reformulation of his thought" (J. Klein, "Hermann Cohen," *RGG*³, I, 1847).

own work as an explicit repudiation of the Neo-Kantian position.[1] It is therefore not sufficient to account for the particularity of Bultmann's Neo-Kantian position simply in terms of the impact of the war. Why did Bultmann tenaciously hold to Natorp's pre-war conceptual schema which Natorp himself felt obliged to re-nounce? Why should Bultmann's participation in the post-war intellectual turmoil of his time leave untouched his pre-war under-standing of reason and its reality?

To answer these questions, one must consider a second factor that entered into the formation of Bultmann's Neo-Kantian position: namely, Lutheran theology as it was mediated to him through Wilhelm Herrmann. At this point I need to be very specific, however and speak not of Lutheran theology in general, but of a Lutheran anthropology adapted to the late nineteenth-century social-cultural situation. For it is this modified Lutheran anthropology that provides the foundation for Bultmann's ontological inversion of pre-war Neo-Kantianism.

The dichotomy between faith and work (in the bourgeois sense of rational-technological achievement for the mastery of nature, not the religious sense of good "works" for the sake of conscience) is fundamental to the Lutheran anthropology developed by Bultmann out of Herrmann. I may describe this modified Lutheranism as follows: in faith, man receives the fulfillment of his being, passively not actively, in *Erlebnis*, not in the *Schaffen* of *Gestaltung*, from God, and not from the world; in work, man struggles to win by his own powers and achievements, especially through reason and his know-ing-controlling relation to nature, a position of security for his own being. The saving resolution to the religious question depends upon the clear distinction between this idea of faith and this idea of work. As Bultmann writes, "Authentic religion is present only in the moments of *Erleben* and even here it is crucial that we distinguish between the idea of faith and the idea of work." [2]

The effect of this anthropology upon Neo-Kantianism was clear and startling. From Bultmann's Lutheran perspective, the self-transcending, world-constituting, objectifying *Geist* suddenly

---

[1] For a lively and brief statement of Heidegger's understanding of his own relation to Neo-Kantianism, see his dialogue with Ernst Cassirer: Guido Schneeberger, *Ergänzungen zu einer Heidegger-Bibliographie* (Bern, Switzerland: A. G. Suhr, 1960), pp. 17-27.

[2] Bultmann, "Religion und Kultur," col. 452.

appeared to be nothing but an enormous extension of man's being in the world in the mode of work. In his later writings, Bultmann explicates in detail this theme of the connection between objectifying reason and the work world. In this early essay, the connection is given implicitly, though not yet fully articulated. Bultmann is clear that the purpose of science and pure mathematics is ultimately to establish man's mastery over the world of nature.[1] In a similar manner, he quotes from Schleiermacher's discussion of the profession and the state, establishing the pattern of relation between the sphere of work and the sphere of belief which may be related to each other only as next to each other, never in or through each other.[2] Culture, with all its science, morality, and art, falls within the sphere of human achievement or work. Salvation is not to be found there or in that mode; but beyond culture, beyond reason, beyond achievement, beyond "all that we might merit or earn is . . . that life, that happiness, which we may only receive as a gift, and never as a prize won." [3]

It is therefore no accident that Bultmann, unlike Natorp, did not apply himself to the task of rethinking the nature of reason or its objectifying activity in the post-war period. It was a question not relevant to the right understanding of salvation. Indeed, there was some advantage for such a theological anthropology in preserving an understanding of work—that is, of reason, objectification, law and culture—that was inimical to the reality of man's existence as a person. The conflict between faith and work was thus made sharper as man was called upon to decide on what grounds he would seek the justification of his own existence. It is also obvious why Bultmann, unlike Heidegger, would not abandon this whole schema of reason and its objectifications, but preserved it through the whole history of his theology. For man comes to salvation, the fulfillment of individuality, or authenticity, not directly, but only indirectly or dialectically: the false understanding of man's being given in and with work becomes the essential negative moment to be overcome for the sake of the true understanding of man's being constituted in faith. Just as the theological function of the law is never eliminated once and for all in Lutheran theology, but is preserved in order to be overcome ever again in the act of faith, so is reason, in its alien and

---

[1] *Ibid.*, col. 450.
[2] *Ibid.*, col. 437.
[3] *Ibid.*, col. 453.

dehumanizing Neo-Kantian form, not eliminated or transformed, but preserved as the expression of the false understanding of existence to be overcome in the realization of true individuality.

The epistemological and ontological dualism, delineated throughout this chapter, is thus fused by Bultmann with a soteriological anthropological dualism. In what mode of being shall man find the fulfillment of that existence which is most genuinely his own: culture or religion, objectification or *Erlebnis*, reason or individuality, work or faith? Bultmann's particular adaptation of Lutheran soteriology and anthropology has found in the dualism of the Neo-Kantian schema a congenial ally. In his hand, Neo-Kantianism becomes a philosophical form used to provide a conceptual matrix for the antinomy of faith and work. Furthermore, in Bultmann's own adaptation of this Neo-Kantian schema, the dialectic of faith and work is clearly preserved through the pattern of subordination and overcoming. Indeed, it is clear that the dualistic pattern described in section three of this chapter, with its absolute antithesis and dialectical movement, corresponds with the pattern of faith, understood in absolute antithesis with works, coming to itself only through the renunciation of works.

Therefore, Bultmann's Neo-Kantian conceptuality may not be separated from his Lutheran theological intentionality. The two are inseparably woven together as the historical and existential-systematic point of departure for his thought. Neither, however, may one dissolve the distinction between these two, and claim for this theological maverick an unbroken continuity with the thought of the Reformation. Rather, one must apprehend both the fundamental philosophical concepts which provide the structure for Bultmann's thought, and the theological motive which informs the direction and purpose of his thought. Bultmann's theological intentionality is described more extensively in Chapter V. For the present, it is sufficient to note the way in which Bultmann's Lutheran anthropology contributes to the particular ontological shape which is distinctive of his version of the Neo-Kantian conceptual schema.

CHAPTER THREE

THE *RELIGIONSGESCHICHTLICHE* FORMULATION OF MYTH

The subject of this chapter consists almost exclusively of Bultmann's "early" discussion of myth. I use the term "early" throughout this chapter in a technical sense to designate that formulation of myth predominant in Bultmann's writings during the years 1920-1933. The year 1920 marks the beginning of this early period for it is in that year that Bultmann publishes his first substantive discussion of myth.[1] The year 1933 marks the end of this early period for, in the following year, Bultmann radically revises his understanding of Hellenistic mythology as a result of the study of Gnosticism worked out by Hans Jonas.[2] In his preface to Jonas' book, Bultmann directly acknowledges the revolution in his own thought occasioned by this work.[3] Beyond Bultmann's own testimony, however, there is ample evidence provided by a comparison of Bultmann's writings before and after 1934 to justify this dating of the fundamental revision in Bultmann's understanding of myth. The purpose in this chapter is thus limited to the task of setting forth that meaning of myth which is the predominant, if not the only, meaning of myth present in Bultmann's writings from 1920 through 1933.[4] The one exception to this chronological principle of

---

[1] Rudolf Bultmann, "Ethische und mystische Religion im Urchristentum," *ChrW*, XXXIV (1920), cols 725-731; 738-743. All citations in this text are to this original edition. The essay has been reprinted in *Anfänge der dialektischen Theologie*, II, 29-47. An English translation is available in *The Beginnings of Dialectic Theology*, ed. James Robinson (Richmond, Virginia: John Knox Press, 1968), 221-235. English translations in this text are my own. Several of Bultmann's writings prior to 1930 refer to the contribution of Richard Reitzenstein's study of Hellenistic mythology to New Testament interpretation: e.g., Rudolf Bultmann, "Die Schriften des Neuen Testaments und der Hellenismus," *ChrW*, XXV (1911), cols. 589-593; "Neues Testament: Biblisch Theologie," *ThR*. XIX (1916), pp. 113-126, esp. pp. 118-120. However, the essay of 1920 offers the first substantive discussion of the theme of Hellenistic mythology and New Testament interpretation.

[2] Hans Jonas, *Gnosis und spätantiker Geist*, Vol. I (2nd ed.; Göttingen: Vandenhoeck & Ruprecht, 1954). The first edition was published by the same firm in 1934.

[3] Rudolf Bultmann, "Vorwort," in Jonas, *Gnosis und . . .*, p. vii.

[4] I use "predominant" as well as "only" to acknowledge the emergence of new motifs in the last half of this early period. By 1926, Bultmann has

delimitation occurs in the concluding section. At that point, I reach beyond the year 1934 in order to establish the fundamental difference between this early formulation of myth and the later concept of myth, and also to identify the elements which continue from this early use of myth into the later concept of myth.

The use of *Religionsgeschichtlich* requires some clarification. First the word is left in the German original since the English equivalent, the history of religions, is grammatically unwieldy. Furthermore, its broad meaning connotes something quite different from the specific focus of the German original. Second, the use of *Religionsgeschichtlich* is more specific than the German *Religionsgeschichtliche Schule* would suggest. When I speak of the *Religionsgeschichtliche* formulation of myth, I do not suppose it possible to construct a single formulation of myth sufficiently comprehensive to include the diversity of positions represented by the dozen or more major theological figures of the *Religionsgeschichtliche Schule*. To discern this diversity, one need only contrast the treatment of myth offered by Gunkel and that presented by Bultmann in the second edition of *Die Religion in Geschichte und Gegenwart*.[1] Therefore, the more specific use of the term is determined strictly by those persons and publications which Bultmann judged as decisive for the *Religionsgeschichtliche* understanding of myth. For him, there are two primary sources, Richard Reitzenstein and Wilhelm Bousset, and the use of the term is limited to the work of these men as Bultmann understood them. Third, this also means that the use of *Religionsgeschichtlich* is somewhat broader than at least some delimitations of the *Religionsgeschichtliche Schule* would allow. For example, Eissfeldt, in his essay on "Religionsgeschichtliche Schule," limits the movement to those men engaged in theological research and, in listing the representatives of this position for a period of three generations, does not include the name of Reitzenstein, since he was

---

introduced a preliminary existentialist approach to mythology; by 1930 he has appropriated the Enlightenment motif in his discussion of myth. The first of these subordinate motifs is considered in Chapter V, section 2; the second in Chapter IV, section 3. As the discussion of these motifs in later chapters will make clear, neither of them alters the predominance of the *Religionsgeschichtliche* formulation during the period 1920-1933.

[1] H. Gunkel, "Mythus und Mythologie: im Alten Testament," *RGG*[2], IV, 381-390. R. Bultmann, "Mythus und Mythologie: im Neuen Testament," *RGG*[2], IV, 390-394.

a classical philologist.[1] Here also, the use of the term follows the direction of Bultmann, as well as contemporary interpreters of the *Religionsgeschichtliche Schule*, who include Reitzenstein and other non-theological scholars within this movement of thought.

The meaning of the *Religionsgeschichtliche* formulation of myth must therefore be specified according to the contributions of Reitzenstein and Bousset. Through Reitzenstein, Bultmann has learned to understand myth as a particular soteriological narrative: namely, the story of the Primal Man or Heavenly Redeemer as this originated in the dualistic religion of Iran and was then appropriated by a variety of Hellenistic religions, mythological traditions, and mystical-speculative writings, including Christianity. Through Bousset, Bultmann has come to understand myth as a phenomenon rooted in the life of the Hellenistic cult: in the history of early Christianity, it is first of all the *Kyrios* cult of the Hellenistic world which appropriates the Primal Man myth as central to the literature and cultic drama of the early Christian community. Through both Reitzenstein and Bousset, Bultmann has come to understand the soteriological intention of myth as inseparably bound up with the cosmic structure and imagery of the narrative. Therefore, I define this *Religionsgeschichtliche* formulation of myth as follows: myth is a soteriological narrative recited in the context of the cult and in the form of a cosmic drama.[2]

---

[1] Eissfeldt, "Religionsgeschichtliche Schule," *RGG*[2], IV, 1898. Cf. Carsten Colpe, *Die religionsgeschichtliche Schule: Darstellung und Kritik ihres Bildes vom gnostischen Erlösermythus* (Göttingen: Vandenhoeck & Ruprecht, 1961).

[2] This formulation of myth is my construct and not Bultmann's. Bultmann's own use of the term in the nineteen-twenties is radically positivistic. Myth means for him the Iranian prototype of the Primal Man, its related Hellenistic stories, and the themes, images, and ideas derived from this (*Infra.*, pp. 94-95). Myth thus does not enjoy the status of a generic concept which could encompass cultic narratives from many periods of history: i.e., primitive and ancient Near Eastern as well as Hellenistic. Thus, when Bultmann does discuss primitive religion and its cult in a general way in 1920, he does not use the category of myth (*Supra.*, pp. 53-54). In this connection, one should also note that his later existentialist formulation of myth is equally restricted to Hellenistic phenomena. While it may be appropriate to ascribe to Hellenistic myths an "entweltlicht" self-understanding, it is necessary to describe primitive myths in an opposite manner, as Mircea Eliade and others have shown. For the present, it is sufficient to show that Bultmann's positivistic use of myth in the nineteen-twenties definitely implies a concept of myth like that proposed above.

The basic texts used in the exposition are the following:

1. "Ethische und mystische Religion im Urchristentum" (1920)
2. *Die Geschichte der synoptischen Tradition* (1921)
3. "Der religionsgeschichtliche Hintergrund des Prologs zum Johannes-Evangelium" (1923)
4. "Die Bedeutung des neuerschlossenen mandäischen und manichäischen Quellen für das Verständnis des Johannesevangeliums" (1925)
5. "Urchristliche Religion (1915-1925)" (1926)
6. Review of *Das Johannesevangelium*, by W. Bauer (1926)
7. "Das Johannesevangelium in der neuesten Forschung" (1927)
8. "Mythus und Mythologie in Neuen Testament" (1930).

Within this chapter, I shall not be concerned with the relationship between Bultmann's philosophical conceptuality, presented in Chapter II, and the early *Religionsgeschichtliche* formulation of myth. For the present, it is sufficient to establish the evidence and clear delineation of a very different use of myth from that characteristic of Bultmann's later writings. These early writings on myth have generally not been discussed in connection with demythologizing or, where they have been touched upon, it has appeared as if Bultmann's early use of myth were of a consistent whole with his later formulations of the concept. It will therefore be sufficient to establish here Bultmann's use of myth which is never identified with either a pre-scientific world view or an objectifying mode of thought, but always and simply with a particular salvation narrative; a use of myth which never proceeds within the context of the history of *Geist*—as if myth were a primitive form of reason or the first expression of a fundamental new self-understanding of *Dasein* —but always proceeds within the context of the history of the cults of the Hellenistic world; a use of myth which is not oriented toward its future appropriation in the philosophy and theology of the Western world, but which is always and persistently directed backwards to the uncovering of the historical origins of the New Testament; a use of myth which is not defined according to its role in the universal sweep of human history, but which is specified as a very definite geographical, historical, and literary phenomenon: limited by the boundaries and centuries of the Hellenistic world, together with its spiritual origins in the East, and limited as the definite story of the Primal Man or Heavenly Redeemer.

1. Sources for the *RELIGIONSGESCHICHTLICHE* Formulation:
R. Reitzenstein and W. Bousset

In "Urchristliche Religion (1915-1925)," Bultmann offers a critical resumé of the literature written during the period 1915-1925 that is of particular significance for understanding the literature and history of the primitive Christian community.[1] Of all the publications of this period, the most important, in Bultmann's judgment, are those which investigate the relationship between primitive Christianity and the myths, religions, philosophy, and speculations of Hellenistic syncretism.[2] Bultmann's animated and enthusiastic style of writing in this section makes it clear that he sees this path of inquiry as constitutive for a "new epoch in biblical studies." [3] In part, the significance of this new research is due to the discovery of new sources. Bultmann here refers to the recent publication by C. Schmidt and I. Wahnberg, "The Conversation of Jesus with his Disciples after the Resurrection," M. Lidzbarski's translation of Mandean texts, and the work of F. W. K. Müller and A. v. Le Coq on Manichean documents. Primarily, however, this new direction in New Testament scholarship has been shaped by the philological research and the historical hypothesis of Richard Reitzenstein. Bultmann is thus clear that it is essentially "the results of Reitzenstein and his fellow workers that provide the foundation for further research." [4]

Bultmann's discussion of Reitzenstein's publications discloses his fundamental agreement with Reitzenstein's basic hypothesis, as well as his high appraisal of the significance of this work for the understanding of the New Testament. The most important contribution of Reitzenstein is his isolation and delineation of the myth of the Primal Man, first set forth in *Poimandres* of 1904. In *Die hellenistischen Mysterienreligionen nach ihren Grundgedanken und Wirkungen* (1910), Reitzenstein has developed the implications of this Primal Man myth for the interpretation of Paul: "with this work he has succeeded in establishing the necessity for under-

---

[1] Rudolf Bultmann, "Urchristliche Religion (1915-1925)," *AR*, XXIV (1926), 83-164.

[2] *Ibid.*, p. 97.

[3] Bultmann had described the contribution of Reitzenstein in an earlier article by this phrase: "Ethische und mystische Religion . . .," *ChrW* (1920), col. 726.

[4] Bultmann, "Urchristliche Religion . . .," *AR* (1926), 105.

standing each fundamental concept [in Paul] through its connection
with the salvation faith of the Primal Man myth." [1] In *Die Göttin
Psyche in der Hellenistischen und frühchristlichen Literatur* (1917),
and *Das mandäische Buch des Herrn der Grösse und die Evangelien-
überlieferung* (1919), Reitzenstein has further substantiated his
basic argument for the Iranian origins of the Primal Man myth.
Again, Bultmann is in full agreement: "the dualistic perspective of
the cosmology and anthropology, together with the individual
details, all point clearly to an Iranian origin." [2] Finally, in *Das
iranische Erlösungsmysterium* (1921), Reitzenstein develops the
diverse forms which this Iranian archetypal myth has assumed
(Mandean, Manichean, Gnostic, and Apocalyptic together with the
speculations of Philo and Paul) and the connections which bind
these later Hellenistic forms of the myth together with their Iranian
source.

In Bultmann's judgment, Reitzenstein has thus succeeded in
delineating the essential structure of this salvation myth, in establishing its pre-Christian origins in Iran and its appropriation in a
variety of Hellenistic cults and speculative writings, and in specifying this myth as the decisive form through which the faith of the
primitive Christian community first came to expression. As a result,
Bultmann's own historical-critical labors during this period of time
consisted, in good measure, in the application, specification, and
extension of Reitzenstein's basic hypothesis.

The second basic source for Bultmann's use of the term myth is
the work of Wilhelm Bousset. In this article, he refers to Bousset's
Hauptprobleme der Gnosis of 1907 as equally basic with Reitzenstein's *Poimandres* of 1904. More frequently, it is Bousset's *Kyrios
Christos* of 1913 which, with the work of Reitzenstein, is cited as the
basis for the newly won understanding of myth in the New Testament. He summarizes the significance of Reitzenstein and Bousset
for New Testament studies as follows:

> One must remember the work of Bousset and Reitzenstein, who
> have performed the great service of making clear, at its key points,
> the total development of early Christianity as an historical religious
> phenomenon. They have rightly recognized the significance of the
> community as a history-creating power, as well as the meaning of
> particular mythical, cosmological, and anthropological traditions.

----

[1] *Ibid.*, p. 105.
[2] *Ibid.*

In short, they have first disclosed in its broad outlines the pre-suppositions for the understanding of the New Testament.[1]

Bultmann does not lightly use such strong language as this. His own work will show quite clearly that he means exactly what he says: namely, that the presuppositions for the understanding of the New Testament have been constituted precisely in the work of Reitzenstein and Bousset.

Reitzenstein's contribution may be specified in relation to two issues. First, Reitzenstein has reconstructed out of a variety of Hellenistic phenomena (or presumed Hellenistic phenomena) an archetypal myth of the Primal Man or Heavenly Redeemer. This reconstructed version of the myth plays such a decisive function in Bultmann's writings of the nineteen-twenties that it is necessary to quote at length Bultmann's resumé of Reitzenstein's reconstruction.

> The fundamental presupposition is a dualistic *Weltbild*: the divine light world and the darkness of chaos stand opposed to each other. Through a dramatic event, which may be a tragic fall or a war-like activity, a part of the light world is thrown into the dark-ness. The heavenly Primal Man, who somehow descends into this darkness, is overcome, captured, and divided up. Only then does it become possible for a cosmos to arise in the sphere of chaos, in which the splintered fragments of light become the cohesive or formative elements, to which the demonic powers enviously cling. For if the light particles were gathered together and freed, and Primal Man were to return again to the light world, the cosmos would return to the chaos of darkness. The light particles captured in matter (the darkness) are nothing other than human souls, whose real home is the light. Each of these bears, to some extent, the Primal Man concealed in themselves. An ambassador from the light world brings them revelation of their origin and home and he teaches them about the heavenly journey and provides the necessary means for this return (the sacraments). After their death, he makes it possible for them to rise again to the light world. The ambassador himself is a form parallel to that of the Primal Man. As with the Primal Man, so it also happens to him, that in his earthly appearance, he is captured and oppressed. His ascent out of this world—in which he dwells as unknown and disguised, in order to deceive the demonic powers—therefore appears as a kind of salva-tion. He is the saved saviour. Since the soul is the image of this Primal Man, it recognizes in the ambassador an exact likeness of itself.[2]

---

[1] *Ibid.*, p. 95.
[2] *Ibid.*, pp. 100-101.

The importance of this particular narrative to Bultmann's early use of myth cannot be overstated. Indeed, in the nineteen-twenties, when Bultmann says myth, he has in mind precisely this story, as a whole or in its derived themes. For this reason I identify the *Religionsgeschichtliche* formulation of myth as being essentially a literary category: it stands for this particular narrative which, when bound together with an historical hypothesis, is understood to be at the root of diverse Hellenistic phenomena. As a literary-historical category, this use of myth is not determined by any particular philosophical tradition or problem. Thus, for example, when Bultmann uses *Weltbild* in the context of this narrative, it is clear that he does not mean a pre-scientific *Weltbild*, or a primitive three-story cosmology. Rather, the notion of *Weltbild* serves simply to specify the cosmic context for the drama of salvation which the myth presents. In a similar manner, when Bultmann works with this understanding of myth and inquires into the mythological origins of the New Testament, he does not use as his norm either a partic-ular view of the world or a particular mode of conceptualizing human existence. Rather, the norm for his use of myth is provided by this narrative. Insofar as any story or concept of the New Tes-tament appears to presuppose, express, or be congruent with this narrative, it is called "mythological." This literary norm for Bultmann's early use of myth must be stated clearly, since readers have become so accustomed to reading this concept of myth in Bultmann in light of quite a different set of norms.

Finally, it is clear from this narrative, as well as from Bultmann's discussion of myth during these years, that this story is something more than a story. In Bultmann's terms of this period, it is a story which does not intend to entertain or explain, but to lay a claim upon man.[1] The story is thus existential and soteriological in its intention; it calls the hearers of the myth to their true home in the light world by disclosing this as their own origin and by presenting the ambassador as the way of return. It is also clear that this soteriological intention appears in the form of a cosmic drama and in the context of the cult, which not only proclaims the story but also provides the sacramental means for its fulfillment. For these reasons, I define Bultmann's early formulation of myth as a definite

-----

[1] Bultmann, "Das Johannesevangelium . . .," *ChrW* (1927), col. 504.

soteriological narrative given in the form of a cosmic drama and in the context of the cult.

Second, Reitzenstein not only reconstructed this parent narrative, but also developed the historical hypothesis which related this original—but only postulated—narrative to its derived—but textually available—versions. Again, I shall cite Bultmann's complex summary of Reitzenstein's argument.

> The proof for the antiquity of this myth, that it extends back to pre-Christian times, is an indirect one. Basically, it consists of this: a variety of sources from the post-Christian period, in which fragments of these speculations occur in the form of a mysterious terminology or conceptual imagery, may be understood in themselves and in their historical context, only if the complete myth is presupposed as a background. This is certainly true for the Christian-Gnostic systems and the speculations of the Mandeans and Manicheans. It is also true, however, for certain parts of the apocryphal Acts of the Apostles, Ode of Solomon, the letters of Ignatius, and the Hermetic literature. It is equally true for writings of the New Testament, like the epistle to the Ephesians and the Gospel of John. Certain motifs in Paul's epistles can now be understood: for example, the famous Christological passage of Philippians 2:6, in which Paul tells of the divine being who came to earth, took on the form of a servant, and was exalted; or, I Corinthians 2:6, in which we read how the world rulers led the Lord of glory to the cross, because they did not recognize him, and so brought about their own downfall. This myth also sheds light on the mysterious figure of the Son of Man, both in the early Christian tradition and in Jewish Apocalyptic. While cut off from its original context, the marks of the Primal Man myth remain obvious here. This Son of Man tradition thus supports, in another direction, the pre-Christian origins of this salvation myth. By reference to this myth, the later Christian notion of the descent into Hell is clarified. For the ambassador brings salvation and revelation, not only to the living, but also to the dead. In the original version, these had their abode, not in an underworld, a Hades, but between heaven and earth, since they were held captive by the demonic powers of the airs (the sphere of the stars). These dead were then freed by the ambassador (so far as they were worthy) with his ascension through the air. In the Jewish tradition, however, the abode of the dead was under the earth. Hence, the necessity, in the Christian tradition, for a further descent of the ambassador, beyond this world to the underworld below.[1]

The genetic function of Reitzenstein's hypothesis is clear from this passage. Having a variety of texts in hand, the historian seeks

---

[1] Bultmann, "Urchristliche Religion . . .," *AR* (1926), 101-102.

for an original text behind all of the known texts which accounts for the motifs which they share in common and provides a total construct in terms of which each of the individual expressions could be interpreted. Bultmann's own use of this literary category of myth is generally consistent with this historical hypothesis, as well as with the literary structure of the narrative. Bultmann thus understands the literature of the New Testament to be grounded in a pre-Christian literary tradition, as are a variety of other Hellenistic phenomena. The task of interpretation, therefore, is to relate a given New Testament story or concept with its probable antecedent source, and thus come to an understanding of that literature in its own historical context.

2. BULTMANN'S EARLY (1920-1933) USE OF THE *RELIGIONSGE-SCHICHTLICHE* FORMULATION IN HISTORICAL-EXEGETICAL STUDIES

In discussing Bultmann's use of the *Religionsgeschichtliche* formulation of myth, I shall delineate a series of expanding circles. I begin with Bultmann's very technical studies into the literary origins of the Gospel of John, then move into a consideration of his use of myth in Synoptic criticism, and then into the criticism of the New Testament as a whole.

In Bultmann's first discussion of John, he proposes an interpretation of the Prologue which arises primarily out of his understanding of the older Jewish tradition of Wisdom literature. In his judgment, Reitzenstein has already shown that this tradition is permeated by a cosmological speculation of Oriental, non-Jewish origins.[1] Bultmann thus reconstructs this "old myth of Wisdom" along essentially the same lines as the myth of the Primal Man, previously cited. Wisdom is with God in the beginning; she seeks a dwelling among men, but is rejected; she returns to the heavenly world, and is now hidden, except to the elect.

> This Wisdom is thus the "Ambassador," who, from time to time, appears on earth embodied in the prophet. Moses is regarded in this way by the Manicheans; John the Baptist by the Mandeans; and the pseudo-Clementine writings regard Adam in the same way.[2]

---

[1] Rudolf Bultmann, "Der religionsgeschichtliche Hintergrund des Prologs zum Johannes-Evangelium," *EUCHARISTERION: Festschrift für Hermann Gunkel*, ed. Hans Schmidt (Göttingen: Vandenhoeck & Ruprecht, 1923), p. 22.

[2] *Ibid.*, p. 19.

On the basis of this bond between Jewish Wisdom literature and the Primal Man myth, Bultmann then develops the parallels between the Wisdom myth and the *Logos* of the Prologue to the Gospel of John. He regards the differentiation of name and sex of the Heavenly Ambassador to be irrelevant (Primal Man, feminine Wisdom, or *Logos*). He is certain that the origin of the myth, in John and Judaism, is not Jewish, but was simply transmitted to Judaism, as it was to Gnosticism, Mandeanism, etc. from Persian mythological origins.[1] He concludes by writing:

> If my suspicion is correct, then the Gospel of John provides further proof for the extraordinarily early impact of Oriental gnostic speculation upon the primitive Christian community.[2]

Throughout Bultmann's analysis of the literary antecedents of the Prologue to John, it is clear that he is dependent upon Reitzenstein's fundamental hypothesis. Myth thus means the narrative of the Primal Man, as this is cast in the feminine form of Wisdom in Judaism and the *Logos* of John. The Prologue to John presupposes this specific literary archetype, mediated to John through Judaism. It is also clear that Bultmann borrows Reitzenstein's historical hypothesis as well as his literary reconstruction. The Primal Man myth is pre-Christian, Iranian (Persian) in its origins, and it appears in the usual collection of related Hellenistic mythological traditions (Mandean, Manichean, Gnostic, etc.).

In this 1927 article on John, Bultmann repeats the same thesis of the earlier essay, supplementing it with new findings in Eastern mythology "whose relationship to John were not clear to me in 1923."[3] His historical argument is the same: John is to be interpreted in the context of a syncretistic Judaism, which has appropriated the Primal Man myth:[4]

> Wisdom is simply one form for the revelation of the Deity, of the savior of the older mythological tradition which, in Christian and non-Christian Gnosticism, more frequently bears the name of Primal Man, or simply Man.[5]

This Jewish tradition must itself be understood in light of the work of Reitzenstein and Bousset, especially in their discussion of Her-

---

[1] *Ibid.*, pp. 19; 21.
[2] *Ibid.*, p. 26.
[3] Bultmann, "Das Johannesevangelium . . .," *ChrW* (1927), col. 505.
[4] *Ibid.*
[5] *Ibid.*

metic literature and its significance for the Prologue to John.[1]
Bultmann does not think it possible to trace back in detail, to any
given mythological tradition, the particular points of the Gospel
of John. He does, however, contend that its pattern as a whole
reflects the Primal Man myth, and sees the probable origin of the
Gospel to be Syria, the meeting point of East and West, the same
context which gave birth to Mandean Gnostic mythology, the Ode
of Solomon, and the work of Ignatius.[2]

Bultmann then extends his earlier interpretation of the Prologue
to include the whole of the Gospel of John. For it is not simply the
Logos in John that is patterned after the archetypal myth, but the
total picture of Jesus.

> The image of Jesus in the Gospel of John, in its general configuration,
> is that of the Ambassador of God, the Revealer, the figure visible in
> the Mandean sources, Manichean texts, the Ode of Solomon, Chris-
> tian Gnosticism, Philo, and Hermetic literature.[3]

The picture of Jesus, as it appears in John, thus conforms to the
literary norm of the Primal Man myth, the Wisdom myth, etc.
Jesus is the "I am," the revealer of the truth and light in a hostile
world, who comes from the Father and returns to him, drawing his
own after him.[4]

Having indicated the lines of continuity between John and the
archetypal redeemer myth, Bultmann then develops some of the
salient points which distinguish John from related mythological
literature. The cosmological motifs are almost completely ignored in
John; so also is the notion of the soul as a pre-existent, banished
light particle. The divinely sent saviour is not the image of the
Primal Man, and the speculation about the heavenly ascent of
souls is also absent.[5] After noting further variations, Bultmann
concludes:

> All of this proves that the older myth has only been used by John
> as a means to bring his Christian understanding of revelation to
> expression.[6]

---

[1] *Ibid.*, col. 504.
[2] *Ibid.*, col. 506.
[3] *Ibid.*, col. 505.
[4] *Ibid.*
[5] *Ibid.*, col. 506.
[6] *Ibid.*

In these studies of John, it is obvious that myth means for Bultmann a definite literary phenomenon, a variant of the Primal Man narrative, which has become the form for John's presentation of Jesus as the Revealer of God. This same use of myth is also determinative for Bultmann's studies of the Synoptic Gospels in this period, especially in his form-critical work, *Die Geschichte der synoptischen Tradition*.[1] Here also one is struck by the absence of the later formulations of myth: myth is never identified with a pre-scientific world view or with an objectifying mode of thought. Perhaps the relationship of miracle stories and myth illustrates this difference most sharply. According to Bultmann's later formulation of myth, the miracle story is essentially mythical because it expresses a pre-scientific understanding of reality in which the world is open to the interference of gods and demons. In *The History of the Synoptic Tradition*, Bultmann also postulates a close connection between miracle stories and the Christ myth. However, he here understands this connection to be of a purely literary-cultic order, not scientific or cosmological. The miracle story is rooted in the understanding of the identity of Jesus given through the Christ myth and in the *Kyrios* cult; the miracle story is thus a literary dependent of the Christ myth. In no sense, however, does the miracle story express a certain understanding of nature which is defined as "mythological."

Bultmann's discussion of the differences between the Gospel of Mark and Q at the point of miracles is illustrative here. While noting the absence of miracles from Q and their abundance in Mark, he rejects as inadequate any explanation of this difference solely on the grounds of the absence of narrative material in Q. Rather, "the deeper reason for their absence is the different light in which Jesus appears."[2] In Q, Jesus is still the eschatological preacher of repentance and salvation, the teacher of wisdom and the law. In Mark, on the other hand, Jesus is presented in terms of the Hellenistic Christ myth, as the Divine Man, or the Son of God walking on the face of the earth.[3] Because of this change in perspective, effected by the introduction of the Christ myth into the Palestinian oral

---

[1] Rudolf Bultmann, *Die Geschichte der synoptischen Tradition* (2nd ed.; Göttingen: Vandenhoeck & Ruprecht, 1931). *The History of the Synoptic Tradition*, trans. John March (New York: Harper & Row, 1963).

[2] *Ibid.*, p. 241.

[3] *Ibid.*

traditions, the miraculous has now become indigenous to the Gospel
of Mark. For both the miracle stories and the cult legends are
connected with the myth through the notion of the "secret epiphany."[1] The feeding of the multitudes, the stilling of the storm, the
walking on the water, the exorcisms and healings are all revelations
of the true identity of Jesus as the Son of God.[2] Thus, Mark has more
miracles than Q because Mark is more mythological: i.e., the literary
structure of Mark is determined by the Primal Man myth, while Q
is not. Because Mark understands Jesus in terms of this myth, the
miracles serve as a natural vehicle to express the heavenly, supernatural origin and destiny of Jesus.

While the discussion of myth is not extensive in Bultmann's
form-critical study, it is clear that the *Religionsgeschichtliche* idea of
myth is a fundamental hypothesis of this work. Two years prior to
the publication of his own form-critical study, Bultmann suggested
this connection between form criticism and myth criticism in a
review of Dibelius' work, *Die Formgeschichte des Evangeliums* (1919):

> In an excellent manner the author handles the relationship of the
> evangelical tradition to myth. That the tradition as a whole cannot
> be reduced to myth is clear through an analysis of the forms which
> are distinctly differentiated from mythical forms. At the same time,
> it is also clear that myth has decisively entered into the tradition.
> It appears in Paul as if there was a Christ myth still unjoined to the
> life of Jesus. In the Gospels, however, a union of these two has been
> effected. This is shown by the structure of the Gospels, in which
> Jesus appears increasingly as an epiphany of the Son of God. It
> also appears in individual pieces of tradition, in sayings and words
> of Jesus. Finally, with John, the whole tradition is transposed into
> the sphere of myth.[3]

This same theme reappears in his own study of the Synoptics. The
fundamental distinction is drawn between the individual pieces of
Palestinian oral tradition and the structure and unity of the Gospels
provided by the Hellenistic Christ myth. It is Mark who first unifies
this Hellenistic Christ myth with traditions of the stories of Jesus.[4]

> The tradition had to be presented as a unity from the point of view
> that in it he who spoke and was spoken of was he who had lived on
> earth as the Son of God, had suffered, died, risen and been exalted

---

[1] *Ibid.*, p. 346.

[2] *Ibid.*

[3] Rudolf Bultmann, Review of *Die Formgeschichte des Evangeliums*, by
Martin Dibelius, *ThLZ*, XLIV (1919), cols. 173-174.

[4] Bultmann, *The History of* . . ., p. 347.

to heavenly glory. And inevitably the centre of gravity had to be the end of the story, the Passion and Resurrection. Mark was the creator of this sort of Gospel; the Christ myth gives his book, the book of secret epiphanies, not indeed a biographical unity, but a unity based upon the myth of the *kerygma*.[1]

As a result of Mark's work as an innovator, the role of myth is stronger in his work than in either of the other two Synoptics.[2] This is true, even though the miraculous is heightened and new mythical motifs are added in the later Gospels. For "in the whole outline [of Matthew and Luke] the Christ myth recedes in favour of the picture of the earthly ministry of Jesus." [3] The only real extension of Mark's style of Gospel occurs in John, "and there of course the myth has completely violated the historical tradition." [4] In all these instances, it is clear that Bultmann means by myth that definite cultic salvation narrative, which had been delineated by Reitzenstein and Bousset, and which is here understood to provide the unifying structure for the Synoptic Gospels.

In his essay on myth in the New Testament for the second edition of *Die Religion in Geschichte und Gegenwart*,[5] Bultmann discusses the relevance of this *Religionsgeschichtliche* understanding of myth for the total body of New Testament literature. The essay itself is a transitional one. It offers one of the last substantive discussions of myth along the lines of the *Religionsgeschichtliche* formulation. It also introduces briefly, and for the first time, the Enlightenment formulation of myth. The themes of interest here are those consistent with the *Religionsgeschichtliche* pattern of the 1920's.

The two primary sources of Bultmann's *Religionsgeschichtliche* formulation of myth find expression here: Reitzenstein's hypothesis of the Primal Man myth, with its Iranian origins and derived multiple Hellenistic forms; and Bousset's understanding of New Testament literature as bound up with the *Kyrios* cult of the Hellenistic Christian community.

In relation to Reitzenstein's hypothesis and its significance for understanding the New Testament, Bultmann writes:

---

[1] *Ibid.*, p. 371.
[2] *Ibid.*, p. 348.
[3] *Ibid.*
[4] *Ibid.*, p. 371.
[5] Rudolf Bultmann, "Mythus und Mythologie im Neuen Testament," *RGG*[2] (Tübingen: J. C. B. Mohr, 1930), IV, 390-394.

> Of all the mythological influences on the New Testament, the strongest is the oriental-gnostic salvation myth which, so far as we can see, goes back to the Iranian myth of the Primal Man.[1]

This old mythological tradition is particularly decisive for the interpretation of John and Paul.[2] Jesus is here most clearly presented in the form of the heavenly ambassador. He is the eternal Son of God, or Word of God; he is with the Father in the beginning; he descends from the heavenly world, is disguised as a man, rejected by the world, and ascends to his Father; through his deeds and death, he overcomes the demonic powers which ruled the world.[3] The influence of this Iranian tradition, however, is not confined to Paul and John. It permeates the New Testament as a whole, and is mediated to the primitive Christian community through its earlier formulations in either the late Jewish or Gnostic traditions.[4] It is particularly at the point of eschatology, so central to the whole of the New Testament, that the Iranian origins of New Testament mythology are most apparent. For here is the dualistic *Weltbild* of Iran, with its Kingdom of Satan, two aeons, and cosmic conflict.[5]

Bousset's understanding of the cult, and its significance for the formation of New Testament mythology, is also developed by Bultmann here. The various honorific ascriptions to Jesus, like Son of God, Lord, Lamb of God, and Servant of God, originate in the cult, and derive their meaning from the life of the cult.[6] The cult has also contributed to the narration of the life of Jesus, especially the cult myths of the baptism of Jesus and his last supper, which perform an etiological function by grounding the sacraments of the cult in the life of its founder.[7] The various epiphany narratives, like the transfiguration story, also disclose the influence of cultically formed myths. Finally, it is the Hellenistic *Kyrios* cult which provides the mythically unifying form for the life of Jesus as a whole. Even the

---

[1] *Ibid.*, col. 393.

[2] For other discussions of the relationship of Paul with the old Oriental mythological tradition, see Chapter V, section two. "It would be saying too little to say that Paul only worked in dependence upon the Hellenistic community, its cult and mythologically-formed concepts. Rather, he must be seen as being one of the chief participants in the Hellenization of Christianity" ("Urchristentum und Religionsgeschichte," *ThR*, IV [1932], 4).

[3] Bultmann, "Mythus und Mythologie . . .," *RGG²*, IV, 393.

[4] *Ibid.*, cols. 391-392.

[5] *Ibid.*, col. 391.

[6] *Ibid.*, col. 393.

[7] *Ibid.*

passion narrative is but a condensed version of this Christ myth.[1]

Bultmann's own work as an historian and exegete of the New Testament discloses the same understanding of myth earlier observed in conjunction with his discussion of Reitzenstein and Bousset. The Gospel of John, the Synoptic Gospels, and the New Testament as a whole repeat, in their own way, the basic motifs of the old Iranian salvation myth. It is this cultic narrative of the Primal Man, as appropriated in diverse forms of the Hellenistic world, which provides the format for the understanding of Jesus in the early Hellenistic community. In light of this historical-literary analysis of the New Testament, the question concerning the theological meaning of myth, its relation to the substance of New Testament faith, became a pressing one. Having completed a survey of Bultmann's historiographical use of the *Religionsgeschichtliche* formulation of myth, I turn now to an examination of the theological use of this formulation of myth in his writings of the twenties.

3. BULTMANN'S EARLY (1920-1933) THEOLOGICAL INTERPRETATION OF THE *RELIGIONSGESCHICHTLICHE* FORMULATION

The discussion of Bultmann's appropriation of the *Religionsgeschichtliche* formulation of myth has been focused thus far upon Bultmann's work as a New Testament exegete. This emphasis is appropriate, since it was primarily in his work as New Testament historian and critic that Bultmann made use of this *Religionsgeschichtliche* formulation of myth. However, Bultmann has never been, at any point of his career, only a New Testament historian and exegete. He has always also addressed himself to the systematic theological issues inherent in the task of interpreting the Christian faith to his own contemporary world. This was as true in 1920 as it was in 1941. It is therefore no accident that Bultmann offers his first substantive discussion of myth in the context of systematic theological problems: i.e., the question of the proper focus of theological reflection and the nature of revelation. In this 1920 essay, "Ethische und mystische Religion im Urchristentum," Bultmann offers a summary of recent New Testament myth studies as a basis for a critique of the theology of later liberalism and Karl Barth. Indeed, this essay might be subtitled: implications of New Testament myth studies for the criticism and reformulation of liberal theology in a non-Barthian manner.

---

[1] *Ibid.*

In order to clarify the meaning of this early theological use of myth, I propose to develop two issues of systematic theology appropriate to Bultmann's discussion of the twenties: 1) the nature of the task of theology as specified by the concept of myth: specifically, the role of the concept of myth in understanding the source, context, and object of theological reflection; 2) the nature of revelation as specified by its dialectical relation with myth: specifically, the role of myth as appropriate for, and belonging to, revelation while absolutely distinct from it. In dealing with these two systematic theological issues, I shall also specify patterns of continuity and change in Bultmann's theological interpretation of myth. In examining Bultmann's early discussion of the nature of the task of theology as stipulated by the category of myth, I shall make explicit the continuity of theological intention which sustains the whole of Bultmann's project, from this 1920 essay through the 1941 demythologizing proposal. In examining the theological dialectic of myth and revelation, I shall describe the differences between this early, and never fully developed, theological usage of myth, and the more recent, developed, and familiar version of this same theme.

I can express the continuity in Bultmann's theological use of myth most simply in the following proposition: theology, defined according to its method rather than its substance, is myth interpretation. This is a central theme in Bultmann's essay of 1920, and it is basic to his 1941 hermeneutical project of demythologizing. Indeed, in a very literal sense, one can say that Bultmann in his project of 1941 has executed in a systematic manner what he proposed in 1920 as the task of theology. At that time, he described his own theological proposal, in contrast with both liberal theology and Karl Barth, as follows:

> One cannot artificially renew an old cult or myth; nor can one artificially create a new one. However, one may creatively reform older priestly or prophetic traditions by entering into the present historical situation, and by unfolding the older tradition in the new situation. To do this one must carefully cut away all that has become obsolete and untrue and join together that which is genuinely urgent. In a matter like this, what is involved is not action: rather, one is concerned to lead self-reflection one step further.[1]

Bultmann does not offer a detailed explication of this theological option in 1920. Therefore, his theological use of myth appears most

---

[1] *Ibid.*, col. 740.

clearly in his critique of the historically oriented theology of A. Ritschl and the Christ-centered theology of Karl Barth. In relation to both, it is the category of myth which provides the clue to the distinctive direction of that theology of revelation which Bultmann proposes.

One factor in determining the nature of the task of theology, at least for Protestantism, is Scripture which serves as the source for theological reflection. It is therefore essential that theology understand the nature of the texts which it would interpret. In Bultmann's judgment, the work of Reitzenstein, Bousset, Wendland, and Heitmueller has made fully clear the mythical sources and presuppositions for the New Testament texts. To these studies of Hellenistic myths, one must add the form criticism of Martin Dibelius, completed by 1920, together with Bultmann's own form-critical work well in progress by this date. As a literary analysis of the sources and structure of the Synoptic Gospels, form criticism had made it impossible to understand these Gospels as if they were histories. What appeared in the Synoptics was not a faithfully remembered, Palestinian-structured biography of Jesus, but rather the Christ myth, rooted in the Hellenistic world. The old focus of liberal theology, which took the historical Jesus as its point of departure, was no longer a possibility on the basis of these historical-literary considerations alone. Therefore, if theology accepts the principle of *sola Scriptura* as determinative for its task, such theology, after the work of the *Religionsgeschichtliche Schule*, must take the form of myth interpretation. For myth constitutes the essential literary form of expression for the substance of the New Testament proclamation of the meaning of Jesus.

Second, the nature of the task of theology is also determined according to the context of theology, and for Bultmann in 1920, the context of theological reflection is given with the Church: the Church not only as an eschatological phenomenon, but the eschatological Church considered also as an historical-sociological phenomenon. Bultmann here draws primarily upon the work of Bousset and Ernst Troeltsch. He thus holds theology accountable to the fact that Christianity became a religion, in the sense of an independent historical movement, only in the Hellenistic world: that is, only when it came to expression in the *Kyrios* cult and Christ myth with its sacred literature and rite. The religion of Jesus and the primitive Palestinian Christian movement must be understood as a sect within the structure of Judaism. Liberal theology, in attempting to focus present faith upon the religion of Jesus, had promulgated an historical and sociological ghost: there never was a religion of Jesus. Not only in its origins, but throughout its history, the Church has found the center of its faith in the Christ myth, and not in the historical Jesus. If liberal theology intends to be a theology of the Church, if it intends to be faithful to its real context of reflection, it will turn its attention away from the religion of Jesus and to the Christ myth of the Hellenistic Christian community.

Finally, the task of theology is determined, not only by its source and context, but also by its object: that is, God in his revelation. What is decisive here is the right understanding of God which holds together in its essential unity the threefold structure: God, who is the eternal, ever newly present, "wholly other" in whom man finds the fulfillment of his existence; his revelation given in the word of Scripture and the continuous preaching of the Church; and the faith which hears this word as the revealing Word of God. In this essay, Bultmann stresses two false modes of understanding this object, center, or theme of theological reflection.

The first is the moralistic distortion of God in liberal theology: the confusion of the transcendent, "wholly other" God, who meets man in the totality and depths of his life and as fulfillment of that life, with the demand of the good and the power for its achievement. Liberal theology has fallen into this error and so it has also converted the revelation theme of the New Testament into a history of Jesus and ignored the proclamation of salvation given in the Christ myth in favor of the ethical teachings of Jesus.

Over against this moralistic misunderstanding of God, Bultmann proposes a theology of revelation. Central to his affirmation of revelation, as the central theme for exegesis and theological interpretation in the New Testament, is his understanding of myth as the fundamental form through which the New Testament gives expression to the meaning of Jesus as the revelation of God. Bultmann finds it no accident that myth occupies such a central place in the New Testament since myth, in its literary structure, cultic context, and salvation theme, is distinctively appropriate to express the idea of revelation. Bultmann is thus quite clear in nineteen twenty that if Protestant theology intends to avoid the pitfalls of moralism, together with psychologism and historicism, it must recover the mythical and cultic origins of faith in the New Testament, and thus discover anew how to speak the word appropriate to the revelation of God in its own time and place. The right understanding of the object of faith, and the theme of the New Testament, thus points to myth as that form decisive to the expression of revelation in the New Testament literature.

Liberal theology misunderstands the object of faith by making God immanent: thus liberal theology moralizes, culturizes, historicizes, and psychologizes the revelation of God. Over against such a this-worldly theology, Bultmann insists, with Karl Barth, upon a theology of revelation. However, Barth also has misunderstood the object of faith by absolutizing one form of God's revelation: i.e., the Pauline Christ myth of the Hellenistic world. Barth thus fails to understand that revelation is always revelation for faith, and so breaks the connection between the eternity of God and the present hearing of faith. Barth fails to understand that God is always God of present history, and may never be identified with any particular person, period, or form of expression of the past, however religiously important it might have been. In misunderstanding the connection between God in his revelation and the present historical reality of faith, Barth makes the same error as old liberalism: while the liberals identified the revelation of God with the historical figure of Jesus, Barth has identified the revelation of God with the Pauline Christ myth.

Bultmann thus formulates his category of myth in specifying his theology of revelation in a double direction. Over against liberal theology, myth serves to designate the literary-cultic form of expression appropriate to the *Sache* of the New Testament. A theology which would speak of the object of faith must be able to speak once more of the revelation of God and find for this reality mythical and cultic forms of expression. Over against Barth, however, Bultmann uses myth as a critical category to distinguish between an historically conditioned form of the past and the revelation of God which found expression in that form and which finds expression again today in contemporary faith. Here Barth has failed to respect the connection between revelation and present history as he has attempted to find the objectiveness of God in a past form of revelation.[1] Myth thus both stands for a form of expression appropriate

---

[1] Bultmann has little empathy for Barth's theological passion for "das Objektive." There is only one way to God: "Inner truth is the only way to faith; the reality of faith can never be made perceptible, and each man must

to revelation and also serves to stipulate the historical particularity of that form of expression.

The theological function of the concept of myth, proposed in 1920, is in many respects confirmed by Bultmann's project of demythologizing in 1941. It is certainly clear in 1941, and in the subsequent discussion of the matter, that demythologizing is born out of reflection upon the task of interpreting Scripture; it is also clear, in spite of the burden of Bultmann's individualistic philosophical apparatus, that demythologizing appears as a phenomenon of the Church. Bultmann repeatedly refers the reader to the context of present preaching as the proper context for understanding his proposal.[1] His sharpest critics, as widely divergent as Karl Barth and Karl Jaspers, recognize his thought as moving within the context of the Church, however they may evaluate this fact.[2] Finally, Bultmann has a resolute passion to speak of the *Sache* of the New Testament: in his exegesis, in his theological essays, and in demythologizing itself, there is always the theological concern to let the word of the Beyond become present in our own time and place.

If theology may be defined according to its method as myth interpretation, it should be clear from our proceeding discussion, that theology defined according to its substance is the interpretation of revelation: specifically, the revelation of God in Jesus Christ for faith. Indeed, the relationship of myth and revelation is such as to qualify, even while illumining, this preliminary statement of the nature of the task of theology. Therefore, to understand Bultmann's early theological use of myth I turn now to the task of clarifying the dialectic of myth and revelation. I may summarize this as follows: myth is appropriate to the reality of revelation: revelation may not be confounded with myth, but neither may revelation be divested of the myth which belongs to it. It is this dialectic affirmation and negation which is decisive for Bultmann's theological use of myth in the nineteen-twenties. I shall present this dialectical relationship in a systematic form of my own, but one which is constructed to account for Bultmann's own theological discussion of myth during this period.

---

make the decision for himself" (Rudolf Bultmann, "Karl Barth's *Römerbrief* in zweiter Auflage," *ChrW*, XXXVI [1922], col. 361).

[1] Rudolf Bultmann, "The Case for Demythologizing," *Myth and Christianity: an Inquiry into the Possibility of Religion without Myth* by Karl Jaspers and Rudolf Bultmann (New York: Noonday Press, 1958), p. 60.

[2] Karl Jaspers, *ibid.*, pp. 55-56; 110-112. Karl Barth, *KaM* II, 121-123.

Myth is appropriate to revelation. By myth, I mean the literary-cultic phenomenon which has been the subject of this chapter. Recalling Reitzenstein's myth of the Primal Man, its appropriateness to the New Testament theme of revelation is obvious enough. Bultmann specifies the affinity between myth and revelation in at least three respects. First, "Myth speaks of God as *Jenseits* in relation to men, even when it speaks of God in a human way."[1] Myth thus stands in sharp contrast with the immanental understanding of God and religion which Bultmann sees to be so characteristic of late liberal theology. Myth knows God as beyond and "wholly other," and it is precisely for this reason that "myth and cult alone are able to be the expression for the living, eternal, supra-historical reality of religion." [2]

Second, myth is appropriate to revelation because "myth knows of the idea of revelation (*der Mythus kennt den Gedanken der Offenbarung*)." [3] Myth is itself the story of the Revealer, the Heavenly Ambassador, and as such is intrinsically related to the message of the New Testament. Third, myth is appropriate to revelation because myth knows of human existence, its lostness and insecurity, and myth speaks to this existence, laying a claim upon it and calling for a decision in relation to the meaning and goal of existence.[4] The existential claim which is manifest in myth is also ethical, as myth sets forth a standard of conduct appropriate to its existential claim.[5]

In each of these ways, Bultmann finds myth to be intrinsically appropriate to revelation. In the spirit of the Gospel of Luke, one might almost designate the resurgence of Hellenistic myths as a decisive factor in determining the right time for the coming of the Gospel.

While myth is thus appropriate to revelation, in no sense may revelation be identified with, or confounded with, myth. Bultmann suggests distinctions between revelation and myth of several different kinds. First, theologically considered, the subject of revelation is God while the subject of myth is man. Therefore, while myth can mediate a knowledge of man, in "his lostness in the world"

[1] Bultmann, "Das Johannesevangelium . . .," *ChrW* (1927), col. 510.
[2] Bultmann, "Ethische und mystische Religion . . .," *ChrW* (1920), col. 739.
[3] Bultmann, "Das Johannesevangelium . . .," *ChrW* (1927), col. 511.
[4] *Ibid.*, col. 504.
[5] *Ibid.*

and as one "who cannot secure himself through his reason," myth
may not give a knowledge of God.[1]

> However, unless God really reveals himself, this [the knowledge of
> man in myth] is only a negative knowledge of God; really it is only
> a form of self-knowledge.[2]

As a result of this fundamental distinction, myth falls consistently
for Bultmann under the rubric of *"Form," "Ausdruck,"* or *"Gestalt"* and as such is set firmly in the history of humanity. "Cult and
myth are not religion but only the necessary forms" and as such,
they are contrasted with "the reality of God" and "his revealing
himself to us." [3]

Second, revelation and myth are to be distinguished, not only
by subject, but also by reference to the specific historical referent of
revelation: for Bultmann, revelation always includes the historical
figure of Jesus of Nazareth. This does not mean that revelation is
differentiated from myth simply because it has any historical referent, in the sense of the *"Dass"* of Bultmann's later discussion. As
Bultmann noted in the twenties, several of the Hellenistic myths
had an historical figure central to them—John the Baptist and the
enigmatic Mani as well as Jesus—and this historical referent did not
make them any less mythical.[4] Rather, what is decisive for the
reality of revelation is not any historicity, but the particular
historicity of Jesus, who ends his life upon the Cross. Apart from
this Jesus and this death, there is no revelation of God for Bultmann.

Bultmann is also clear that the primitive Christian understanding
of Jesus is thoroughly mythical and that no history of Jesus may
be written today because of the essential mythical structure of his
life as given in the New Testament.[5] However, while recognizing
this, he does insist that the figure of Jesus may not be reduced to a
"poetic creation developed out of mythology." [6]

---

[1] *Ibid.*, cols. 510-511.
[2] *Ibid.*
[3] Bultmann, "Ethische und mystische Religion . . .," *ChrW* (1920), col. 739.
[4] Bultmann, "Der religionsgeschichtliche Hintergrund des Prologs . . .,"
EUCHARISTERION . . ., p. 19.
[5] Bultmann, "Mythus und Mythologie im Neuen Testament," *RGG*[2], IV,
393.
[6] *Ibid.*, col. 394.

> While the Christ myth gives the life of Jesus its formal unity, this form is still the secondary element: the primary element consists of the individual pieces of narrative from the older tradition.[1]

Revelation may not be reduced to myth, since revelation includes within it, and is decisively determined by, the particularity of the historical reality of Jesus.

Third, the distinction between revelation and myth also appears as a hermeneutical principle: one may not interpret the texts of the New Testament as if they were simply myth without regard to the intention of the author to speak of the revelation of God. Thus, in discussing the Gospel of John, Bultmann insists that the whole apparatus of historical-mythological criticism is to be understood as only a preamble, albeit a necessary preamble to the real task of theological exegesis, which is the exposition of the revelation of God in Jesus.[2] This preliminary myth analysis of the Gospel allows the interpreter to understand its speech, and makes him familiar with its conceptual presuppositions, but does not lead him to the content of the Gospel. This hermeneutical distinction is necessary if the interpreter is to be faithful to the intention of the author of the Gospel of John.

> For the Gospel of John is in itself no mythology ... but it only uses with sovereign confidence the form of expression of myth (just as it also uses forms of the older evangelical tradition) in order to bring to expression its apprehension of the revelation of God in Jesus.[3]

The difference between a theologically informed hermeneutic and a purely myth-oriented hermeneutic appears in Bultmann's critique of the concrete interpretation of New Testament texts developed by his colleagues in the *Religionsgeschichtliche Schule*. For example, Bultmann regards Bousset's interpretation of Paul as simply

---

[1] *Ibid.* Bultmann is thus highly critical of the effort by A. Drews to prove that Jesus is simply a fabrication out of the traditions of Hellenistic mythology (*Das Markusevangelium als Zeugnis gegen die Geschichtlichkeit Jesu* by A. Drews). Over against the contention of this book, Bultmann cites the consensus of New Testament myth studies: "While all this research shows that the Christian faith expressed the meaning of the historical appearance of Jesus through a mythology of oriental origins, nevertheless, none of the scholars discussed come to the conclusion that the historical figure of Jesus can be dissolved into myth (Bultmann, "Urchristliche Religion ...," *AR* (1926), p. 108).

[2] Bultmann, "Das Johannesevangelium ...," *ChrW* (1920), col. 510.

[3] *Ibid.*

incorrect because it fails to recognize the centrality of the cross of Christ as the revelation of God's forgiveness in the whole thought of Paul.[1] Bousset has attempted to interpret Paul consistently and only in the context of Hellenistic mythological traditions, and thus has failed to recognize that which is decisive to the meaning of the Pauline texts. An adequate interpretation of any text takes account of the intent of the author, and in the case of the New Testament, this includes the understanding of Jesus and his cross as the point of God's revelation for faith.

Myth, appropriate to revelation, nevertheless may not be confounded with revelation; but neither may revelation be divested of myth, for myth belongs to revelation. Bultmann is clear in 1927 that the relationship of myth and revelation may not be construed in terms of an accident of history.

> One would falsely understand the Gospel [of John] if one were to regard its use of myth as a purely historical, causally determined accident.[2]

The connection between revelation and myth, as its form of expression, is much more intrinsic and organic than such a purely historical view of the matter would disclose. In this connection, Bultmann develops the characteristics of myth which we have previously considered under the category of appropriateness. The author of John says what he says in the form of myth because the form of myth allows him to express his intention: namely, to speak of God as transcendent, now revealed in Jesus, and exercising a claim upon man concerning the meaning and goal of his existence and the conduct of his life. The error of liberal theology is that it attempted to sunder myth from revelation, and thus was left with no revelation of God but simply the moralizing historical Jesus. Over against Barth, Bultmann insists upon a flexible and critical appropriation of myth; one may not simply repeat the Pauline Christ myth as the norm for the spiritual life of modern man. However, the word which theology must speak is one continuous with myth as a form of expression, even as it is a changing expression appropriate to ever new historical situations. For this reason, Bultmann can chide his liberal theological colleagues: they shall simply be a passing episode in the life of the Church unless they can

---

[1] Bultmann, "Urchristliche Religion . . .," *AR* (1926), p. 108.
[2] Bultmann, "Das Johannesevangelium . . .," *ChrW* (1927), col. 510.

learn to speak again the word of myth and cult, for this alone is able to express the reality of revelation.[1]

Myth is appropriate to revelation; revelation is distinct from myth, though revelation may not be divested of myth, since myth belongs to revelation.

In Bultmann's later essays, this theological dialectic of myth and revelation recedes into the background and is replaced by a philosophical dialectic with quite a different pattern. I may briefly distinguish here between these two formulations of the relation of myth and revelation, even though I shall not develop the philosophical form of the dialectic until Chapter V.

The theological dialectic of revelation and myth leaves the relation of the two fundamentally open, to be resolved in the act of interpretation and proclamation. Bultmann thus admonishes the modern theologian to recover the mythical origins of Christian faith in order to speak again in this form of expression in our age, even as Paul and John did in their own age. Theology is thus concerned with myth, not as an end in itself nor as an historical accident of the New Testament past, but as the original and continuing form of expression appropriate to, and belonging to, the reality of revelation. At the same time, the word of proclamation always transcends the confines of myth, even while using it "with sovereign confidence," in order to speak anew of God as revealed in Jesus for faith. Myth is thus always present, even as it is always overcome, and both present and overcome for the sake of revelation.

According to the philosophical form of the dialectic, the relation of revelation and myth has been already decisively resolved. There is no longer a continuing bond between the two since, in the movement of the *Geist* of history, myth as a form of expression has been overcome once for all in a new conceptuality, a new form of expression adequate to the original intention of revelation and myth itself. Myth was once the form of expression for the meaning of revelation, in a past moment of the history of *Geist*; it remains as a problematic point of departure for interpretation which, in the present moment of the history of *Geist*, recovers the original meaning of myth in the new existentialist conceptuality even while rejecting the original form of expression. Myth thus does not really belong to revelation; myth belongs essentially to the archaic world

---

[1] Bultmann, "Ethische und mystische Religion . . .," *ChrW* (1920), col. 740.

of the past, and it became joined to revelation only through its juncture with revelation in a particular moment of the past.

It would be tempting to speculate on the shape of Bultmann's project of demythologizing, had it followed the direction indicated during the twenties. In this theological use of myth, Barth's new theology of revelation is joined with the new myth studies of the *Religionsgeschichtliche Schule*. Bultmann's theological use of myth did not follow this pattern, of course. To understand his later project of demythologizing, one may not take either the theology of Barth or the historical studies of the *Religionsgeschichtliche Schule* as a basic point of departure, but must return to the fundamental conceptuality of Bultmann's Neo-Kantian origins.

4. HISTORICAL CRITICISM AND PHILOSOPHICAL REVISION OF THE
RELIGIONSGESCHICHTLICHE FORMULATION : H. JONAS AND
BULTMANN

Throughout this chapter, the *Religionsgeschichtliche* use of myth has been described in terms of the definite historical phenomenon to which it refers—or, at least, a limited body of literary phenomena bound together by an historical hypothesis. A series of Hellenistic religious and quasi-philosophical texts were understood by Reitzenstein and Bultmann to be rooted in an original Iranian myth of Primal Man. There never was any textual evidence to support the existence of a pre-Christian, archetypal redeemer myth, and there were unresolved problems in the dating and origins of the texts that were cited as evidence for this hypothesis. As a result, Reitzenstein's hypothesis soon fell under sharp criticism.

A thorough discussion of the historical critique of Reitzenstein's hypothesis appears in the work of Carsten Colpe, *Die religions-geschichtliche Schule*.[1] Colpe concludes that the so-called pre-Christian Iranian myth of the Heavenly Redeemer is actually a post-Christian creation.[2] He understands the hypothesis to have developed out of no firmer a base than an analogical extrapolation from Old Testament research: just as there were pre-biblical creation myths, so there must be pre-Christian redeemer myths. Without accepting all of Colpe's conclusions, it does seem necessary to

---

[1] Carsten Colpe, *Die religionsgeschichtliche Schule: Darstellung und Kritik ihres Bildes vom gnostischen Erlösermythus* (Göttingen: Vandenhoeck & Ruprecht, 1961).

[2] *Ibid.*, pp. 15 ff.

accept the general consensus among New Testament scholars concerning the indefensability of Reitzenstein's historical hypothesis concerning the pre-Christian Iranian myth of the Primal Man or Heavenly Redeemer.[1]

This historical critique of the *Religionsgeschichtliche* myth hypothesis is not new, but was already developed, in good part, in the thirties, especially in the work of H. Lietzmann. Bultmann reviewed Lietzmann's critique of Reitzenstein's interpretation of the Mandean texts, and concurred with Lietzmann's basic conclusions.[2] He acknowledges his own error in the dating of the Mandean texts.[3] He also agrees that these texts cannot be used to establish the pre-Christian origins of the Primal Man myth; they now appear to be the product of a Syrian, syncretistic version of Christianity. However, he does not accept Lietzmann's basic conclusion: "In the Mandean tradition we are able to study the Christianizing of an oriental *gnosis*, not the gnostic foundation of early Christianity." [4] For Bultmann, the relationship between Christianity and an independent older oriental myth tradition remains unresolved, even though some of the Mandean textual questions have been clarified.[5]

While it is necessary to take note of this historical critique of the *Religionsgeschichtliche* myth hypothesis, it is equally necessary to note that this criticism was not decisive for Bultmann's reformulation of myth.

He continued to employ Reitzenstein's basic historical hypothesis throughout his later writings and, to the best of my knowledge, has never rejected it. His emphasis has changed from speaking of the several sources (Mandean, Manichean, Ode of Solomon, etc.) to the two sources decisive for the pre-Christian salvation myth: the Jewish apocalyptic Son of Man and the Heavenly Redeemer of Gnosticism. Similarly, the key to the interpretation of these

---

[1] Cf. Richard Nelson Frye, "Reitzenstein and Qumran Revisited by an Iranian," *Harvard Theological Review*, LV (1962), pp. 264-265: James Robinson, Review of *Die religionsgeschichtliche Schule* by Carsten Colpe, *JBL*, LXXXI (Sept. 1962), pp. 287-289.

[2] Rudolf Bultmann, Review of *Ein Beitrag zu Mandäerfrage* by H. Lietzmann, *ThLZ*, LVI (1931), 577-580.

[3] *Ibid.*, p. 577.

[4] Hans Lietzmann, *Ein Beitrag zu Mandäerfrage*, as quoted by Bultmann in his review, *ThLZ* (1931), p. 578.

[5] *Ibid.* Cf. Bultmann, Review of Reitzenstein, *Historische Zeitschrift* (1932), p. 375; also Rudolf Bultmann, Review of *The Fourth Gospel* by C. H. Dodd, trans. W. G. Robinson, *Harvard Divinity Bulletin*, XXVII (1963), 12.

Hellenistic phenomena has ceased to be Reitzenstein's reconstructed Iranian prototype myth and become instead Jonas' *Geist* of Gnosticism. Therefore, in order to understand the shift from Bultmann's early to later formulations of myth, it is necessary to understand, not the historical criticism of Reitzenstein's hypothesis, but the philosophical interpretation of Hellenistic thought which appeared in the work of Hans Jonas.

The revolutionary significance of Jonas' work for Bultmann's thought appears in Bultmann's own testimony from his preface to *Gnosis und spätantiker Geist*, Vol. I:

> Therefore I should say that I, who have devoted for many years a large part of my work to the study of Gnosticism, have not learned as much from any other inquiry in this sphere—and there are certainly enough of them—for a real knowledge of the *geistesgeschichtlichen* phenomenon of Gnosticism as I have learned out of this one. Indeed, the meaning of this phenomenon, in its full extent, has been first disclosed to me in this work. While this work stands clearly in the line of earlier research, there has been demonstrated here for the first time—or so it appears to me—the ordered connection of Gnosticism with the history of late antiquity, Thus, it has become clear what Gnosticism means in the turn of world understanding from the ancient world to the Christianity of the West. Thus, the question of the relationship between Gnosticism and Christianity now appears in a new light. It is no longer a matter of concern limited to individual phenomena of the New Testament and ancient church history, but concerns the total understanding of the world and salvation in Christianity. The method of the author, that of apprehending the authentic meaning of an historical phenomenon through the principle of existentialist analysis, appears to me to have proven its fruitfulness here. I am certain that this work will fructify the *geistesgeschichtliche* research in many respects, not the least of which will be in the sphere of New Testament interpretation.[1]

The constructive significance of Jonas' work for Bultmann's interpretation of myth appears in a later chapter. At this point, I only intend to describe Jonas' philosophical critique of the *Religionsgeschichtliche* understanding of myth and the impact of Jonas' philosophical perspective on Bultmann's position.

First, the *Religionsgeschichtliche* formulation of myth was concerned primarily with the question of "origins," in the precise

---

[1] Rudolf Bultmann, "Vorwort," in *Gnosis und spätantiker Geist*, by Hans Jonas (2 vols.; 2nd ed. of Vol. I; Göttingen: Vandenhoeck & Ruprecht, 1954), p. vii.

sense of a genealogical line of descent. The Iranian hypothesis of
Reitzenstein, or Bultmann's discussion of *Logos*, as was derived
from the figure of Wisdom in Jewish literature, clearly illustrates the
direction of their orientation. Jonas, however, is concerned with the
determination of the essence of Gnosticism, not its genealogical
origins. He describes his own task as that of delineating a "Gnostic
principle" which he comes to identify with a particular "*entweltlicht*" understanding of human existence. The self is here understood as isolated, in relation to society, and placed in an alien and
threatening world. The God who is known and worshipped is a
radical world-transcending God, as is the self, and is as alien to this
world as is the self.[1] Salvation thus is tantamount to being cut free
from the alien world, free to be that which the self was originally
and will be again, as restored to its unity with a transcendent God
and freedom from an encumbering world. It is this existentialist
analysis of the anthropological essence of Gnosticism that constitutes the center of Jonas' contribution.[2]

Second, the central category of the *Religionsgeschichtliche* interpretation of the Hellenistic religious and mythological phenomena
was "syncretistic." Jonas rejected this concept, common to Bultmann and the *Religionsgeschichtliche Schule*.

> Syncretism is a chemical image, a perfect correlate to an objectifying,
> thingifying perspective. It grasps the matter only from the outside
> ... in its functional role and in an objective causal structure. The
> principle of syncretism was appropriate to the older *religions-
> geschichtliche* research, which was concerned with the causal relation-
> ships of the materials of Gnosticism. ... However, if one would
> reach another goal, the new question must be stated at the outset:
> namely, what is the ultimate principle of unity in this many-sided
> phenomenon?[3]

Bultmann concurred with Jonas' critique of the "syncretistic"
image, and the need to explore the question in terms of a fundamental inner unity. Thus, in a review of H. Lietzmann's book,
Geschichte der alten Kirche, published in the same year (1934),
Bultmann praises Lietzmann for moving beyond the old error of

---

[1] *Ibid.*, pp. 18ff.
[2] Cf. Carsten Colpe, *Die religionsgeschichtliche Schule*, p. 201. Colpe
proposes the concepts of "origin" and "essence" as descriptive of the distinction between the *Religionsgeschichtliche* interpretation of Gnosticism and
that offered by Jonas.
[3] Jonas, *Gnosis und spätantiker . . .*, I, p. 11.

Harnack, who had understood Gnosticism as a Hellenized form of Christianity.[1] However, he cannot agree with Lietzmann's own positive treatment of Gnosticism and its relationship to the early Church:

> I cannot agree with the author in his judgement concerning Gnosticism and its significance for the history of the early Church. It appears to me as if it is not important to apprehend Gnosticism as a syncretistic phenomenon, that the relationship of Christianity to *Gnosis* is not rightly seen, as a result of the author's apprehension of *Gnosis* as a syncretistic phenomenon. Rather, I believe that in it a new understanding of *Dasein* breaks forth, new in relation to both the Old Testament and to Greek thought. This is developed and unified in its own structure, however much its mythological and theological speculation may be a syncretistic by-product.[2]

Bultmann then proceeds to characterize this unified self-understanding as a devaluation of the world (*Abwertung der Welt*) and a "deworldlizing" of *Dasein* ("*Entweltlichung*").[3]

Third, the shift of inquiry from origin to essence, from the objectifying perspective of syncretism to the existentialist perspective of self-understanding, also brought about a corresponding change of context of interpretation. For Bultmann's earlier discussions of myth, it was Bousset's work that elucidated the decisive context for the interpretation of myth: namely, the cult of the Hellenistic world. For Jonas, however, the emergence of a radical new understanding of human existence could not be confined to the cultic context. For, as Jonas was to demonstrate in his second volume, this same new understanding of existence was determina-

---

[1] Rudolf Bultmann, Review of *Geschichte der Alten Kirche* by Hans Lietzmann, *ZKG*, III (1934), 629.

[2] *Ibid.* Bultmann offers a similar point in discussing the same Lietzmann volume two years later:

> Lietzmann has in his history of the ancient church shown that *Gnosis* did not first develop on the ground of Christianity, as its acute Hellenizing (Harnack) but that it is a general phenomenon of the Hellenistic period. However, he still apprehends it as a syncretistic phenomenon. Over against this is the work of Hans Jonas, of which the first volume has now appeared. Jonas shows that in *Gnosis* there is developed a complete and unified understanding of *Dasein*, which is genuinely new, both in relation to the Old Testament and to the Greek world (Rudolf Bultmann, "Neueste Paulusforschung," *ThR*, VIII [1936], 19).

Cf. Rudolf Bultmann, "Geleitwort," *Das Wesen des Christentum* by A. Harnack (Stuttgart: Ehernfried Klotz Verlag, 1950), pp. x-xi.

[3] Bultmann, Review of *Geschichte der Alten Kirche*, *ZKG* (1934), 629.

tive for the development of the philosophical thought of the late Hellenistic world.[1] In any case, the *Sache* of the Hellenistic myths was not of the order of the history of cultic phenomena, but of the order of the history of *Geist*. The myths of the Hellenistic world were therefore to be interpreted in the context of a particular stage in the unfolding of a radical new self-understanding of *Dasein*, namely the beginning or point of transition, and not as the final product of this history of a *mythos* developing from Iranian origins to a final Hellenistic end product.

Fourth, I may stipulate this same difference by reference to the direction of interpretation. The *Religionsgeschichtliche* concern with myth was characteristically oriented backwards from the Hellenistic world to more primitive origins; Jonas' concern with myth was oriented forwards, from the Hellenistic myths through the history of medieval thought into Luther and Kierkegaard in the West. Gnosticism was therefore not to be understood as an end product, a complex and highly developed synthesis of the old Hellenic world and the old Eastern mythologies. Rather, Gnosticism was a new beginning. Jonas expressed this character of Gnosticism as follows:

> Now it is important to recognize that in these events we are dealing, not with a reaction of the *old* East, but with a novel phenomenon which at that crucial hour entered the stage of history. The "Old East" was dead. The new awakening did not mean a classicist resuscitation of its time-honored heritage. Not even the more recent conceptualizations of earlier oriental thought were the real substance of the movement. Traditional dualism, traditional astrological fatalism, traditional monotheism were all drawn into it, yet with such a peculiarly new twist to them that in the present setting they subserved the representation of a novel spiritual principle; and the same is true of the use of Greek philosophical terms. It is necessary to emphasize this fact from the outset because of the strong suggestion to the contrary created by the outer appearances, which have long misled historians into regarding the fabric of thought they were confronted with, except for its Christian part, as simply made up of the remnants of older traditions. They all do in fact appear in the new stream. ... But syncretism itself provides only the outer aspect and not the essence of the phenomenon. ... Though these

---

[1] Hans Jonas, *Gnosis und spätantiker Geist*, Part II, First Half (Göttingen: Vandenhoeck & Ruprecht, 1954). This volume is sub-titled: "Von der Mythologie zur mystischen Philosophie," and focuses upon Philo, Plotinus, and Origen. While not published until 1954, the copy was placed in the hands of the printers prior to 1934, as Jonas states in the "Vorwort."

syncretistic associations are by no means irrelevant, we can discern a new spiritual center around which the elements of tradition now crystallize, the unity behind their multiplicity; and this, rather than the syncretistic means of expression is the true entity with which we are confronted. If we acknowledge this center as an autonomous force, then we must say that it makes use of those elements rather than that it is constituted by their confluence; and the whole which thus originated will in spite of its manifestly synthetic character have to be understood not as the product of an uncommitted eclecticism but as an original and determinate system of ideas.[1]

Bultmann shares this new perspective on Gnosticism. In it there emerges a novel spiritual principle which provides the point of transition from the old world of the Greek city state and Old Testament to the new understanding of world and self which appears in the history of the West. In reviewing several studies of the relationship of Christianity to the ancient world, Bultmann writes:

> Both books should have made an attempt to understand Gnosticism as a whole: that is, as an authentic salvation faith and myth expressing both an understanding of man and the world. Hans Jonas' presentation of Gnosticism has made clear the epoch-making character of Gnosticism, which brought to an end the old Greek world, so that Gnosticism and Christianity are parallel phenomena. What is decisive in either case is the problem of *Dasein* and its self-understanding. The self-understanding and the world relationship, which had been predominant in the classical world of Greece and Rome, have here become questionable. The world is no more the home of man, and he is in error to understand himself in terms of the world, whether this be in terms of the cosmos objectified in thought, of which he is a member and in reference to which he understands himself, or whether it be in terms of the political and social worlds of the Greek city-state.[2]

Fifth, in light of these changes of perspective, it was also necessary to reconsider the relationship of Hellenistic myths in general, or Gnosticism in particular, to the interpretation of Christianity. In Bultmann's use of the *Religionsgeschichtliche* tradition, it is axiomatic that the Hellenistic myth studies are relevant to the interpretation of the New Testament only as a preliminary mode of inquiry, and only at the point of clarifying the meaning of particular concepts and images. The use of Hellenistic materials is therefore

---

[1] Hans Jonas, *The Gnostic Religion* (2nd ed.; Boston: Beacon Press, 1963), pp. 24-25. Cf. *Gnosis und spätantiker Geist*, I, 74-75.
[2] Rudolf Bultmann, "Zum Thema: Christentum und Antike," *ThR*, XVI (1944), 19.

limited to the level of form, rather than substance, and to partic-
ulars, rather than to the understanding of the meaning of the text
as a whole. Bultmann expresses the nature of the exegetical role of
Hellenistic myth materials clearly in his 1927 essay on the Gospel of
John:

> The newest form of research in the Gospel of John might be called
> —if one wishes a title for it—the mythological-historical. However,
> one should not be deceived by this name: it suffices only as a pre-
> liminary study for exegesis. To be sure, this preliminary study is
> indispensable and has decisive meaning, for it makes it possible to
> understand the language of the Gospel as it unfolds its conceptual
> presuppositions.[1]

The role of this myth criticism is to assist the New Testament
interpreter in understanding particular concepts and expressions of
the New Testament:

> That Paul brings this to expression with the help of the oriental
> salvation myth is not irrelevant, since the knowledge of the myth
> helps to explain more certainly his individual expressions.[2]

In Jonas' study of Gnosticism, however, there appeared a relation
between Christianity and the myths of the Hellenistic world which
was of a quite different order. It was no longer a question of cross
influences, which would appear in particular images or ideas, but
rather a question of the common origin of Christianity and Gnostic
mythology in a common *Geist*. For Christianity and Gnosticism
were products of the same epoch, and, according to the philosophy
of *Geist*, "were formed out of the same powers of an all embracing
movement of *Geist*." [3] Christianity is therefore not to be understood
as borrowing elements foreign to itself from Gnosticism, but as
itself participating in the same fundamental transformation of the
understanding of *Dasein* which appeared also in Gnosticism. It is
thus axiomatic for Jonas that "Christianity and extra-Christian
phenomena must be understood as arising out of this more common
fundamental ground." [4] The study of Gnosticism is therefore determinative for the understanding of Christianity, not simply at the
level of forms of expression; rather, Gnosticism "sheds real light

---

[1] Bultmann, "Das Johannesevangelium . . .," *ChrW* (1927), col. 510.
[2] Rudolf Bultmann, Review of *Die Auferstehung der Toten* by Karl Barth,
GV, I, 53 [originally published: *ThBL*, V (1926), 1-14].
[3] Jonas, *Gnosis und* . . ., I, 82.
[4] *Ibid.*, p. 81.

upon the inner development of Christianity because it stands in an
inner relationship to it." [1] They share common origins in a common
Geist.

While Bultmann does not explicitly appropriate the philosophical
presuppositions and technical philosophical categories which are
intrinsic to Jonas' interpretation of Gnosticism and Christianity,
he does accept the basic conclusion reached. As he wrote in the
foreword to the volume by Jonas:

> Thus the question of the relationship between Gnosticism and
> Christianity now appears in a new light. It is no longer a matter
> of concern limited to individual phenomena of the New Testament
> and ancient church history but concerns the total understanding of
> the world and salvation in Christianity.[2]

The level of discussion has now shifted from "individual elements"
to the whole, and also from the level of "forms of expression" to the
fundamental substance, the "total understanding of the world and
salvation in Christianity." From this point on, Bultmann shall
describe Gnosticism and Christianity as expressing, in their distinct
forms, the one fundamental new spiritual principle which broke
forth into history at this particular moment. The content of this
Gnostic principle is the "deworldlizing" of human existence: the
understanding of human existence as absolutely different from all
worldly existence.

> For the essence of Gnosticism does not lie in its syncretistic mythol-
> ogy, but rather in a new understanding—new in the ancient world—
> of man and the world; its mythology is only the expression of this
> understanding ... the utter difference of human existence from
> all worldly existence was recognized for the first time in Gnosticism
> and Christianity and thus the world became foreign soil to the
> human self.[3]

While Bultmann always insists upon the distinction between
Gnosticism and Christianity, it is also clear that he shares with
Jonas the same fundamental view of the nature of the relationship
of these two historic phenomena: in their spiritual origins, they are
one, bringing to expression the same new understanding of human
existence. The hermeneutical role of Gnosticism, in relation to the

---

[1] *Ibid.*
[2] *Ibid.*, p. vii.
[3] Rudolf Bultmann, *Theology of the New Testament*, trans. Kendrick
Grobel (2 vols.; New York: Charles Scribner's Sons, 1951-1955), I, 165.

literature of the early Christian movement, is obviously quite different on these grounds than it was on the older *Religions-geschichtliche* basis.[1]

These, then appear to be basic points at which Bultmann breaks away from the *Religionsgeschichtliche* tradition in his understanding of the Hellenistic world and its myths as a result of Jonas' 1934 study of Gnosticism. Having delineated the sharpness of this break and the mediating role of Jonas, several qualifications need to be noted. First is the biographical fact that Jonas was himself a pupil of Bultmann's. He came to know the world of Hellenistic religions and myths through Bultmann, and himself appropriated the basic conclusions of the *Religionsgeschichtliche Schule* as the point of depar-ture for his own work.[2] Second, by 1934, Bultmann had himself begun to move toward an existentialist interpretation of Hellenistic myths. While he never attained the clear and systematic formula-tion of the "Gnostic principle" which he first found in Jonas, it is nevertheless true that he understood himself, and his *Religions-geschichtliche* colleagues also, as moving toward the delineation of this principle. Thus, in a 1932 retrospective review of Reitzenstein, he could write:

> Regarding the great theme of the change in the self-understanding of man and his corresponding understanding of the world and God, which has resulted from the meeting of East and West, one may say that there have been few writings of comparable importance to the work of the author [Reitzenstein].[3]

Third, in emphasizing the contribution of Jonas, one need re-member that Bultmann consistently appropriated for his own thought only that which was consistent with his own fundamental philosophical-theological conceptuality. This is true for his theolog-ical relationship with Barth as well as his philosophical relation-ship with Heidegger. In this connection, one cannot overlook the close connection between the *"entweltlicht"* anthropology, which appears as "the Gnostic principle," "the new autonomous spiritual movement," in Jonas, and the concept of individuality, as this is

---

[1] For an example of Bultmann's insistence on the use of the Gnostic principle in the interpretation of New Testament literature, see his Review of *The Fourth Gospel* by C. H. Dodd, *Harvard Divinity Bulletin*, XXVII (January, 1963), 10-12.

[2] Cf. Carsten Colpe, *Die religionsgeschichtliche* . . ., p. 60.

[3] Bultmann, Review of Reitzenstein, *Historische Zeitschrift* (1932), p. 375.

determined by its negative epistemological relationship to any rational-objective world form and the social-existential mood of postwar Germany. From the perspective of the *Religionsgeschicht-liche Schule*, Bultmann looked at the myths of the Hellenistic world and could only discern their essential strangeness, bound up as they were with the cult and with a cosmic form of salvation. From the perspective of Jonas' Gnostic principle, however, Bult-mann could look at these same phenomena and discern there— albeit in the inadequate and confused form of expression of myth—a much more familiar understanding of man, isolated in his indi-viduality before a radically world-transcending God and in the midst of a hostile culture. The roots for this reformulation of myth are in Bultmann's own thought, even if the formulation of an appropriate systematic conceptual expression has been developed only by his pupil, Hans Jonas.

I may summarize the discussion of this discontinuity as follows:

1. As a member of the *Religionsgeschichtliche Schule*, myth criticism meant for Bultmann an historical form of inquiry into the origins of particular New Testament literary motifs (i.e., the *Logos* of the Johannine Prologue); after Jonas, myth criticism became a form of existentialist analysis which attempts to determine the new understanding of human existence which is fundamental to the New Testament as a whole.

2. As a member of the *Religionsgeschichtliche Schule*, Bultmann understood myth to mean a particular salvation narrative present in several related texts (Mandean, Manichean, Ode of Solomon, etc.), unified in terms of a common Iranian prototype, and to be interpreted in the context of the cult of the Hellenistic world; after Jonas, myth comes to mean a particular form of expression (objectifying) of a radical new self-understanding (*entweltlicht*), present in a variety of Hellenistic texts but deci-sively disclosed at the point of Gnosticism, and to be interpreted in the context of the history of *Geist*.

In all these ways, Bultmann's *Religionsgeschichtliche* formulation of myth recedes into the background. In order that this transition be fully understood, however, it is now necessary to note the motifs of the old *Religionsgeschichtliche* use of myth which continue to be present in Bultmann's later discussion of the subject. For with Bultmann, it is a general rule, that old ideas never die, they just slip into the background. Thus, while Bultmann moves out of this basic formulation of myth, he continues to preserve selected motifs of that usage in his later discussion of the subject.

For example, Bultmann never rejects Reitzenstein's basic hypothesis concerning the old Iranian prototype myth; he simply alters the point of emphasis. He is still free, in discussing Christianity or Jewish apocalyptic, to refer to the decisive role of "Iranian speculation" or "Iranian dualistic mythology" or "Persian mythology." [1] More often, however, he simply cites the familiar collection of Reitzenstein's Iranian derivative myth traditions as constituting a family of traditions, "whatever historical connections may underlie this kinship." [2] Bultmann still insists upon speaking of a "pre-Christian redeemer myth," only now it is no longer Reitzenstein's myth of the Primal Man from Iran, but more simply the pre-Christian Gnostic myth of the Heavenly Redeemer. [3]

As a result of these changes, Bultmann's later use of *Religionsgeschichtliche* data often acquires a positivistic character. Myth comes to be defined by reference to a certain body of literature, all of which are generally known to be examples of myth, without being given any determinate essence according to genealogical derivation. Thus, Bultmann writes:

> It is evident that such conceptions [apocalyptic pictures of the end] are mythological, for they were widespread in the mythologies of the Jews and Gentiles, and then were transferred to the historical person of Jesus. Particularly the concept of the pre-existent Son of God who descended in human guise into the world to redeem mankind is part of the Gnostic doctrine of redemption, and nobody hesitates to call this doctrine mythological. [4]

Not only is the relationship between the myths of the Hellenistic world and Christianity treated in this positivistic manner, but the numbers of myths are greatly reduced: characteristically, it is only Jewish apocalyptic and Gnosticism that come to expression as

---

[1] Rudolf Bultmann, Review of *Reich Gottes und Menschensohn* by R. Otto, *ThR*, IX (1937), 7; Bultmann, *Theology of the New Testament*, I, 172; Rudolf Bultmann, *History and Eschatology: The Presence of Eternity* (New York: Harper & Brothers, 1962), p. 26.

[2] Bultmann, *Theology of the New Testament*, I, 132.

[3] Rudolf Bultmann, *Das Evangelium des Johannes* (Göttingen: Vandenhoeck & Ruprecht, 1950), p. 12; Bultmann, Review of *The Fourth Gospel* by Dodd, *Harvard Divinity Bulletin* (1963), pp. 10; 17-18; Rudolf Bultmann, "The Christological Confession of the World Council of Churches," *Essays: Philosophical and Theological*, trans. James C. G. Greig (London: SCM Press Ltd., 1955), pp. 279.

[4] Rudolf Bultmann, *Jesus Christ and Mythology* (New York: Charles Scribner's Sons, 1958), p. 17.

examples of the common genus, myth. The historical grounds for Bultmann's use of myth, in conjunction with the literature of the New Testament, thus comes to be the cosmological, anthropological, and soteriological motifs which it shares in common with these two traditions.

The fact that this original *Religionsgeschichtliche* hypothesis of myth has been thus weakened does not have any significant effect upon Bultmann's fundamental argument for demythologizing. For the project of demythologizing itself was not born until after this historically oriented use of myth had already fallen into the background. In demythologizing, it is the discipline of philosophy, rather than that of history, which provides both the presuppositions and context for its usage. The older use of myth then serves simply to provide evidence of a circumstantial character with a very indirect relationship to the actual project of demythologizing. Indeed, the clearest testimony to the independence of Bultmann's later concept of myth from the early *Religionsgeschichtliche* formulation is the fact that the serious criticism of Reitzenstein's historical hypothesis has had no impact upon the theological project of demythologizing.

It should be obvious from Bultmann's discussion of this period, and the description of this literary-cultic formulation of myth, that this use of myth was basically alien to the dualistic philosophical conceptuality set forth in the preceding chapter. Cosmos and existence; individual and community; salvation and morality; self-understanding and world-understanding; literary form and existential meaning: these are here bound together in an insep-arable unity. It is therefore no accident that Bultmann as theolo-gian quickly moved beyond this formulation of myth which he had borrowed as New Testament historian. In the following chapters, we shall begin to see the development of a concept of myth more consistent with the dualistic philosophical conceptuality examined in the previous chapter.

CHAPTER FOUR

THE ENLIGHTENMENT FORMULATION OF MYTH

The conclusion of the preceding chapter described the transition from the early *Religionsgeschichtliche* formulation of myth to Bultmann's later discussion of the subject by reference to the existentialist studies of the Hellenistic world developed by Hans Jonas. It would thus appear as if one should move directly to a consideration of the existentialist formulation of myth. Such, however, is not the case. For Bultmann's thought does not simply move from the *Religionsgeschichtliche* use of myth to the existentialist use of myth, but rather moves from the one to the other only by way of a third. This third element in Bultmann's later concept of myth I call "the Enlightenment formulation of myth." I choose the historical period of the Enlightenment as a name for this formulation of myth because it was born in the seventeenth-century French Enlightenment and first appropriated into biblical studies in the eighteenth-century German Enlightenment. Beyond this consideration of literal, chronological origins, this formulation of myth is appropriately called by the name of the Enlightenment since it expresses so well the essence of the Enlightenment spirit: man's discovery of his past as discontinuous with the life of reason he knows in the present.

I might also call this an epistemological formulation of myth. For myth is here apprehended, in its essence and by definition, as a false form of knowledge of the world. More properly, one should speak of an historico-epistemological formulation of myth. For the issue is not simply one of false knowledge, but the falseness of the knowledge is understood to be grounded in the underdeveloped capacity for knowing characteristic of man at a certain stage of history. Man *necessarily* has a false knowledge of his world because he has not yet developed the powers of reason, with its capacities for observing, relating, abstracting, testing, and logic, which are the preconditions for true knowledge. In a brief form, I define this Enlightenment view of myth as a primitive (naïve, pre-rational pre-critical, pre-logical, etc.) mode of thought expressing a pre-scientific (pre-modern, pre-Enlightenment, etc.) view of the world. The concept of "primitive" is used in the sense of a developmental philosophy of history, and the concept of "scientific" in terms of its popular association with a view of reality as determined by the laws of causality.

It is the examination of this particular formulation of myth, in its original sources and in the thought of Rudolf Bultmann, that constitutes the subject matter of this chapter. Unlike the previous chapter, however, this inquiry may not be delimited according to a definite period of Bultmann's writings. While this formulation of myth never appears in Bultmann's writings prior to 1930, after that date it is increasingly present in Bultmann's discussion of myth, and by 1941, it has become an integral part of his total concept of myth. This means that the Enlightenment formulation of myth is developed by Bultmann simultaneously with his existentialist formulation of myth until, by the fusion of the two with the remnants of the *Religionsgeschichtliche* tradition in 1941, he has constructed that stable concept of myth which provides the semantic kernel for demythologizing. As a result of the close interpenetration of the Enlightenment tradition with the total concept of myth, I shall have to extract this particular use of myth from any given text under consideration.

The most important sources for the chapter are those essays which constitute the central core for Bultmann's later discussion of myth and the demythologizing proposal:

1. "Neues Testament und Mythologie" (1941)
2. "Zu J. Schniewinds Thesen, das Problem der Entmythologisierung betreffend" (1948)
3. "Zum Problem der Entmythologisierung" (1952)
4. "Die christliche Hoffnung und das Problem der Entmythologisierung" (1953)
5. "Antwort an Karl Jaspers" (1953)
6. *Jesus Christ and Mythology* (1958)
7. "Zum Problem der Entmythologisierung" (1961) [1]

---

[1] I may note at this point some bibliographical information on these publications. I shall not attempt to note all of the editions and translations of these works, but simply that information of possible help to the reader.
1) "Neues Testament und Mythologie," as previously noted, first appeared as a portion of *Offenbarung und Heilsgeschehen*. Above, Chapter I, p. 1.
2) "Zu J. Schniewinds Thesen . . .," has been translated by Reginald Fuller and appears, together with "Neues Testament und Mythologie," in *KaM*, I.
3) The last two sections of "Zum Problem der Entmythologisierung" (1952) have also been translated by Fuller and appear under the title "Bultmann Replies to His Critics" in *KaM*, I. Fuller apparently followed Bultmann's judgment, expressed in Chapter I of this study, concerning the peripheral

I shall also consider Bultmann's 1930 *RGG* essay, "Mythus und Mythologie im Neuen Testament," together with a variety of reviews and essays relevant to the Enlightenment formulation of myth. Beyond these Bultmann texts, I shall also examine the important essay of the late seventeenth-century French author, Bernard Fontenelle, *De l'origine des fables*, together with portions of J. G. Eichorn's *Einleitung ins Alte Testament* (1780-1783) and D. F. Strauss's *Das Leben Jesu* (1835-1836).

The Enlightenment motifs in demythologizing have caused considerable intellectual confusion and theological embarrassment. It is not immediately apparent how Enlightenment rationalism may be reconciled to the Christian faith and it is even less clear why an existentialist theologian of the twentieth century would resuscitate a somewhat obsolete eighteenth-century view of myth. As a result, many early Bultmann studies have treated the Enlightenment motifs in his thought as a surd, to be exaggerated by enemies

---

role of the discussion of myth in the demythologizing debate. At least he has omitted the first section of the essay, in which Bultmann addresses himself to the specific issue of myth, from the English translation. This first section is available only in the German original, *KuM*, II, 179-190.

4) "Die christliche Hoffnung ..." was originally published in *Unterwegs*, VII (1953). It then was published as a separate volume under the same title (Stuttgart: Evangelisches Verlagswerk, 1954). This volume includes the three essays by G. Bornkamm, R. Bultmann, and F. K. Schumann, together with their concluding conversation. All future references are to this single volume edition of "Die christliche Hoffnung..." More recently, this essay has been published (without concluding dialogue) in *GV*, III, 81-90.

5) "Antwort an Karl Jaspers" first appeared in *Schweizerische Theologische Rundschau*, III-IV (1953), 74-106. The German text is most easily found in *KuM*, III, 49-60. It is also available in an English translation in two editions: 1) *Myth and Christianity: An Inquiry into the Possibility of Religion without Myth*, by Karl Jaspers and R. Bultmann (New York: The Noonday Press, 1958), 2) *KaM*, II, 181-194. Future references are to the Noonday Press edition, unless otherwise specified.

6) Originally presented as lectures in English, *Jesus Christ and Mythology* appeared as a separate volume (New York: Charles Scribner's Sons, 1958).

7) "Zum Problem der Entmythologisierung" (1961) was first presented as a paper at an international colloguy on demythologizing held under the auspices of the Istituto di Studi Filosofici, Universita di Roma, in January, 1961. It was first published in German in the volume, *Il problema della demitizzazione*, ed. Enrico Castelli (Rome: Archivio di Filosofia, 1961), pp. 19-26. It has since also appeared in *KuM*, VI-1, 20-27. S. Ogden has translated the essay into English under the title: "On the Problem of Demythologizing," *JR* XLII (1962), 96-102. References are to the Castelli edition, or the Ogden translation, as specified.

9

and dismissed or ignored by friends.[1] However, from the perspective of Neo-Kantian epistemology, it is possible to give an account of this Enlightenment understanding of myth as a clear and consistent expression of Bultmann's thought.

1. SOURCES FOR THE ENLIGHTENMENT FORMULATION: B. FONTENELLE, J. G. EICHORN, AND D. F. STRAUSS

It is neither possible nor necessary to establish a direct historical antecedent for Bultmann's appropriation of the Enlightenment formulation of myth. By the end of the eighteenth century, to say nothing of the beginning of the twentieth century, this concept of myth had been well assimilated into a variety of cultural traditions of the modern western world.[2] By the middle of the nineteenth century, it was firmly established as a central category of critical biblical studies.[3] Bultmann first introduces this idea of myth into his discussion of that subject matter in his essay, "Mythus und Mythologie im Neuen Testament." [4] Prior to this, he never uses myth with an Enlightenment sense of meaning. In part, he rejects the Enlightenment meaning of the term when he writes, in 1927, that myth is not to be understood as "a primitive explanation of the world or a philosophy in embryo." [5] However, since he offers a similar critique of this formulation of myth in 1942, after he has himself espoused the position, one may not take too seriously this critique. What is clear, however, is that during the period of 1915-1929, in which there are abundant references to myth in Bultmann's publications, none of these suggest, or could be construed along the lines of, the Enlightenment meaning of the term.[6]

---

[1] Above, pp. 12-13.

[2] For a comprehensive survey of this idea of myth as developed by a variety of eighteenth-century thinkers, see: *The Eighteenth Century Confronts the Gods* by Frank E. Manuel (Cambridge, Mass.: Harvard University Press, 1959).

[3] For a study of the extensive use and development of this concept of myth in nineteenth-century biblical studies, see *Die Ursprung des Mythosbegriffes in der modernen Bibelwissenschaft*, Christian Hartlich and Walter Sachs (Tübingen: J. C. B. Mohr, 1952).

[4] Rudolf Bultmann, "Mythus und Mythologie: III B. Im NT," *Die Religion in Geschichte und Gegenwart* (2nd edition; Tübingen: J. C. B. Mohr, 1920), v. IV, cols. 390-394.

[5] Bultmann, "Das Johannesevangelium . . ." (1927), col. 510.

[6] Carsten Colpe has recognized the distinction between the *Religionsgeschichtliche* formulation of myth and the earlier use of myth in nineteenth-century biblical studies (*Die religionsgeschichtliche Schule*, p. 59). While the

The date of the appearance of this motif may be specified, though not any specific source from which Bultmann received this motif.

I describe the Enlightenment formulation of myth in terms of three fundamental presuppositions:

1) A developmental philosophy of history. The development of history in its totality is understood as analogous with the development of the individual human being. The age in which men make myths is related to the age of reason as childhood is related to maturity.

2) A theory of primitive mentality. There is a certain type of mentality, universally present in the history of man and qualitatively different from modern mentality, which is the source of myths.

3) A scientific view of reality as a unified cause-effect nexus. In the primitive stage of history, in which the capacity for reason was not yet fully developed, man could not know the nature of reality. Hence, the pre-scientific world view, defined according to its antithesis with a scientific world view, came to be the essential criterion for the definition of myth.

The central core of this concept of myth is the fusion of a developmental hypothesis with an Enlightenment perspective on history. It was Augustine, not the Enlightenment, who first likened the history of humanity to the history of the individual man. Man, including his reason, does not appear in the fullness of his humanity at the beginning of history. He must undergo a process of growth in order that, through Christ, he might come to that fullness of humanity for which he was destined.[1] As wedded to an Enlightenment view of history, however, this original Augustinian analogy lost the essential dimension of the future, and became a simple formula for relating the past to the present. Primitive man—indeed, the whole of pre-Enlightenment history with the exception of the Greeks— came to be the child; the Enlightenment man was the mature man,

---

Religionsgeschichtliche concern with myth, in terms of its specific literary motifs and their historical genesis, did not exclude a philosophical concern with myth as a pre-scientific phenomenon, neither did it encompass nor demand such an hypothesis.

[1] A still earlier theological form of this developmental perspective is offered in Irenaeus, for whom Adam is child and Christ is fully mature man, the eschatological goal of all humanity.

Bultmann never attempts to recover the theological origins and eschatological perspective of this developmental hypothesis. Indeed, since all of history and its development falls within the sphere of reason, he feels compelled to allow the secularity of the Enlightenment reformulation to stand, regardless of its theological and existential inadequacies.

the man come of age. The decisive turning point of history was the Enlightenment itself, for it was here that the Age of Reason was born. Little wonder, in such a realized eschatology, that the past uncovered by the Enlightenment historian and designated by the concept of myth was a past essentially alien to the rational man of the Enlightenment, a past from which he could profit little except as Fontenelle suggested, "to study the history of the errors of the human spirit." [1]

For a guide in the exposition of this Enlightenment view of myth, I shall follow out the thought of Bernard Fontenelle as presented in his early work, *De l'origine des fables*.[2] For it is Fontenelle who

---

[1] Bernard Fontenelle, *De l'origine des fables*, ed. J. R. Carré (Paris: Libraire Felix Alcan, 1932), p. 40.

[2] The original date of publication is 1724. J. R. Carré, who has prepared the critical edition of Fontenelle's work, argues that *De l'origine* ... must have been written prior to 1680, though withheld from publication until the later date of 1724. Carré bases this argument on a consideration of internal evidence, provided by a comparison of this work with later publications, and the external evidence provided by correspondence between Fontenelle and friends. In the latter, there are references to a document such as *De l'origine* ..., as early as 1688 (*ibid.*, p. 4). It is on the basis of Carré's argument that I have selected Fontenelle, rather than Pierre Bayle or others, as the first exponent of this idea so prevalent in the Enlightenment world. (Cf. Manuel, *The Eighteenth Century* ..., pp. 42 ff.)

Regardless of the validity of Carré's dating of the Fontenelle text, it is nevertheless clear that one is dealing here with a phenomenon that is considerably earlier than the eighteenth-century texts of C. G. Heyne. As Manuel wrote:

> One must understand that the genius of a Fontenelle lies in his understanding of myth as an integral and essential moment in the development of man. Myth is thus not primarily an exported and culturally transmitted product perpetuated by some power group like the priests. Myth-making was a stage in the history of reason common to all people. At this point, Fontenelle, Vico, Boulanger, Hume, de Brosses, and Herder would be in accord, for their very conception of a universal human nature made it possible for them to dispense with the migrating gods required by the previous generation (*ibid.*, p. 46).

It is thus clear that by the last quarter of the eighteenth century, this formulation of myth has become the common property of the intellectual tradition of the West. Thus, Manuel includes only a brief discussion of Heyne in conjunction with Herder's conception of myth.

> The Herder conception of myth received its most significant scholarly application in the classical studies of Christian Gottlob Heyne ... Heyne established interesting distinctions between the *sermo mythicus*, the original spontaneous outburst of *Volk* feeling, and the *sermo poeticus*, the elaboration of the myth by the conscious creative artist. His scholarship was impeccable, his editing of texts in the great tradition,

first develops the basic themes of this Enlightenment theory of myth. While he uses the term "fable" and not "myth," it is quite clear from his discussion of "fable" that he does not mean the product of the freedom of the imagination, but rather the necessary product of the pre-rational mind customarily designated by myth.[1]

The distinctive contribution of Fontenelle was to first propose a unified and total theory of myth. No longer were myths to be understood by reference to particular circumstances: i.e., climatic conditions, ethnic traits (e.g., the exaggeration of the Oriental), or cultural transmission. However different the peoples might be, all myths were to be understood in the same manner. Greece, Persia, China, Arabia, the Indians of the New World: Fontenelle freely selects examples from all of them, and all of them display the same characteristics. "The conformity between the fables of the American Indians and the Greeks is astonishing." [2] In delineating the homo-geneity of the total past of humanity, Fontenelle is even willing to extend his hypothesis to include undiscovered nations of men: "even if we were to find a new people living on one of the poles, their first histories would be fables."[3] Fable making, or myth making, thus comes to be understood as a universal phenomenon in the history of humanity, and not as an activity characteristic of a particular people or region.

The reason for the universality of this phenomenon was not difficult to discern. As Fontenelle observed, it was a demanding task for a cultivated person of his own age to write a true history of

---

but for all the appurtenances of learning the spirit which animated him and generations of German *Gelehrte* was the same romantic Hellenism which possessed his literary compatriots in the eighteenth century (Manuel, *The Eighteenth Century* . . ., p. 302).

While Heyne's work was of great significance for the early theological use of the Enlightenment formulation of myth, Manuel offers a more accurate estimation of his significance in the total development of this concept of myth than the work of Hartlich and Sachs, who argued that Heyne recognized myth as a universal form of thought for the first time, *Die Ursprung* . . ., p. 4.

[1] Fontenelle distinguishes between the essential "ignorance" of the savage and his free use of imagination and embellishment. The former is the root of "fables," not the latter; it is because of this essential ignorance that fables are a universal and necessary product in the history of humanity. The imaginative exaggeration is something added onto what is already a fable narrative posing as history (Fontenelle, *De l'origine* . . ., pp. 20-21). Cf. *ibid.*, p. 32.

[2] *Ibid.*, p. 32.

[3] *Ibid.*, p. 30.

events, and even now all too few could recognize the difference between true history and false history or fable.[1] Little wonder, then, that the men of earlier ages all told their histories in the form of fables. For their "power of reason" was not yet developed.[2] In their mental capacity, they were to be compared with children and peasants. The myths or fables of the past were the necessary product of this primitive and undeveloped intellect, qualitatively distinct from the "higher powers of abstraction so remarkably concentrated among members of the French academies."[3] All men understood the nature of the world in terms of their own experience. The *"pauvres sauvages"* understood the nature of their world in terms of their immediate concrete experience: therefore, the primitive projected his feelings into the world of nature.[4] This was his only mode of world-explanation, since "the *pauvres sauvages* did not know of weights, levers, or the laws of the physical world."[5] The *"grossière philosophie"* of the primitive ages was thus the result of the limited experience and capacity of reason of primitive man.[6] It is this mental deficiency, rather than any imaginative powers, that is to be understood as the root of the fable.[7]

Because of the quality of necessity intrinsic to fable making, two conclusions followed. First, one could not impute malice or deception to the author of fables. "The falsification of history which occurs in fables . . . is due to the mental powers of the author, not his character or will."[8] Fontenelle was not the typical French anti-clerical mythophile who made the priests responsible for the creation and preservation of the myths of antiquity. The authors of these false narratives from the past wrote them within the limits of the mental capacities available at that stage of history, and could not be blamed for their results.[9] Second, one could not impute great

---

[1] *Ibid.*, p. 24.

[2] *Ibid.*

[3] Manuel has coined this phrase to describe the norm for the theory of primitive mentality (Manuel, *The Eighteenth Century* . . ., p. 44).

[4] Manuel makes the point that the fundamental idea of projection—the explanation of nature in terms of human feelings as a result of which the gods are born—was first developed by Fontenelle, though later appropriated by Vico, Hume, and most recently, Freud (*ibid.*, p. 44).

[5] Fontenelle, *De l'origine* . . ., p. 16.

[6] *Ibid.*

[7] *Ibid.*, p. 20.

[8] *Ibid.*, p. 21.

[9] Fontenelle did hold the primitive responsible for his "prodigious exaggerations" and for his persistence in ignorance in the light of truth. However,

moral or spiritual truths to fables. Fontenelle thus rejected the
allegorical method of interpretation, which purported to find
"great thoughts relevant to morality or the physical world disguised
in the images of fables." [1] Nor would he accept the attitude of
awe or respect for the great truths of the past age as appropriate to
their real offerings. In the thought of the men of antiquity, one finds
neither malice of will nor depth of wisdom, but simply the mind of
man in a very early stage of its development.

The essential mark of the fable was its false view of the nature of
the world. It is a world of gods and demons, creatures like man
himself only of greater power; above all, it was a world of miracles,
in which these supernatural powers cause unexpected happenings.[2]
This view of the world was a product of primitive man's projection
of feelings, on the one hand, and absence of knowledge—"ignorance"—of the laws of nature, on the other hand. In any case, it
was the laws derived from the science of nature which provided
Fontenelle, like his followers, with the essential criterion for distinguishing between *"l'histoire fabuleuse des premiers siècles et l'histoire
vraisemblable ou véritable des siècles qui ont suivi."* [3] The distinction
between true history or real history and false history or fable and
myth is thus constituted firmly on the grounds of the criteria
provided by the sciences of nature in their description of the world.

Fontenelle thus formulated the three essential characteristics of
the Enlightenment idea of myth: the developmental schema of
history with its theory of primitive mentality as this is recognized
in the pre-scientific world view. In turning to the early biblical
studies of the nineteenth century, one finds the same elements
determinative for the meaning of myth. At this point, it is J. G.
Eichorn who must be acknowledged as the father of historical myth
criticism as well as literary source criticism. Both of these break-
throughs in critical biblical studies appeared in his 1780-1783
edition of *Einleitung ins Alte Testament*.[4] Eichorn's use of this

---

these character defects did not constitute the source of fables, but only their
accompanying traits (*ibid.*).

  [1] *Ibid.*, p. 40.
  [2] *Ibid.*, pp. 13, 19.
  [3] *Ibid.*, p. 46.
  [4] J. G. Eichorn, *Einleitung ins Alte Testament* (2nd edition.; Leipzig: Erben
und Reich, 1787). In a later writing, Eichorn recounts how C. G. Heyne
presented him with the fundamental dilemma which the universal Enlightenment theory of myth posed to a biblical scholar: "Either all nations enjoyed

concept of myth remained, however, limited in its scope of application, and it was not until the work of David Friedrich Strauss that
the whole of biblical literature was systematically considered in
terms of this Enlightenment category of myth.[1] In considering the
work of Eichorn and Strauss, I shall not be concerned with the
history of the concept of myth from Eichorn to Strauss, or with the
differences in their use of the term.[2] I shall limit my attention to the

---

a special relationship with celestial beings during their stage of infancy, or
none did" (cited, D. F. Strauss, *The Life of Jesus Critically Examined*, trans.
Marion Evans [4th edition; New York: Calvin Blanchard, 1955], p. 22). Thus,
it was the universal theory of myth that marked the end of the special
biblical hermeneutic of old orthodoxy. (Cf. Hartlich und Sachs, *Die Ursprung* . . ., pp. 87-90.)

[1] Strauss' own contribution was made in the New Testament. However,
by this time, W. M. de Wette, and others had completed the analysis of myth
in the materials of the Old Testament. (Cf. *ibid.*, pp. 118-120).

[2] Hartlich and Sachs have demonstrated the essential continuity between
Eichorn and Strauss in their use of myth. They have thus insisted that
Strauss' use of myth is thoroughly historico-critical and in no sense Hegelian
in its formulation or presuppositions. As they write:

> The concept of myth basic to Strauss' critical *Life of Jesus* is free from
> Hegelian presuppositions. Strauss is in no way here dependent upon the
> premises of Hegelian speculation, but rather applies criteria of a pure
> critical rationality . . . as had been characteristic of the earlier school of
> myth critics (*ibid.*, pp. 121-122).

As evidence for the intent of this judgment, I refer to Strauss' lengthy
discussion concerning the formulation of criteria for the recognition of myth.
At one point, he proposes for consideration the Hegelian view of the Absolute as a possible criterion for the recognition of myth.

> It [the idea that a god has a history] is irreconcilable with our idea of the
> Absolute to suppose it [the Absolute] subjected to time and change,
> to opposition and suffering; and therefore when we meet with a narrative
> in which these are attributed to a divine being, by this test we recog-
> nize it as unhistorical or mythical (Strauss, *Life of Jesus*, pp. 77-78).

He rejects such a Hegelian criterion for myth as inappropriate to the presentation of God in the biblical literature, and proposes instead the familiar
world view—not the idea of the Absolute—as the proper criterion for myth.

> Admitting that the biblical history does not equally with the heathen
> mythology offend our idea of Deity, and that consequently it is not in
> like manner characterized by this mark of the unhistorical, we are met
> by the further question whether it be not less accordant with our idea
> of the world, and whether such discordancy may not furnish a test of
> its unhistorical nature (*ibid.*, p. 78).

While accepting the intent of Hartlich and Sachs' judgment, it is also
necessary to reject the formulation of the statement itself as a gross over-
simplification of the problem. Any reading of Strauss makes it clear that
his use of myth has a religious-Hegelian presupposition as well as a rational-
critical formulation. One need only note his criticism of Eichorn, the positive

delineation of the basic elements of the Enlightenment theory of myth which they shared in common as a critical tool of biblical scholarship.

For Eichorn, the universal theory of myth came to provide a hermeneutical principle, determining the context within which the biblical literature was to be understood. Understanding of the book was possible only as the reader broke free from the expectations of his own modern rational age and entered once again into the spirit of the childhood of humanity.

> Read the Bible as two historical works of the old world; breathe therein the air of its age and country. Forget the age you live in, and the knowledge it affords you; and if you cannot do this, dream not that you can enjoy the book in the spirit of its origin. The youth of the world which it describes demands a spirit that has descended to its depths. The first rays of the glimmering light of reason do not harmonize with the clear light of broad noon. Without a close intimacy with the manner of thinking and speaking in the uncivilized world (obtained by a knowledge of Greece in its earliest ages, and of the uncultivated nations of modern times), you easily become a traitor to the book, when you would be its deliverer and interpreter. Above all, in this book, it is like the world in its childhood. It is often destitute of comprehensive general expressions, and therefore it must mention the parts of things to furnish an idea of the whole.[1]

The literature of the Hebrews was to be understood as the product of "the lowest stage of civilization," "the days of infancy," "an intellect limited to puerile representations." [2] The reason of man is so limited in this period of human history that one can hardly speak of it. Eichorn grants that the prophets were a partial exception to this common primitive mentality, but they were so few as to be easily overcome by "the great mass too rude and wild to be susceptible of more than common ideas" and the priests who served this "great mass." [3]

---

use of myth as a primitive expression of the ideal in an unconscious corporate form, and the conversion of myth into dogma to recognize the firm Hegelian ground upon which the historical project rests (*ibid.*, pp. 80-81; 770-777).

[1] Cited, Wilhelm Martin de Wette, *A Critical and Historical Introduction to the Canonical Scriptures of the Old Testament*, trans. Theodore Parker (Boston: Little and Brown, 1850), v. II, p. 32.

[2] Johann Gottfried Eichorn, *Introduction to the Study of the Old Testament*, trans. G. T. Gallop (London: Spottiswoode and Co., 1888), pp. 4, 36.

[3] *Ibid.*, pp. 6; 38.

> He who would expect from a nation which had remained so nearly
> in the state of its primitive organization and so little changed as to
> that of its intellect a multifarious literature of many aspects...
> must be ignorant of what is possible to the human mind in its
> various states and conditions and make demands in which history
> will not bear him out.[1]

Eichorn thus sets the biblical texts in the early stage of human
history prior to the full development of man's power of reason. So
he understands the claims of special revelation and of supernatural
happenings as a product of this primitive mentality. Like Fontenelle, Eichorn also regards the projection of man's feelings into the
world of nature to be a salient characteristic of this myth-making
mentality. It is no accident that the primitive mind has populated
his world of nature with "ghosts, demons, divinities, and other such
beings . . . to account for the terrible changes of nature, such as
thunder, lightning, hail, tempests, etc." [2] Strauss makes a similar
point in his discussion of the origins of religion. He defines religion
as being essentially the objectification of feeling, and it is only in
certain primitive tribes, like the Eskimos, that religion has not
developed beyond the level of purely immediate and subjective
feeling.[3]

> As it progresses, the religious principle loses more and more of this
> indefiniteness, and ceasing to be subjective, becomes objective.
> In proportion as the significance given to these objects [the sun,
> moon, stars, etc.] is remote from their actual nature, a new world
> of mere imagination is created, a sphere of divine existences whose
> relations to one another, actions and influences can be represented
> only after human analogy, and therefore as temporal and historical.[4]

There is thus born, out of the projection of the primitive, myth-
making mind, the whole new world of the supernatural and the
miraculous. "It is in this mental condition that the biblical history
was written." [5] Every change in nature or the human mind was
attributed to some supernatural cause.[6]

The whole process of myth-making is understood by Eichorn and
Strauss to be a product of a definite "mental condition" which was

---

[1] *Ibid.*, p. 4.
[2] *Ibid.*, p. 36.
[3] Strauss, *Life of Jesus*, p. 62.
[4] *Ibid.*
[5] *Ibid.*, p. 59.
[6] *Ibid.*

determinative for a particular stage in the development of human history. As a result of this hypothesis it is therefore possible to speak of the falsity of mythical accounts in the biblical literature without attacking the integrity of that literature. Eichorn is clear that myth is not to be confused with fable, premeditated fiction, or willful falsehood.[1] As Strauss expressed this same point:

> [In the biblical text] we have neither miracles to wonder at, nor deceptions to unmask, but simply the language of a former age to translate into our own.[2]

While myth may not be construed as a deception, neither may it be understood as a repository of hidden depths of wisdom. With Fontenelle, Eichorn and Strauss reject any allegorical mode of interpretation for myth.[3] Myth is not a form of communicating

---

[1] Cited, *ibid.*, p. 28.

[2] *Ibid.*, p. 22. Relevant to this same point, Strauss later cites with approval Otfried Müller:

> This reasoning brings us to the conclusion, that the idea of a deliberate and intentional fabrication, in which the author clothes that which he knows to be false in the appearance of truth, must be entirely set aside as insufficient to account for the origin of *mythus*. There is a certain necessity in the connection between the idea and the real, which constitutes the *mythus*; that the mythical images were formed by influences of sentiments common to mankind; and that the different elements grew together without the author's being himself conscious of their incongruity (*ibid.*, pp. 62-63).

[3] Strauss places Eichorn in the naturalistic-historical school of myth interpretation over against the moral-spiritualistic allegorizing mode of interpretation. Strauss defines the relationship between his own mythical view and the older allegorical view as follows:

> The mythical and the allegorical view equally allow that the historian apparently relates that which is historical, but they suppose him, under the influence of a higher inspiration known or unknown to himself, to have made use of this historical semblance merely as the shell of an idea—of a religious conception. The only essential distinction between these two modes of explanation is, that according to the allegorical, this higher intelligence is the immediate divine agency; according to the mythical, it is the spirit of a people or a community. Thus, the allegorical view attributes the narrative to a supernatural process, whilst the mythical view ascribes it to that natural process by which legends are originated and developed. The allegorical interpreter may with the most unrestrained arbitrariness separate from the history every thought he deems to be worthy of God, as constituting its inherent meaning; whilst the mythical interpreter, on the contrary, in searching out the ideas which are embodied in the narrative, is controlled by regard to conformity with the spirit and modes of thought of the people and of the age (*ibid.*, p. 43).

hidden teachings, adapted to the simplicity of the people of that age, but myth is itself simply the product of the mind of "an infantile and unscientific age." [1]

Strauss and Eichorn also agree in establishing a particular world view as the decisive form of expression of the mythical mind. This is the world that has not yet become determined according to the laws of the natural sciences. Eichorn can identify the emergence of the intellect out of its "puerile condition" with the recognition of the ultimate and infinite connection of all things by law.

> The farther we go back into the time of the old world the narrower do we find the knowledge of men with regard to the nature of things and the causes of their changes, destruction, renovation, and return. It cost thousands of years to enable the human intellect to comprehend that all changes are connected with one another like the links of a long chain, and to form an idea of eternally immutable laws by which all the workings of Nature are regulated. [2]

Strauss makes a similar point when he describes the "progress of mental cultivation as consisting mainly in the gradual recognition of a chain of causes and effects connecting natural phenomena with each other." [3]

It is precisely this scientific world view which provides the criterion for the recognition of myth, and thus the distinction of what Fontenelle called *"l'histoire fabuleuse"* from *"l'histoire véritable."* In Strauss, myth is synonymous with the "unhistorical"; this, in turn, is defined according to its antithetical relationship with the apprehension of the world as a unified cause-effect system. Strauss is clear that, apart from such a world view, no real concept of history is possible.

> No just notion of the true nature of history is possible, without a perception of the inviolability of the chain of finite causes, and of the impossibility of miracles. [4]

Note that the criterion for the distinction of the "mythical view" from the "allegorical view" is fidelity to the historical context of thought, not to the text itself. Bultmann's use of allegory is thus consistent here with that of Strauss. By allegory, he means the non-historical spiritualistic, moralistic or dogmatic interpretation of the text. While his own interpretation also establishes the meaning of the text behind the text itself, it is nevertheless "non-allegorical" since it is an interpretation congruent with the Hellenistic historical context of the text.

[1] *Ibid.*, p. 22.
[2] Eichorn, *An Introduction . . .*, p. 36.
[3] Strauss, *Life of Jesus*, p. 12.
[4] *Ibid.*, p. 55.

With this basic concept of history, it is then possible for Strauss to specify the criteria for myth in terms of four groups of laws:

1. The known and universal laws which govern the course of events.
2. The laws of historical succession ... that a course of events follow in a certain order of sequence, of increase and decrease.
3. Psychological laws which render it improbable that a human being should feel, think, and act in a manner directly opposed to his own habitual mode and that of men in general.
4. The law of contradiction, that an account cannot be inconsistent with itself and with other accounts.[1]

It is this scientific, law-connected view of reality which provides Strauss with the basis for his use of myth in relationship to the biblical literature. Strauss acknowledges that the concept of myth cannot be applied to the Bible on the basis of its conformity with heathen mythology. Judged by this standard, Strauss admits that "the Hebrew religion has no mythology," for it is singularly free from the accounts of the births and deaths of gods and worlds that are so characteristic of a heathen mythology.[2] However, the foundation for the use of the concept of myth does not lie at this point. It is, rather, the modern, scientific view of reality which provides the norm for the determination of the mythical, and it is in light of this standard that the concept is used in biblical studies.

These, then, are the three essential characteristics of the Enlightenment formulation of myth: the developmental schema of history, the theory of primitive mentality, and the normative status of the scientific world view. These three motifs are as decisive for the use of the concept in the critical biblical studies of Eichorn and Strauss as they were in Fontenelle's early study of fables. In all of them, myth is used as an historico-epistemological category, designating the "false history" or false knowledge of the world which is the product of the underdeveloped reason determinative for man's thought at a particular stage of history.

2. Bultmann's Appropriation of the Enlightenment Formulation (1930—).

Bultmann's appropriation of the Enlightenment formulation of myth is limited in several respects: the developmental motif and the theory of primitive mentality are not present in his thought.

---

[1] *Ibid.*, p. 70.
[2] *Ibid.*, p. 59.

However, there are a variety of themes in Bultmann's discussion of myth that are continuous with the Enlightenment tradition; namely the Enlightenment periodization of history as definitive for the use of myth, the identification of myth with a particular form of thought characteristic of a given age of history, and the essential criteria for the recognition of myth defined according to a particular world view (i.e., a world view defined negatively by its antithetical relationship with a scientific lawful world view and positively by reference to projections, miracles, and the objectification of supernatural beings).

Previously, Bultmann's appropriation of the Enlightenment periodization of history was described as intrinsic to his understanding of the autonomy of modern culture.[1] At that time, however, Bultmann was not yet using myth in the Enlightenment meaning of the term. In 1920 he did not once use this category in distinguishing the autonomy of modern culture from the religious and cultic dependence of earlier cultures. By 1941, however, Bultmann is using myth in accordance with this Enlightenment schema of history. In this later formulation of myth, he consistently presupposes the absolute distinction between "the epoch of mythical thinking and the epoch of the Enlightenment."[2] As a result, he is completely consistent in refusing to use myth to describe any phenomena which occur in the post-Enlightenment period of history. The use of the term is necessarily limited by the historical schema definitive for it.

Since 1941 Bultmann has consistently presupposed the Enlightenment periodization of history as a criterion for his use of myth. However, he did not originally make this an explicit theme of his discussion. As a result, much of the discussion of his 1941 proposal on demythologizing was confused because Bultmann's readers had not grasped his historically circumscribed use of the concept of myth. In retrospect, however, it is clear that this motif was present in his thought from the very beginning of his proposal to demythologize. Thus, in a footnote to the 1941 essay, Bultmann noted that "there are people alive today ... who are primitive enough to qualify for an age of mythical thought."[3] However, he continued:

----

[1] Above, Chapter II, pp. 53-54.
[2] Bultmann, *Die christliche Hoffnung . . .*, p. 47.
[3] Bultmann, *KaM*, I, 5.

There are also many varieties of superstition. But when belief in spirits and miracles has degenerated into superstition, it has become something entirely different from what it was when it was genuine faith. The various impressions and speculations which influence credulous people here and there are of little importance, nor does it matter to what extent cheap slogans have spread an atmosphere inimical to science.[1]

The point made here is clear enough: myth-like phenomena of our contemporary age are not to obscure the fundamental distinction between the age of science and the age of myth. Indeed, when phenomena characteristic of the mythical mind appear in the context of the modern world, they are properly regarded as "superstition" and not as "myth." In a second footnote of this same essay, Bultmann makes the same point.

Myth is not used in that modern sense, according to which it is practically equivalent to ideology.[2]

Whatever resemblance ideology may have to myth, the former stands on the other side of the historical threshold of the Enlightenment and so may not be confused with myth itself.

However, it was only in the later writings, as Bultmann was called upon to clarify his use of myth in the original 1941 essay, that he made explicit the Enlightenment periodization of history. Thus, he chides J. Schniewind for describing natural science as being mythological: "you are using the word 'myth' in an improper sense." [3] Schniewind is also incorrect in suggesting that "philosophers can speak of ultimate questions only in mythological terms." [4] Their speculations may be "hypothetical," but in no sense may such an inquiry be termed mythical. In a footnote to his 1952 explanation of demythologizing, Bultmann repeats these same points:

It is obviously meaningless to say that the world understanding of science may also be a "Myth." One may call it an ideology, a fiction, or whatever one likes. What matters, however, is to make clear the fundamental distinction between mythical thinking and scientific thinking. Also, one should not think of myth in terms of *Mythos des 20. Jahrhunderts* in order to determine the meaning of the concept.[5]

---

[1] *Ibid.*
[2] *Ibid.*, p. 10.
[3] *Ibid.*, p. 103.
[4] *Ibid.*
[5] Bultmann, *KuM*, II, 180.

By these later writings of the demythologizing debate, Bultmann had made it very clear that he was using the concept of myth strictly as limited by the Enlightenment periodization of history. The term was not properly used to describe any contemporary phenomenon, whether it be superstition, ideology, or a hypothetical speculation; nor could it be properly used to describe any phenomenon which was not historically circumscribed, such as religion or a total view of reality.

Certainly the clearest statement of the Enlightenment criteria definitive for Bultmann's use of myth appeared in his essay of 1952, "Zum Problem der Entmythologisierung." In the first paragraph of this discussion of myth, Bultmann wrote as follows:

> I understand by "Mythos" a very definite historical phenomenon (*ein ganz bestimmtes geschichtliches Phaenomen*) and by "Mythology" a very definite mode of thought (*eine ganz bestimmte Denkweise*).[1]

Having already examined the meaning of myth as a "definite historical phenomenon" as stipulated according to the Enlightenment periodization of history, I now turn to a discussion of the nature of mythology as a definite mode of thought. The exact meaning of this phrase, *eine ganz bestimmte Denkweise*, must be determined according to the context of its use, as it has a double meaning for Bultmann. Sometimes, the mythical *Denkweise* refers to an objectifying mode of self-understanding which requires hermeneutical correction; sometimes, the mythical *Denkweise* refers to a primitive form of world explanation which requires epistemological criticism. In the present stage of the argument, I am only concerned with the latter use of the term: namely, as a traditional Enlightenment category used to specify the false form of world knowledge characteristic of a particular epoch of history.

Bultmann's explication of the definition cited above makes it clear that in this use of *Denkweise* it is the Enlightenment meaning of the term which is intended. In his effort to clarify this phrase, he never mentions the distinction between an objectifying and an existentialist mode of understanding human existence, but focuses solely upon the contrast between a mythical and scientific form of world explanation. Thus he sets forth the rubric for the explication of a mythological *Denkweise*: "Mythical thinking is the opposite of

---

[1] Bultmann, *KuM*, II, 180.

scientific thinking." [1] The nature of this opposition is one familiar from the earlier Enlightenment description of mythology as a mode of thought. Scientific thinking explains world phenomena only within the perspective of "the closed connection of cause and effect." [2] Scientific thinking is thus defined as being in accordance with the principle of law (of causality or logic) and as being an absolute unity (in the sense of being both coherent and all-inclusive).[3] It presupposes the lawful ordering of all events in the world and it is born with the question concerning the *arche*, the unifying origin of the multiplicity of the world.[4] Mythological thinking is defined as the opposite of this. In contrast with the lawful structure of scientific thought, it is characterized by arbitrariness and is expressed in "the unrelatedness of mythical narratives." [5] In contrast with the closed cause-effect unity of scientific thought, mythological thought regards the world as open to the entrance of otherworldly powers.[6]

While mythological thought is thus defined primarily in terms of its antithetical relationship with scientific thought, there is also here the positive characterization of mythology: namely, the projection or objectification of supernatural powers and forces, especially as these arise out of man's immediate emotional response to his natural environment.

---

[1] *Ibid.*
[2] *Ibid.*
[3] *Ibid.*, pp. 180-181.
[4] *Ibid.*, p. 180.
[5] *Ibid.*, p. 181.
[6] *Ibid.* At one point, Bultmann attempts to offer a description of scientific thought that follows more along empirical lines, referring to the "experiment," the "laboratory," and "adequate research" as being the decisive characteristics of science. In a citation from Hartlich and Sachs, that is an obvious response to the criticism of Bultmann's own definition of science in terms of the closed, unified world view, the attempt is made to free "modern scientific thinking" from the world view that is its content or conclusions, and found it strictly upon methodological considerations. The crucial difference does not lie at the point of the conflicting world views, but "the unbreachable gulf between mythological and scientific thinking lies in the distinction between an uncritical-unconscious judgment and a critical conscious judgment." This view of the matter, however, appears only briefly in Bultmann, and then is never fully developed. It is far more characteristic of him to define scientific thinking in terms of the two principle characteristics of the scientific world view: the all-embracing unity of the world and the law of cause-effect connection (*ibid.*).

> Mythological thinking objectifies the divine activity and projects it on the plane of worldly happenings.[1]

The result of this naïve projection of the imagination upon the screen of nature is the construction of the familiar three-story world, populated with its spirits, demons, and gods, busily moving from one sphere to another and always disrupting man in his daily course of affairs with their miraculous deeds.[2] The root of this projection in mythological thinking is the immediate, felt response of man to that which is striking in his environment.

> They [etiological myths] are significant in the present context only insofar as they permit us to understand mythological thinking as something that arises out of astonishment, fright, and questioning and that thinks in terms of the connection of cause and effect.[3]

In regarding myth as a mode of thought and in describing that mode of thought, in its negative relationship with science and its positive movement in projection out of immediate feeling, Bultmann is consistent with the basic Enlightenment formulation of myth first examined in Fontenelle, Eichorn, and Strauss.[4]

Still another point of continuity between Bultmann and the Enlightenment tradition appears in his discussion of the similarity of myth with science. For the Enlightenment regarded myth as sharing a common intention with science: namely, that of explaining the causes of worldly phenomena. Without some such continuity of intention, there would have been no justification for describing myth as a pre-scientific mode of thought. One would not describe, for example, primitive poetry as "pre-scientific." Myth, in contrast, was understood to be scientific in its intention, if not in its execution. The motives of science—a curiosity to understand and

---

[1] Bultmann, *KaM*, I, 197.

[2] *Ibid.*, pp. 1-2.

[3] Bultmann, "On the Problem of Demythologizing," *JR* (1962), p. 100.

[4] While characterizing the mythical mode of thought in a manner consistent with the Enlightenment tradition, Bultmann does not develop a theory of primitive mentality to account for the phenomenon. Concerning the characteristic Enlightenment speculation as to the origin of myths, he wrote as follows:

> Myths about the end of the world are found among many peoples—of the destruction of the world by water or fire or by some other catastrophe. It may be left undecided whether all these myths spring from the same kind of thinking, and whether natural catastrophes created in primitive peoples the impression of the end of the world (*History and Eschatology* [New York: Harper and Brothers, 1957], p. 23).

a practical need to control the environment—were also deemed to be
the motives of myth. The relationship of myth and science was,
therefore, not simply one of opposition, but also of continuity.
Insofar as myth was a primitive expression of that quest for knowledge which came to full expression in science, it was rightly
regarded as continuous with science and hence, as "scientific," in
some qualified sense of that term.

The Enlightenment tradition expressed this continuity between
myth as primitive science and real science in the form of its developmental hypothesis. Bultmann never proposes the developmental
hypothesis in conjunction with his discussion of myth. However,
he does characterize the relationship of myth and science in the
same manner as that intended by the earlier developmental schema:
1) a relationship of continuity in terms of intention, the "putting
of the question," and the thought form, and 2) a relationship of
historical succession, science having taken the place of myth for
these particular human functions. The fundamental intention, which
is fully developed in science and only partially and confusedly
present in myth, is rooted for Bultmann in the human phenomenon
of work, and comes to expression in the effort to explain (in order
to control) the world of nature.[1] The questions posed by myth and
science are also similar: the question of why, in the sense of causality; what made this happen?

> It is often said that mythology is a primitive science, the intention
> of which is to explain phenomena and incidents which are strange,
> curious, surprising, or frightening, by attributing them to super-
> natural causes, to gods or to demons. So it is in part, for example,
> when it attributes phenomena like eclipses of the sun or of the
> moon to such causes. ...[2]

As a result of this congruence, Bultmann can describe mythological
thinking and scientific thinking as similar forms of thought, both of
which move in the categories of cause and effect.[3] Or again, their

---

[1] Bultmann, *KuM*, II, 180. "This is the reality (represented in objectifying
vision) in which man finds himself, in which he orients himself by standing
over against it, and with whose continuum of happenings he reckons in order
to master it and thereby to secure his life. This way of looking at reality
is fully developed in natural science and in the technology it makes possible."
Cf. Bultmann, "On the Problem of Demythologizing," *JR* (1962), p. 96.

[2] Bultmann, *Jesus Christ and Mythology*, p. 18.

[3] Bultmann, *KuM*, II, 182.

similarity appears in the fact that both are objectifying modes of thought.[1]

While there is thus this element of continuity which runs from myth to science, it is also clear that Bultmann, like his predecessors, relates the two as historically successive forms of world explanation. Myth is thus a "primitive form of science," and as such is defined by its historically prior relationship to science.[2] As Bultmann writes, with a slight note of irritation at some of his critics who cannot see the obvious,

> In the conflict between the objectifying thinking of myth and the objectifying thinking of science, the latter remains self-evidently the victor.[3]

Mythology is thus the defeated historical antecedent of science, sharing with science a similar intention, question, and form of thought.

Finally, Bultmann, in continuity with the Enlightenment tradition, employs the category of *Weltbild* as the decisive criterion for the recognition of myth. Bultmann's total concept of *Weltbild* is very complex, and requires special discussion later in this chapter. For the present, it is sufficient to note his continuity with the Enlightenment tradition in his use of "scientific *Weltbild*" together with the decisive role which this concept enjoys in his presentation of the total project of demythologizing.

Thus, Bultmann describes the original impetus for demythologizing as rooted in the conflict between the scientific *Weltbild* and the mythological *Weltbild* of the Bible.[4] Furthermore, it is the scientific *Weltbild* which provides the decisive criterion for the recognition of any phenomenon as mythological.

> This conception of the world we call mythological because it is different from the conception of the world which has been formed and developed by science since its inception in ancient Greece and which has been accepted by all modern men.[5]

Finally, it is the successful excision of this mythical *Weltbild* that

---

[1] *Ibid.*

[2] Bultmann, "On the Problem of Demythologizing," *JR* (1962), p. 100. Cf. Bultmann, *KuM*, II, 182; Bultmann, *Jesus Christ and Mythology*, p. 18.

[3] *KuM*, II, 184.

[4] *Ibid.*, p. 207.

[5] Bultmann, *Jesus Christ and Mythology*, p. 15.

constitutes the norm for determining the successful completion of
the project of demythologizing.

> Are there any mythological remnants [in this existentialist inter-
> pretation of the New Testament]? Certainly, there is for anyone
> who calls something mythology if it speaks of the deed of God, of
> his decisive eschatological deed. However, such mythology is, in
> any case, no longer mythology in the old sense which has been
> denigrated with the passing of the mythical *Weltbild*.[1]

One may still choose to call an existentialist interpretation of the
Gospel mythological, but for Bultmann it obviously is not mythological, for it has been freed from any connection with the obsolete
mythological *Weltbild*. The concept of *Weltbild* thus serves to
specify the beginning, middle, and end of the project of demythologizing.

The concept of the mythical *Weltbild*, delineated in the Enlightenment tradition as the opposite of the scientific, law-structured
Weltbild, is thus central to the original argument of Bultmann's
essay of 1941. He begins with a description of the mythical *Weltbild*
which the New Testament presupposes, and concludes with his
judgment concerning the totality of his demythologized interpretation on the basis of this same mythical *Weltbild*.[2] It is necessary
to state here that Bultmann's use of the *"mythische Weltbild"* may
not be dismissed as a mere polemical motif in his thought, or as an
excess of the passionate plea offered in the original essay of 1941.
Bultmann uses "mythical *Weltbild*" and "scientific *Weltbild*" as
precise, technical concepts, not vague epithets. He assumes full
responsibility for the decisive role of these concepts in his characterization of myth. Thus, in his dialogue with Schumann, Bultmann
acknowledges that the distinctive thrust of his thought in differentiation from Schumann appears precisely in his use and understanding of the mythical *Weltbild*.[3] The concept of the "mythical

---

[1] Bultmann, *KuM*, I, 48.

[2] *Ibid.*, pp. 15-20; 48.

[3] In a dialogue between Bultmann and Schumann, Schumann says:

> The fundamental difference between you and me appears to consist of
> this: according to your understanding, mythological speech today has
> become, if not basically impossible, then at least unbelievable, because
> its sphere, the mythical *Weltbild*, has been dissolved by the *Weltbild*
> of modern science.

To this, Bultmann replies, "*Jawohl.*" (Bultmann, *Die christliche Hoffnung* . . .),
p. 45.

Weltbild" is rooted in the Neo-Kantian foundations of his thought, and it never loses its central role in his description of the project of demythologizing.

In accordance with the Enlightenment tradition, the mythical *Weltbild* is described primarily according to its antithetical relationship with a scientific, law-structured *Weltbild*. Bultmann acknowledges the revisions in modern science which would allow for a greater element of indeterminacy in the structure of causality, but he does not see these corrections as having any fundamental effect upon the nature of the scientific world view and its essential opposition with the mythical world view.

> In this modern conception of the world the cause and effect nexus is fundamental. Although modern physical theories take account of chance in the chain of cause and effect in sub-atomic particles, our daily living, purposes, and actions are not affected. In any case, modern science does not believe that the course of nature can be interrupted or, so to speak, perforated, by supernatural powers.[1]

Such specific scientific conclusions do not affect the substance of Bultmann's argument because, in his judgment, they do not affect "our daily living" or the fundamental distinction between the *Weltbild* of science and myth. This basic distinction Bultmann can describe in terms of the categories of "closed" and "open."

> For mythical thinking, the world and world events are open—open namely to the entrance of other-worldly powers, therefore infringing upon the point of view of scientific thinking. For it, the world and world events are closed, closed against the entrance of unworldly powers. . . .[2]

To understand the concept of a "closed *Weltbild*" one needs to recall Bultmann's earlier Neo-Kantian discussion of the autonomy of thought, grounded in reason alone.[3] To say that the scientific view of the world is closed is to say that it is autonomous: that is, it is wholly grounded in reason, its constructs are lawfully connected relationships, with nothing falling outside the bounds of reason. Thus, the concrete results of scientific research in no way affect Bultmann's concept of the scientific *Weltbild*, or its opposite, the mythical *Weltbild*, since these are constituted solely on the grounds of reason and are not dependent upon particular empirical results.

---

[1] Bultmann, *Jesus Christ and Mythology*, p. 15.
[2] Bultmann, *KuM*, II, 181.
[3] Above, Chapter II, section 2.

The main point, however, is not the concrete results of scientific research and the contents of a world view, but the method of thinking from which world views follow. For example, it makes no difference in principle whether the earth rotates around the sun or the sun rotates around the earth but it does make a difference that modern man understands the motion of the universe as a motion which obeys a cosmic law, a law of nature which human reason can discover. Therefore *modern man acknowledges as reality only such phenomena or events as are comprehensible within the framework of the rational order of the universe.*[1] [Italics mine.]

In this rationalistic interpretation of science, in attributing to it a total, causally connected, closed and unified *Weltbild*, in making such a scientific *Weltbild* definitive for the recognition of the phenomenon of myth, and in giving to this category of *Weltbild* a central role in the total discussion of myth, Bultmann betrays his close affinity with the earlier Enlightenment discussion of the subject.[2]

The basic continuity of Bultmann's later formulation of myth with the earlier Enlightenment tradition is thus apparent: the appropriation of the Enlightenment periodization of history to provide the chronological brackets for the use of the term; the identification of mythology with a particular mode of thought, together with the description of that thought as the opposite of scientific, law-determined thinking and characterized as a projection rooted in an immediate emotional response to environment; the description of the relationship of mythology and science in terms of the similarity of their intentions in a schema of historical succession; and finally, the construction of a rationalistic concept of scientific *Weltbild* with its antithetical mythical form as central to the total discussion of myth. It is thus clear that Bultmann's understanding of myth, together with the problem of biblical interpretation implicit in this category, stands firmly in the tradition of that older use of myth characteristic of early nineteenth-century biblical studies.

---

[1] Bultmann, *Jesus Christ and Mythology*, pp. 37-38.
[2] For a critique of the rationalist, non-empirical understanding of science in Bultmann, see K. Jaspers, "Myth and Religion," *Myth and Christianity* by Jaspers and Bultmann (New York: The Noonday Press 1958), pp. 4-7; G. Crespy, "Science et mythe chez Bultmann," *Etudes théologique et religieuses* XXXIII (1958), pp. 129-141.

3. The Subordinate but Autonomous Role of the Enlightenment Formulation in Demythologizing

Because of the confusion intrinsic to Bultmann's many-sided concept of myth, it has been necessary to bring together here, in a single historical and systematic pattern, those motifs of Bultmann's thought which are congruent with the Enlightenment formulation of myth. However, to close the discussion at this point of the argument would constitute a gross distortion of Bultmann's true position. For one may not reduce Bultmann's discussion of myth to the Enlightenment formulation, nor may one even argue that this formulation is determinative for Bultmann's total concept of myth. For an adequate understanding of Bultmann's appropriation of the Enlightenment formulation, one must therefore proceed to examine Bultmann's critique of this view of myth, and to inquire into the role of this one motif in his total myth concept. For the sake of clarity, I abstracted this Enlightenment formulation out of the total context of Bultmann's discussion of myth; now I need to reinsert this one formulation into Bultmann's larger and more complex meaning of myth.

In an attempt to win an understanding of the role of this Enlightenment formulation of myth in the larger context of Bultmann's thought, I shall begin by considering his critique of this tradition. His 1927 rejection of any view of myth which regards it merely as a primitive form of science or philosophy has already been noted.[1] An even stronger rejection of this Enlightenment formulation appears in Bultmann's 1942 review of *Vom Mythos Zum Logos* by W. Nestle.[2]

> It appears to me that the author fails to grasp in a creative way either *Mythos* or *Logos*. In his designation of mythical notions and logical thinking as opposites, it is clear that he understands this opposition only as relative, since for the author mythical imagery is only a primitive thinking which has the same object as rational thought, namely reality. It is understandable, even self-evident, that mythological thinking must in the course of time give way to the rational, so long as one does not consider the real point at which the issue lies: namely, wherein at any given moment is reality seen. The author does not inquire into the concept of reality or the concept of being which is presupposed in Greek sciences from the outset. Hence, he has given no account of the fact that myth is

---

[1] Above, Chapter IV, p. 130.
[2] Rudolf Bultmann, Review of *Vom Mythos zum Logos* by W. Nestle, *ThLZ*, LXVII (1942), 146-147.

not primarily concerned with a primitive explanation of the world
... but that there lies hidden in it an understanding of reality fundamentally opposed to that of rational thinking. The struggle between
Mythos and *Logos* must appear in a completely different form when
it is seen as a struggle between two possibilities for the understanding
of being.[1]

It is quite clear that Bultmann understands Nestle to be presenting
that basic interpretation of myth described as the Enlightenment
formulation. The opposition of *Mythos* and *Logos* is seen to be of an
historically relative and successive order, a theme characteristic of
Bultmann's own discussion of the subject. In reducing the problem
to such a level, however, Nestle has failed to see "the real point at
which the issue lies." This is the point of the understanding of being.
Properly understood, the relationship of *Mythos* and *Logos* is to be
understood, not in terms of an historically relative and successive
form of opposition, but rather in terms of a timeless conflict between two opposing understandings of being.

In this critique of Nestle, Bultmann speaks out of his own existentialist interpretation of myth, which apprehends in myth a new
understanding of being. He would thus appear to reject in its
entirety the Enlightenment formulation of myth as a pre-scientific
mode of thought or world view. Yet, he has himself preserved these
same Enlightenment themes and in writings contemporaneous with
this critique of Nestle. Our task now is to relate these two sides of
Bultmann's position.

I propose to describe Bultmann's relationship to the Enlightenment formulation of myth as a dialectual one: that is, one of affirmation and negation. As a preliminary sketch, it is possible to
describe this position as a dialectic of whole and part: Bultmann
affirms the Enlightenment formulation of myth as a partial truth
or essential element in myth, but rejects it as inadequate to express
the whole meaning of myth. Thus, for example, in each of his
descriptions of myth as a primitive form of science, Bultmann
explicitly and carefully qualifies this description of myth.

One often calls myth a primitive science. That is correct *insofar
as* ...[2]

It is often said that mythology is a primitive science. ... So it is
in part, for example when it attributes phenomena like eclipses of

---

[1] *Ibid.*
[2] Bultmann, *KuM*, II, 182.

the sun or of the moon to such causes; *but there is more than this in mythology*.[1]

> They [etiological myths] are significant in the present context of discussion *only insofar as* they permit us to understand. ... Such thinking can be characterized as a form of primitive science, and *many researchers in fact seek to reduce it to just such terms*.[2] [Italics mine].

The dialectical pattern is clear here. It is certainly true that myth is a primitive form of science, as "it is often called," or as "is often said." Bultmann accepts the validity of this position, but does not identify himself with it, ascribing it simply to the nameless others. At the same time, the partiality of this view of myth is made clear: this is true in part, or "only insofar as." Bultmann's critique of those researchers who reduce the whole of myth to this partial element is as implicit in these passages as it is explicit in his review of Nestle. Bultmann is consistently clear that "the real intention," the "original meaning," the "authentic purpose" of myth may not be understood in terms of the partial Enlightenment understanding of myth, but must be developed only in terms of the more adequate and comprehensive existentialist understanding of myth.

I may also describe the relationship of the Enlightenment formulation to the existentialist formulation of myth as a dialectic of subordination and autonomy: that is, the Enlightenment interpretation of myth is made radically subordinate to the existentialist understanding of myth; however, this subordination in no way entails a radical undoing of the Enlightenment hypothesis in light of the new existentialist perspective. Quite the contrary. The Enlightenment view of myth is allowed to stand in its original form as an autonomous motif and a sufficient expression of the meaning of myth in many uses of the term. In order to establish this dialectic of subordination and autonomy, I shall first delineate the history and structure of the concept of *Weltbild* as this discloses Bultmann's anthropologically grounded revision of the earlier Enlightenment tradition. Then, I shall examine the use of demythologizing in the later essays. My purpose here is to establish the autonomy of the Enlightenment formulation by showing those uses of demythologizing which may be understood with *only* an Enlightenment meaning.

---

[1] Bultmann, *Jesus Christ and Mythology*, pp. 18-19.
[2] Bultmann, "On the Problem of Demythologizing," *JR* (1962), p. 100.

Like almost every concept in the structure of Bultmann's thought, *Weltbild* has the character of a palimpsest: new meanings are added, but the old ones are never discarded. The concept of *Weltbild* first appears in conjunction with Bultmann's discussion of myth in a 1926 review article.[1] The term here was used only to designate the perspective of a soteriological dualism that was characteristic of the myth of the heavenly redeemer. There was no suggestion of a three-story cosmology involved; simply the two conflicting powers of light and darkness, etc. Nor was there any suggestion that *Weltbild* was used to designate a total mythical view of reality over against a modern scientific view of reality.[2]

By 1930, the concept of *Weltbild* has moved beyond the very limited use and meaning of the nineteen-twenties. In his essay on myth in the New Testament, written for the second edition of *Die Religion in Geschichte und Gegenwart,* Bultmann develops the concept of *Weltbild* in its specific Enlightenment meaning and as definitive for the meaning of mythology. This text is significant for understanding the total meaning of *Weltbild* in that it provides the first occasion in which Bultmann discusses mythology in the terms of the Enlightenment tradition and, correspondingly, is also the first instance in which *Weltbild* is used as a technical Enlightenment category.

In the opening paragraph of this essay, Bultmann characterizes a variety of New Testament phenomena as expressing "the mythological understanding of the primitive Christian community."[3] In its eschatology, the community understands its future mythologically; in its account of the death and resurrection of Jesus, the community understands its past mythologically; and in the interpretations of its present life (miracles, sacraments, etc.) it is also determined by a

---

[1] Bultmann, "Urchristliche Religion (1915-1925)," *AR* (1926), p. 100. Above, Chapter III, p. 93.

[2] Bultmann never lost sight of this original soteriological-existential meaning of the mythical *Weltbild.* When he was later criticized for confusing a three-story primitive cosmology with a distinctively mythical understanding of reality, Bultmann replied by reminding his critics that the spheres above and below the earth were both numinous spheres—the dwelling of an other-worldly reality, whether this be divine or demonic. He acknowledged that not every three-story universe need be considered mythical, but insisted that this particular three-story cosmology was properly regarded as mythical because it retained a soteriological meaning (Bultmann, *KuM*, II, 183).

[3] Bultmann, "Mythus und Mythologie im N.T.," *RGG²*, IV, 390.

mythological form of understanding.¹ Bultmann concludes this pargraph as follows:

> In this sense the early Christian thought is wholly determined by mythology. ... This is understandable because the presupposition of early Christian thought is the old mythological *Weltbild*.²

In identifying mythology with a particular form of understanding and with its corresponding *Weltbild*, Bultmann has clearly taken up the Enlightenment formulation for the first time in his discussion of the subject. Furthermore, it is clear here, as it was in the essay of 1952 previously discussed, that by a "mythological form of understanding," he does not refer to the distinction between an existentialist and objectifying understanding of human existence, but rather to the distinction between a scientific and a primitive explanation of a given world phenomenon. Bultmann defines here a mythological mode of understanding in the characteristic Enlightenment terms. Positively, any event is understood mythologically if it is attributed to a divine or transcendent power, and hence regarded as a "miraculous and supernatural accomplishment." ³ Negatively, one may say that any understanding of an event is mythological if it does not attribute that event to "a result of historical development" or "to worldly powers or human activities." ⁴ Mythology is thus understood not as a particular interpretation of transcendence, but rather as a particular explanation of the world and worldly events. In this regard, it is the concept of the pre-scientific *Weltbild* that determines most succinctly the meaning of mythological: i.e., any understanding of a given event as not arising out of the closed context of worldly powers and human deeds.⁵ To summarize the nature of this *Weltbild*, which is the presupposition for early Christian thought and which makes its mythological character understandable, Bultmann need only write: "This general *Weltbild* . . . is not scientific but mythological."⁶

By the time of the 1941 essay, the concept of *Weltbild* has acquired a third meaning. Not only is it a religious concept indicating the dualistic context of salvation characteristic of the

¹ *Ibid.*
² *Ibid.*
³ *Ibid.*
⁴ *Ibid.*
⁵ *Ibid.*, Col. 391.
⁶ *Ibid.*, Col. 390.

heavenly redeemer myth and an epistemological concept denoting a false, pre-scientific form of world understanding, but it has also become a universal anthropological category. A *Weltbild* is now understood to be essential to man's being in the world, grounded in his practical care for that world, and determinative for the possibilities of his relationship to that world. It is this last stage in the history of the unfolding of the concept of *Weltbild* that is of concern here, for it is at this point that one sees most clearly the way in which Bultmann's existentialist tradition limits and modifies the Enlightenment formulation of myth.

As a universal anthropological category, *Weltbild* is not a term more appropriate to one period of history than another. The literal meaning of the term might suggest a pictorial form of world representation, and hence a naïve, primitive stage of world understanding: i.e., the picture of the three-story universe which Bultmann finds in the New Testament. Bultmann, however, also speaks of the modern *Weltbild*, and of the change in this *Weltbild* affected by Copernicus and the atom theory.[1] *Weltbild* is to be understood as any form of world understanding, pictorial or propositional, and as characteristic of man in any period of history, mythical or modern.

> I am of the opinion that every man, whether he lives in a mythical age or an enlightened age, has a *Weltbild*, lives in a *Weltbild*, by which I naturally do not mean that this *Weltbild* must be a closed and systematic *Weltbild*.[2]

While *Weltbild* as a category is a universal, essential to man's being in the world, no particular *Weltbild* can claim for itself this status. This is as true for the scientific *Weltbild* as it was for the earlier mythological one. Bultmann was clear as to the changing, relative character of every *Weltbild* from the time of his programmatic essay of 1941:

> Naturally it [the scientific *Weltbild*] is not unchangeable, and the individual can even contribute towards its reformulation. Thus could the *Weltbild* change as a result of the Copernican discovery or the atom theory.[3]

In 1953 and again in 1958, he made this same point, specifying

---

[1] Bultmann, *KuM*, I, 17.
[2] Bultmann, *Die christliche Hoffnung* . . ., pp. 46-47.
[3] Bultmann, *KuM*, I, 17.

explicitly the historically relative character of any *Weltbild*, including the scientific *Weltbild*:

> It is not at all relevant if one points out that the *Weltbild* of natural science is different from what it was in the nineteenth century. Whoever stands in this [scientific] tradition knows that all results of science are relative and that no *Weltbild* developed in the past, present, or future can ever be final.[1]
> The science of today is no longer science as it was in the nineteenth century, and to be sure, all the results of science are relative, and no world view of yesterday, today, or tomorrow is definitive.[2]

While every *Weltbild* is relative and not absolute, nevertheless, for the men of any given age, every *Weltbild* is experienced as of the order of necessity, not of freedom. This appears, for example, in Bultmann's frequent assertion that it is impossible, as well as unnecessary and irrelevant, to revive the obsolete *Weltbild* of the New Testament because "no man can adopt a *Weltbild* by his own volition—it is already determined for him by his place in history." [3] This characteristic of necessity or impossibility is not of an ontological order, as if the scientific *Weltbild* were synonymous with ultimate reality, but of an ontic order: every and any *Weltbild* has this character of necessity, including the modern one. At this point, it is helpful to differentiate between Bultmann's understanding of *Weltbild* and *Weltanschauung*. A *Weltbild* is not what a man chooses in the sphere of his freedom. A *Weltbild* is the practical organization of the world which precedes one in any given historical situation and which prescribes the necessary form for dealings with that world.

> That man can tend to his daily affairs and communicate with his fellow man presupposes that a definite *Weltbild* is self-evident to him.[4]

A *Weltanschauung*, in contrast, has more the character of an option; it is chosen by a man in order thereby to understand himself in his world. Thus, it is not necessary for theology to consider the various *Weltanschauungen* which occupy modern men; for these do not arise with necessity out of the situation of modern man. "We are

---

[1] Bultmann, *KuM*, II, 181.
[2] Bultmann, *Jesus Christ and Mythology*, p. 38. Bultmann is so consistent at this point that there should be no need for accusing him of absolutizing the historically relative *Weltbild* of the present.
[3] Bultmann, *KaM*, I, 3.
[4] Bultmann, *Die christliche Hoffnung . . .*, p. 47.

still free to adopt it [a biological *Weltanschauung*] or not as we choose." [1] A *Weltbild*, however, is the presupposition for a range of *Weltanschauungen* in a given period, and this is relevant to the theological criticism of the New Testament.[2] In describing *Weltbild* under the rubric of necessity, Bultmann is clearly extending into the modern epoch that category of "necessity" which Fontenelle first employed in his description of the world view of the *"pauvres sauvages."*

The meaning of *Weltbild* as an anthropological category appears through its contrast with *Weltanschauung*, but also through its contrast with *Weltverständnis*. As Bultmann uses this term, *Weltverständnis* is not an expression of man's practical concern for the world, but his theoretical attempt to explain the world. Most characteristically used in relation to scientific man, Bultmann can also speak of a mythical *Weltverständnis* "insofar as mythical thinking can be characterized as a primitive form of scientific thinking, as an inquiring mode of thought dealing with cause and effect." [3] *Weltbild*, however, does not have this theoretical character, but is born out of man's practical concern for his world. Thus, the scientific *Weltbild* is in no sense limited to a scientific elite engaged in the process of theory formation and experimentation.

> The thinking of modern man is determined by science, regardless of whether or how far he actively participates in scientific research or understands its methods.[4]

Nor is the actualization of this *Weltbild* associated so much with the laboratory, as it is with "the school, the press, the wireless, the cinema and all the other fruits of technical progress."[5] It is just because of this social and practical function of a *Weltbild* that Bultmann can offer his famous argument of "the man listening to the radio":

> It is impossible to use electric light and the wireless and to avail ourselves of modern medical and surgical discoveries and at the same time to believe in the New Testament world of demons and spirits.[6]

---

[1] Bultmann, *KaM*, I, 7.
[2] *Ibid.*
[3] Bultmann, *KuM*, II, 182.
[4] Bultmann, *Die christliche Hoffnung* . . ., p. 24.
[5] Bultmann, *KaM*, I, 5.
[6] *Ibid.*

This social and practical *Weltbild*, which is a product of and tool for man's work world, is as different anthropologically from the Enlightenment original concept as it is metaphysically. For the Enlightenment, the scientific *Weltbild* was not regarded as the property of the masses. Most often, the "peasant" was judged to be of the same mentality as his primitive ancestors. The acquisition of a true understanding of the real nature of the world was regarded as the high and difficult attainment of an intellectual aristocracy.[1] For them, however, it represented a form of cultural salvation, by freeing men for the first time in history from the morass of error, superstition, and ignorance in which they had been held captive; in no sense, could this attainment of reason be reduced to the status of a craftsman's tools, regarded as the common property of the men of an age. Furthermore, in its original Enlightenment form, the modern *Weltbild* was apprehended not only as a true description of the world, but as the most reliable guide to the understanding of the nature of being itself. Thus, when theology appropriated this Enlightenment hypothesis, it did so, not simply at the level of world understanding, but as a basis for the understanding of the being of God and of man. In both Eichorn and Strauss, there is a close connection between the development of the understanding of the world as a unified causal system and the emergence of monotheism, the understanding of God as First Cause active in his world through this system of secondary causes.[2]

For Bultmann, the scientific *Weltbild* could never enjoy such a positive ontological and theological status. As in his treatment of the Neo-Kantian concept of reason in 1920, in which he reinterpreted the meaning of reason from an anthropological perspective which stripped it of any ontological substance or value, so in the treatment of the scientific *Weltbild* in his more recent writings, he affirms this older tradition but within the limits of his own anthropological perspective. He thus acknowledges that, as a matter of fact, demythologizing does employ the modern world view as a norm for the interpretation of Scripture.[3] However, it is a norm only in the limited sense that "scientific thinking has destroyed the

---

[1] For a discussion of the social extension of the Enlightenment category of primitive mentality, see Manuel, pp. 178; 203.

[2] Cf. Eichorn, *Introduction . . .*, p. 12; Strauss, *Life of Jesus*, p. 59.

[3] Bultmann, *KuM*, II, 184.

mythological *Weltbild* of the Bible." [1] In no sense, may this modern
Weltbild be construed as providing a positive norm providing the
fundamental categories for the interpretation of Scripture.

> The expressions of Scripture, which speak out of existence and to
> existence, do not need to be justified before the forum of an objec-
> tifying science.[2]

It is, rather, the intention of Scripture itself that will provide the
norm for its interpretation.[3] The goal of demythologizing, therefore,
is not to win the freedom of Scripture from the mythological
Weltbild only to hand Scripture over to the scientific *Weltbild*.

> Rather, will demythologizing win an understanding of Scripture
> which is free from any *Weltbild*, as an objectifying thinking projects
> it, whether this be the *Weltbild* of myth or whether this be the
> *Weltbild* of science.[4]

Bultmann's modifications of the Enlightenment use of *Weltbild*
disclose the fundamental dialectical pattern of his thought. On the
one hand, he agrees with the Enlightenment tradition concerning
the meaning and use of "scientific *Weltbild*" as a necessary norm for
the criticism of myth in the biblical writings; on the other hand, he
will not give a positive theological function to this *Weltbild* in the
interpretation of the meaning of Scripture or the understanding of
the being of God and man. The categories appropriate to the intentionality of Scripture are not those of the objectifying thinking of
science, but rather those borrowed from the existentialist anthropology of Martin Heidegger. Bultmann thus subordinates the
Enlightenment tradition to the anthropological perspective central
to his own thought, even as he preserves the Enlightenment formulation of myth as an autonomous motif in his own thought.

Having examined the subordinate status of the Enlightenment
formulation in Bultmann's total concept of myth, I turn now to
discuss the autonomy of this motif in his thought. If the analysis of
Bultmann's concept of myth in terms of three historically and
logically independent traditions is correct, one would expect
Bultmann's actual use of the term to reflect a composite of the
meanings of these divergent traditions. The various meanings of

---

[1] *Ibid.*
[2] *Ibid.*, p. 187.
[3] *Ibid.*, p. 184.
[4] *Ibid.*, p. 187.

myth, from "salvation narrative in cultic context" through "pre-scientific mode of thought expressed in a primitive world view" to "a particular understanding of human existence in an objectified form" characteristically blend in with each other, so that it is often difficult to specify one meaning, to the exclusion of others. If, however, Bultmann's concept of myth is the kind of hybrid described, one should also expect to find persistent uses of the term which express only one tradition of meaning and demand the exclusion of the other two. This, in fact, is the case. Examples of the use of myth with only the meaning of the *Religionsgeschichtliche Schule* have been cited in the previous chapter. In the next chapter, it will be clear that Bultmann frequently uses myth to mean only "objectified form of particular self-understanding." At this point, therefore, I will examine selected uses of myth which reflect only the Enlightenment meaning of that term. Since the persistent independence of this tradition has been most neglected in Bultmann studies, and since it has been characteristic to reduce Bultmann's concept of myth to the distinctive and predominant existentialist formulation of the concept, it is particularly important to recognize the continuing autonomy of this formulation of myth in Bultmann's thought.

Because demythologizing employs only the existentialist and Enlightenment meaning of myth, the relevant question for the determination of the meaning of any given use of the term is this: does mythology mean a particular form of understanding human existence and God, i.e., an objectifying rather than an existentialist form of understanding; or, does mythology mean a particular form of explaining world events, i.e., in accordance with a primitive, rather than a scientific, world view or mode of thought? In the former case, to demythologize would mean: to de-objectify, to take away a conceptuality inadequate for the expression of the existential intention of the text; in the latter case, to demythologize would mean: to strip away the antique *Weltbild* and its corresponding false form of world explanation. While it is clear that these two meanings of "demythologize" do not contradict each other, but supplement each other, it is also clear that they are logically independent of each other. One does not necessarily entail the other. Eichorn could "demythologize" in the latter sense, without any concern for an existentialist conceptuality. It is just as plausible that a contemporary theologian might demythologize, in the sense of developing one step further that tradition of conceptualizing initiated in the biblical literature in order to express the intention of that tradition, without any commitment to the scientific *Weltbild* as a critical norm. It is therefore essential, in the present stage of discussion of demythologizing, to recognize the autonomy of these two fundamentally independent uses of the term.

Bultmann quite clearly uses the concept of demythologizing frequently in only the Enlightenment meaning of that term. This appears especially clearly when he identifies demythologizing with modes of thought which are, by his own declaration, objectifying modes of thought. Thus, for example, natural science has played a particularly prominent role in demythologizing the Bible.[1] This is obviously not meant to impute an existentialist, de-objectifying interpretation to natural science, but simply to recognize its role as the destroyer of the antique *Weltbild*.

> As such, it [natural science] of necessity demythologizes because it excludes the working of supernatural powers about which myth speaks. ... A thorough-going natural science has no need of the "God hypothesis" (Laplace) because it understands the forces that govern natural processes to be immanent within them. Likewise, it eliminates the idea of miracle as an event that interrupts the causal continuum of the world process.[2]

In a similar manner, "history necessarily demythologizes to the extent that it views the historical process in an objectifying way and thus understands it as a closed continuum of events." [3] For the historian "cannot allow that the continuum of historical happenings is rent by the interference of supernatural powers; nor can he acknowledge any miracles in the sense of events whose causes do not lie within history itself." [4] Like natural science, so the science of history demythologizes, not because it takes away an inappropriate objectifying conceptuality, but precisely because it insists upon regarding the past in a way consistent with its own objectifying perspective.

Beyond these classical enemies of mythology, Bultmann also discovers a host of other allies who have also demythologized the New Testament: sacramental theology, Hegel, Marx, Luther, the

---

[1] Bultmann, "On the Problem of Demythologizing," *JR* (1962), p. 96.
[2] *Ibid.*
[3] *Ibid.*, p. 99.
[4] *Ibid.*

Social Gospel, Karl Immerman, etc.[1] If one asks what unites such a motley group as this in the common venture of demythologizing, there is obviously only one answer: all have stripped away, by one means or another, the antique *Weltbild* from the New Testament proclamation. In this use of the term, the historical dialectic of Marx and the theological objectivism of sacramental theology furnish as clear examples of demythologizing as does Bultmann's existentialist theology.

Finally, it is also clear that Bultmann can use the criterion of the mythical *Weltbild* as determinative for the stipulation of the project of demythologizing at each stage of its formulation. The concept of the mythical *Weltbild* thus provides the occasion, the critical principle, the material point of departure, and the final criterion for the success of the program of demythologizing: in brief, the whole of the project of demythologizing may be formulated only with reference to the Enlightenment criterion. Thus, it is the discrepancy between the mythological *Weltbild* of the Bible and the scientific *Weltbild* that provides the occasion and the motive for the project of demythologizing.[2] The modern *Weltbild* provides the norm (*Massstab*) or the criterion for the project of demythologizing.[3] Finally, it is the total absence of the mythical *Weltbild* in a theological interpretation of the New Testament which established the successful completion of the project of demythologizing. It is thus possible for Bultmann's total program of demythologizing to be stated within the limits of the Enlightenment formulation of myth.[4]

4. NEO-KANTIAN EPISTEMOLOGY AND ENLIGHTENMENT HISTORIOGRAPHY

Why does Bultmann suddenly adopt the Enlightenment formulation of myth in the nineteen-thirties? It is clearly not an expression of his historical-literary biblical studies, for as a biblical critic Bultmann's use of myth was determined by the *Religionsgeschichtliche* meaning of the term. While Bultmann was also developing an existentialist interpretation of myth during the nineteen-thirties, no one would argue that the Enlightenment formulation was particularly congenial to the existentialist anthropology of Martin

---

[1] Bultmann, *Die christliche Hoffnung* . . ., pp. 27 ff.
[2] Bultmann, *KuM*, II, 207.
[3] *Ibid.*, p. 184; Bultmann, *Jesus Christ and Mythology*, p. 35.
[4] Bultmann, *KuM*, I, 48.

Heidegger. Indeed, Heidegger unqualifiedly repudiated the Enlightenment understanding of myth.[1] Nor does Hans Jonas employ
this version of myth in his idealist-existentialist interpretation of
Hellenistic mythology. It almost appears as if this Enlightenment
version of myth suddenly drops into the midst of Bultmann's work
without any organic connection to the significant intellectual origins
and developments of his thought—if one ignores the Neo-Kantian
origins of demythologizing.

However, from a Neo-Kantian perspective, Bultmann's appropriation of Enlightenment motifs appears not only consistent with
his thought, but essential to it. For the basic structure of Bultmann's Neo-Kantianism was the dualism of reason and individuality.
Therefore, in coming to terms with mythology, Bultmann needs to
develop a schema of interpretation which takes account of both
sides of this dualism. Jonas' idealist dialectic accounts for the
transition from mythology to the existentialist conceptuality of
Heidegger in correspondence with the Neo-Kantian category of
individuality. But for Bultmann, that is only one-half of the
problem. He also needs to account for the transition from mythology to science in correspondence with the Neo-Kantian category
of reason. The Enlightenment formulation fits this purpose perfectly,
and thus enables him to develop demythologizing as a double-
sided myth hermeneutic in correspondence with his Neo-Kantian
dualism.

The similarities between Neo-Kantianism and Bultmann's
Enlightenment discussion of myth are striking.

First, the concept of science and the scientific *Weltbild*, developed
in the later essays on demythologizing, is thoroughly consistent with
the concept of reason developed in the early Neo-Kantian writings.
In both cases, the stress is laid upon the all encompassing unity of
reason and its determination according to the principle of law.
Thus, science for Bultmann in 1941 is no more empirically oriented
than the reason of mathematical science was for him in 1920.
Because of this, he traces the history of science, in 1941 as in 1920,
as beginning with the Greek philosophical quest for the *arche*.
Modern science appears as the phoenix of Greek reason born out of
the ashes of the medieval world. He never acknowledges the dis-

---

[1] Below, pp. 210-211.

tinctive novelty of modern science, which differentiates it from
Greek reason and relates it to a biblical understanding of reality.[1]

Theology is called upon to recognize the autonomy of science in
1941 as in 1920. Any language of faith is objectionable if "it in-
fringes upon the point of view of science." [2] The result of this
autonomous, self-grounded reason is the closed context of objectification and lawful connection which constitutes the scientific world
view. The "conceptualist" or constructionist character of science is
as present in 1941 as it was in 1920. The scientific world view is the
objectification of reason and therefore this world view shares the
characteristics of scientific reason itself: namely, its unity and lawfulness.[3] Since the world is regarded by scientific man as the construct of reason in accordance with law, it is a thoroughly rational
world: only that is acceptable to modern man which is comprehensible within the limits of a rational world order.[4] The autonomy,
self-sufficiency and unity of modern man, expressed in his self-
understanding, appears simply as the correlative microcosm to the
macrocosm of his scientific world.[5]

The fundamental activity of objectifying a total world, as the
basic expression of a trans-individual *Geist* or *Vernunft*, is understood by Bultmann in 1941 as in 1920 to be a universal phenomenon
of human history. It only follows that the individual does not enjoy
a relationship of freedom to this *Weltbild*, but is related to it in the
mode of necessity. He may contribute to its further development,
as the point for the self-unfolding of reason, but he may not exercise
any sovereignty in relationship to it.[6] Thus, it is no accident that
when Bultmann reinterprets the Enlightenment meaning of the
scientific *Weltbild*, from its original ontological-theological role to an
anthropological category, he nevertheless does not confine this
anthropological category to the modern period of history but
understands it as a universal category. In every period of human
history, the *Geist* objectifies a world construct in terms of which the
individual man orders his daily affairs. Mythology is as clearly a

---

[1] For a critique of Bultmann's view of science in the form of a history of
modern science, see Alan Richardson, *The Bible in the Age of Science* (Philadelphia: The Westminster Press, 1961).
[2] Bultmann, *KuM*, II, 180.
[3] *Ibid.*, pp. 180-181.
[4] Bultmann, *Jesus Christ and Mythology*, p. 39.
[5] Bultmann, *KaM*, I, 6-7.
[6] Bultmann, *KuM*, I, 17.

product of this objectifying activity as is science. The difference between them falls, in 1941 as in 1920, at the epistemological point of law and the historical point of the Enlightenment. Modern thought since the Enlightenment objectifies in accordance with the principle of law while mythological thought of the primitive period objectifies in accordance with factors of an individual character: e.g., fear, surprise, threat, etc.

Furthermore, it is also clear in Bultmann's essays after 1941 that the status of the Enlightenment formulation in relation to the existentialist interpretation of myth corresponds exactly with the Neo-Kantian dialectic of reason and individuality. One need only compare the dialectic of reason and individuality, developed in Chapter II, with the dialectic of whole and part, of subordination and autonomy, developed in this chapter. The scientific *Weltbild* is radically deontologized just as the Neo-Kantian concepts of reason and culture were in 1920. In both cases, reason was given a new ontological status by being given a specific and limited anthropological function. In both cases, however, the radical subordination of reason and its objectified construct did not entail any rejection or substantive modification of the original understanding of reason or science. Bultmann's fidelity to the original Enlightenment hypothesis is thus comparable with his fidelity to Natorp's rejected pre-war epistemology. In neither case, will Bultmann take science or reason seriously, that is, with conviction and as related to that which matters. He is therefore free to criticize the Enlightenment hypothesis which he himself espouses when it is taken seriously by a colleague just as he concludes his 1920 essay with a critique of the Neo-Kantian understanding of reason and culture which he has accepted. Some matters are true, but not really true, not true for being or existence; there are, if you like, throw-away truths, which one espouses for the sake of reason and its world but rejects for the sake of existence and its historicity. Hence, Bultmann's ideal, in 1941 as in 1920, is to be related to the world of objectifying reason "as if it were not." While he has not yet appropriated this Pauline phrase as his *Stichwort* in 1920, he clearly understands it to be the theme of New Testament eschatology even then.

Bultmann's use of the Enlightenment formulation discloses once again the fundamental cleavage between thought and being. Being is that which occurs in the becoming of the individual; thought is that which determines the structure of the total social, natural objective world in which man finds his existence. *Tertium non datur*. It is thus clear why it is necessary for Bultmann to develop two interpretations of myth as the twin foundations for demythologizing: the one, which considers myth as a form of thought and dispenses with it as obsolete; the other, which considers myth as an expression of existence and interprets it in new existentialist categories in order to communicate its original existential meaning.

It is thus no accident that Bultmann recovered as central to his own reflection on myth this Enlightenment formulation in the nineteen-thirties. For it is precisely in this period that he is beginning to develop his own existentialist interpretation of myth. It is precisely in this period that he is beginning to reinterpret the meaning of myth, so that it is no longer a borrowed, primarily historiographical category, alien to the foundations of his own thought, but rather a theological category, central to his own work of New Testament interpretation, and expressive of the foundations of his thought. In the course of this transition, however, it would not have been sufficient to have developed only an existenialist interpretation of myth. For that should have expressed only one-half of the dualism of reason and individuality. It was necessary, simultaneously, to formulate an understanding of mythology as "false reason" and it was for this purpose that Bultmann appropriated the old Enlightenment tradition. His use of this concept of myth is therefore not be understood as a mark of his continuity with the liberal-critical tradition of the nineteenth century, for he did not initially use this concept of myth in his work as a biblical critic. Rather, his use of the Enlightenment formulation is to be seen as a necessary element in the construction of a total concept of myth which is able to bring to expression as a critical concept of systematic theology the Neo-Kantian origins of his thought.

CHAPTER FIVE

THE EXISTENTIALIST FORMULATION OF MYTH

Several preliminary comments are necessary concerning the use of the term existentialist and the meaning of the phrase "existentialist formulation of myth" in this chapter. The use of both of these is determined by the results of historical-exegetical inquiry. As a result, the meaning of these "labels" are established according to the texts under consideration, and the ideas expressed in them, rather than in accordance with their general, popular usage. Indeed, these terms can be used as descriptive for the content of this chapter only if first freed from their popular usage, which includes certain historical misconceptions, and determined strictly in accordance with the subject under consideration.

1) The meaning of "existentialist." I am not concerned here to develop the important, but by now familiar, distinction between "existential" and "existentialist."[1] I use the term "existentialist" to refer to a particular philosophical conceptuality occupying a distinct role in the history of philosophical and theological thought. However, in the context of the history of thought, my use of the term "existentialist" is both more specific and more general than is customary.

First, I do not use the term "existentialist" to refer to a total philosophical movement: i.e., from Kierkegaard through Sartre. I have no particular objection to such a usage of the term, but it is far too general for this specific historical inquiry. While dispensing with such a general use of the term, however, I also reject the very specific use of "existentalist" which had become prevalent in theological discussion: namely, a movement of thought that is constituted in, or defined by reference to, the early philosophical writings of Martin Heidegger.[2] Such a use of the term, which would

---

[1] See Martin Heidegger, *Sein und Zeit* (9th ed.; Tübingen: Max Niemeyer Verlag, 1960), p. 13.

[2] The identification of existentialist with *Sein und Zeit* in theological discourse is primarily a result of Bultmann's own work. Karl Jaspers offers just this critique of Bultmann's position (Karl Jaspers, "Myth and Religion," *Myth and Christianity*, p. 8). It is also a practice that has been extended through Bultmann studies: e.g., John Macquarrie, *An Existentialist Theology: A Comparison of Heidegger and Bultmann.*

make Heidegger's *Sein und Zeit* the norm for the meaning of "existentialist," is irrevelant to a study of Bultmann's existentialist formulation of myth because it presumes a simple, direct, conceptual continuity between Heidegger's philosophy and Bultmann's existentialist myth hermeneutic which simply does not exist. In no sense is it possible to speak of Bultmann's existentialist formulation of myth if the norm for the meaning of existentialist is taken to be *Sein und Zeit*. Therefore, the meaning of the term must be broader than a strict Heideggerian reference would allow.[1]

By "existentialist," I therefore mean a movement of thought, of which Rudolf Bultmann and Hans Jonas are the chief exponents, which is specifically hermeneutical-historiographical in its inception, which is formulated in relation to the texts of the Hellenistic period of history, and which presupposes certain anthropological categories from *Sein und Zeit* while re-interpreting these in accordance with an idealistic philosophy of history and (for Bultmann) a Lutheran theology of *sola fide*. I apologize for such a definition, which makes so complex such a traditional category in the history of thought. It seemed clear, however, that the label "existentialist" had become inseparably bound up with Bultmann's formulation of myth and furthermore, I knew of no viable alternative to propose in its place.

---

[1] I do not propose this distinction between the use of "existentialist" and *Sein und Zeit* on the basis of discussions of Heidegger's philosophy. It is true that the application of the label of existentialist to his philosophy, early as well as late, has become increasingly dubious. (For example, see the essay by James Robinson, "The German Discussion," *The Later Heidegger and Theology*, esp. pp. 60-70.) The basis for this distinction, however, has been the re-interpretation of the early *Sein und Zeit* in the light of later philosophical writings. My grounds for insisting upon the distinction between the use of "existentialist" and the thought of *Sein und Zeit* are of quite a different order. I wish to reserve the use of "existentialist" for that determination of thought which finds expression in the existentialist formulation of myth as this is constituted in the writings of Rudolf Bultmann and Hans Jonas during the years 1925 through 1934. The particularity of thought which comes to expression here presupposes Heidegger, but Heidegger may not be construed as being consistent with it. Therefore, if the term "existentialist" is to be defined by Heidegger, I must abandon its usage in conjunction with Bultmann's formulation of myth; or, the other possibility which I have chosen to follow is to provide a more comprehensive and appropriate textual foundation for the actual meaning of the term.

There is, quite obviously, a convergence in the conclusions of Heidegger studies, which would dissociate *Sein und Zeit* from the existentialist perspective, and my own historical-exegetical studies, which define "existentialist" primarily according to the texts of Bultmann and Jonas, rather than Heidegger.

In such a situation, it seemed best to preserve the conventional name, while defining it in accordance with the results of an historical-exegetical inquiry.

In the use of the term, "existentialist" refers primarily to neither an ontology nor an anthropology, but to a hermeneutic: a hermeneutic, not in the comprehensive use of that term—as the meaning of the language of being—but in the more specific sense of a method of interpretation directed to texts of the past.[1] This is why I use the qualifying phrase: 'historiographical'. The existentialist hermeneutic with which I am concerned is primarily a tool of historiography, even while it is also a hermeneutic of *Dasein*. It is necessary to stress this historiographical dimension in the use of existentialist since the particular contribution of Bultmann and Jonas emerges in response to the particular problems which they encountered as interpreters of texts of the Hellenistic world. While they bring to this task a Heideggerian anthropology, their particular myth hermeneutic is determined by the question of the meaning and nature of history, on the one hand, and the question of the meaning of these specific Hellenistic texts, on the other hand. Heidegger provides them with an answer to neither of these questions.

It is also clear that this use of existentialist is defined essentially by reference to the relevant texts of Bultmann and Jonas. The relationship of Heidegger's *Sein und Zeit* to the existentialist formulation of myth is therefore analogous to the relationship of the message of Jesus to New Testament theology, as Bultmann has described this: that is, Heidegger's thought is the essential presupposition for the formulation of an existentialist myth hermeneutic, but it may not be construed as a part of that movement of thought. As in Bultmann's discussion of New Testament theology, so here, both sides of the proposition must be stressed. Heidegger's work is genuinely essential to this formulation of myth; apart from *Sein und Zeit*, one cannot imagine such a conceptual creation. Both Bultmann and Jonas are dependent upon the creative impetus of *Sein und Zeit*, even when they are not consistent in their use of Heidegger's categories. However, Heidegger is not a part of this venture. The concepts of objectifying, myth, self-understanding, world, authentic and inauthentic, together with the schema of history in which myth is set, may not be derived from Heidegger

---

[1] James Robinson, "Hermeneutic since Barth," *The New Hermeneutic*, pp. 39-77.

or set in agreement with him. In these essential concepts, the existentialist formulation of myth is inconsistent with the corresponding concepts in Heidegger's writings of the same period. It is for this reason that it is necessary to define the use of existentialist, not in relation to Heidegger, but in relation to Bultmann and Jonas.

Finally, there is the further complication of introducing alien philosophical and theological motifs into the meaning of "existentialist." When I introduce the element of nineteenth-century historical idealism into the meaning of existentialist, I do not do this on the grounds of those Heidegger studies which purport to demonstrate the similarity between Hegel and Heidegger.[1] Rather, when I speak of historical idealism, I refer specifically to the interpretation of history as the history of *Geist*, the *Geist* whose dialectical movement is expressed in the *Stichwort*: thesis, antithesis, and synthesis. Accroding to this schema of history, the Hellenistic period comes to play a crucial role in the dialectical movement of *Geist*. On the one hand, the Hellenistic literature marks the "turn" from one epoch to another, as a fundamental new self-understanding breaks forth in history; on the other hand, this new self-understanding—as the first fruits of *Geist*—appears in a form antithetical with its own intention and thus must be recovered, in the present moment of history, in a new conceptuality appropriate to its original intention. The interpretation of the Hellenistic literature within this idealistic schema of history and as fused with Heidegger's *Daseinanalytik* is the particular contribution of Hans Jonas.

When I speak here of the theological contribution of the Lutheran *sola fide*, I do not mean this is the sense of a repristination of a Reformation doctrine. I mean Bultmann's version of Luther's *sola fide*, which is necessarily a *sola fide* whose meaning is deternined by the Neo-Kantian dialectic of reason and individuality as well as by the dialectic of faith and works. Nevertheless, since it is primarily the Lutheran interpretation of justification, with its antithetical relationship to works, that enters into this existentialist formulation, it may properly be considered under this rubric.

2) The meaning of 'existentialist formulation of myth.' This phrase also has a very technical meaning. In no sense may it be made equivalent to a general movement of thought which considers myth in accordance with an existentialist perspective or body of

---

[1] Jan Van Der Meulen, *Heidegger und Hegel oder Widerstreit und Widerspruch* (Meisenheim/Glan: Westkulturverlag Anton Hain, 1953).

categories. It is a very specific formulation of myth which I define as follows: myth is an expression of a particular understanding of existence in an objectifying form. This formulation is obviously based upon Bultmann's discussion of myth in the essays on demythologizing after 1941, although it is first developed in Jonas' studies of Augustine and Gnosticism in 1930 and 1934. The major task of the chapter is to clarify the meaning of this existentialist formulation of myth by establishing its connections with older philosophical and theological motifs. However, some preliminary comments on the meaning of this phrase are in order within the scope of this introduction.

This formulation of myth consists of two elements: 1) "a particular understanding of human existence" which is the content of myth—its "real intention," "abiding meaning," "original purpose," etc.—and 2) the objectifying (*objektivierend*) form of expression which is both essentially alien to the real intention of myth and essential to the nature of the total phenomenon as its own distinctive form of expression. In his use of the phrase, "particular understanding of human existence," Bultmann intends to specify a definite material content of myth. He thus does not use this phrase in the sense of a formal methodological principle designating nothing more than a form of question or perspective of inquiry appropriate to the subject matter of myth. Rather, he means by this phrase one very definite possibility of understanding human existence which was first actualized in human history in myth.

In a similar manner, the concept of "objectifying" is given a very particular and limited meaning in the context of the existentialist hermeneutic. It is especially necessary to emphasize this point, since I have previously used the concept of "objectifying" as rooted in Neo-Kantian epistemology. While the existentialist hermeneutical concept is continuous and assimilated with the older Neo-Kantian epistemological concept—as all of Bultmann's concepts are formed through an accretion of layers of meaning—nevertheless, the meaning of "objectifying" in the existentialist myth hermeneutic is genuinely new and must be clearly differentiated from the older Neo-Kantian layer of meaning. The surest sign of the specificity and novelty of the existentialist meaning of objectifying is this: Bultmann does not employ myth as a systematic hermeneutical concept until he receives the technical existentialist concept of "objectifying" from Hans Jonas, even though he has always had available to him the Neo-Kantian concept of "objectifying." The concluding section of Chapter VI discusses the close connection between this existentialist concept of objectifying and the Neo-Kantian foundations of Bultmann's theology. However, this line of connection may not obscure the distinct subject matter which is under consideration here as "objectifying" and which must be differentiated from that discussed under the same word in Chapter II.

The structure of this chapter varies considerably from the two previous chapters which are its counterparts. This is due primarily to the complications involved in winning an accurate understanding of the historical origins and conceptual presuppositions of this formulation of myth. I am not here examining a tradition of myth usage developed independently of Bultmann, which he then appropriated and modified, as was done in the previous two chapters. I therefore do not begin with a section on the sources for this formulation of myth, since Bultmann is himself one of its primary sources. At the same time, however, I am not able to begin only with Bultmann, as if his writings were in fact the only or even decisive source for this formulation of myth. In a very real sense, Bultmann is every bit as dependent upon the work of others for this existentialist formulation of myth as he was for those uses of myth derived from the *Religionsgeschichtliche Schule* or the Enlightenment tradition. The organization of the chapter must therefore make apparent the complex and subtle relationship between Bultmann and Jonas in the history of this formulation of myth: Bultmann, the elder and professor of Jonas, who brings together in a partial and tentative way the anthropological categories of Heidegger with the *Religionsgeschichtliche* understanding of myth; Jonas, who has been introduced into Hellenistic studies by Bultmann, who constructs a new philosophical hermeneutical concept of objectifying, and who demonstrates to Bultmann the historical fecundity of that hermeneutical concept in his study of Gnosticism; Bultmann, who then appropriates into his own thought from Jonas, the technical existentialist concept for which he has himself prepared the way.

Still another difficulty intrinsic to the discussion of the existentialist formulation of myth arises out of the widespread error in historical interpretation which has become determinative for the whole of this discussion: namely, the notion that Bultmann develops the existentialist formulation of myth in direct dependence on Heidegger, or, that the general formulation of his existentialist theology is equivalent with the development of the technical existentialist formulation of myth. Both of these opinions are false, but special care must be taken in the organization of the materials to correct this historical error while showing the complexities inherent in the actual connections of the texts.

1. 'OBJECTIFYING' AS AN ANTHROPOLOGICAL-THEOLOGICAL CONCEPT: W. HERRMANN, M. HEIDEGGER, AND BULTMANN (1925-1933)

The concept of objectifying is obviously basic to Bultmann's hermeneutical project of demythologizing. Like the concept of myth, however, objectifying cannot be considered as a single entity, but must be analyzed in terms of its component elements. The Neo-Kantian epistemological use of 'objectifying' was examined in Chapter II. In this section, the focus falls on a second dimension of meaning of this concept: namely, objectifying as equivalent with an inauthentic or sinful self-understanding.

This anthropological-theological meaning of objectifying is developed by Bultmann in a series of "early" existentialist essays: from 1925 through 1933. In 1925 Bultmann first began to use Heidegger's existentialist vocabulary and formulated that theological anthropology which was to continue as the center of his existentialist theology.[1] 1933 provides a clear cut-off point prior to the publication of Jonas' volume on Gnosticism in 1934 and is also the publication date of *Glauben und Verstehen*, I. The essays in this volume express Bultmann's theological-anthropological use of

---

[1] Bultmann obviously learned his Heidegger through his teaching relationship with him, including joint teaching assignments, rather than through *Sein und Zeit*, which was published two years later in 1927. In light of the earlier discussion of Bultmann's anthropologized Neo-Kantianism, it should prove interesting to re-examine these formative years in the relationship of Bultmann and Heidegger, especially in the context of post-war Neo-Kantian thought. It may well be that we should have to correct our older picture of Bultmann's dependence upon Heidegger, either as a faithful and correct interpreter of his thought or as the perpetrator of a partial and incorrect appropriation. The relationship may well entail a far greater degree of reciprocity than has characteristically been assumed to be the case: Bultmann's own understanding of existence from the perspective of a religiously conceived individuality providing the stimulus to Heidegger's formulation of the existentialist interpretation of *Dasein* as the point of departure for a radical new ontology. Such an inquiry, however, does not fall within the scope of this inquiry.

'objectifying,' and are written before Bultmann has available Jonas' hermeneutical formulation of 'objectifying.' [1]

The significance of this period (1925-1933) as the creative center for Bultmann's total theological career cannot be overestimated. In these years, Bultmann appropriated the Heideggerian categories and deployed them through the full range of his work as a system-

---

[1] While the date of 1934 appears to be decisive for Bultmann's appropriation of a technical existentialist interpretation of myth, it is not the decisive date for the development of the existentialist interpretation of myth in the writings of Hans Jonas. The following bibliographical information, made available to the author in a personal conversation with Dr. Jonas, is relevant to the discussion of the historical origins of the existentialist formulation of myth.

1) *Der Begriff der Gnosis* (Göttingen: Hubert & Co., 1930). This was published in limited circulation as the *Teildruck* of Jonas' doctoral dissertation. It appears in substantially the same form as: "Einleitung: Zum Problem der Objektivation und ihres Formwandels," *Gnosis und spätantiker Geist*, II, 1 (Göttingen: Vandenhoeck & Ruprecht, 1954). This is the methodological portion of Jonas' study of Gnosticism and has as its theme the relation of the objectivation of myth to the existential root of myth.

2) *Augustin und das paulinische Freiheitsproblem: ein philosophischer Beitrag zur Genesis der christlich-abendländischen Freiheitsidee* (Göttingen: Vandenhoeck & Ruprecht, 1930). This includes the appendix: "Über die hermeneutische Struktur des Dogmas." This appendix is one of the most important texts in any consideration of the existentialist formulation of myth and is considered in section three of this chapter. Jonas originally did the work on the Augustine volume as part of a seminar project with Heidegger in 1927. The volume has been republished with an introduction by James Robinson.

3) *Gnosis und spätantiker Geist*, I (Göttingen: Vandenhoeck & Ruprecht, 1934).

4) *Gnosis und spätantiker Geist*, II, 1 (Göttingen: Vandenhoeck & Ruprecht, 1954). While published in 1954, the book was written before 1933: "Vorwort" (*ibid.*, pp. vii-viii). Indeed, pages 17-112 were set and printed before 1934; pages 112 through 121 were set, though not yet printed. The departure of Jonas from Germany in 1933 and the later ban on the publications of Jewish emigrés made the appearance of the work impossible until after the war.

While Jonas had developed the technical existentialist formulation of myth as early as 1928 and 1930, and while these publications were available to Bultmann, it was not until Jonas proved the historical fruitfulness of this existentialist hermeneutic for the Hellenistic literature that Bultmann really took notice of it. The earlier publications had been primarily methodological and philosophical; it was only with the 1934 volume on Gnosticism that Jonas showed the power of this hermeneutic for the interpretation and ordering of the data of the Hellenistic world. It was Jonas' work as an historian of Gnosticism that make his myth hermeneutic convincing to Bultmann, and not Jonas' philosophical and methodological formulations of the matter.

atic and exegetical theologian. An existentialist theology, as a systematic position, is born in these years, from the initial, *existentielle* position of "Welchen Sinn hat es, von Gott zu reden? " to the more complete, critical, and properly existentialist position of "Die Geschichtlichkeit des Daseins und der Glaube: Antwort an Gerhardt Kuhlmann" (1930). [1] This is also the time in which an existentialist historiography is born, in *Jesus* of 1926. The fundamental existentialist theological interpretation of Paul is developed in the *R.G.G.* article on "Paulus" for 1930 as is the basic interpretation of John in "Die Eschatologie des Johannes-Evangelium"of 1928.[2] One need only compare the interpretations of Paul and John developed in these essays with the corresponding material in the later *Theology of the New Testament* to appreciate the significance of this period.[3] It is not simply that the foundation for an existentialist theology is established during these years, but the whole edifice is built, requiring only minor corrections and additions in the later years of Bultmann's thought.[4]

---

[1] Rudolf Bultmann, "Welchen Sinn hat es, von Gott zu reden?" *GV*, I, 26-37. Originally published under the same title in *Theologische Blätter*, IV (1925), pp. 129-135. Rudolf Bultmann, "Die Geschichtlichkeit des Daseins und der Glaube: Antwort an Gerhardt Kuhlmann," *ZThK*, XI (1930), pp. 329-364. Translated by Schubert Ogden as "The Historicity of Man and Faith," *Existence and Faith* (New York: Meridian Books, Inc., 1960), pp. 92-110.

[2] Rudolf Bultmann, "Paulus," *RGG* [2], IV, 1019-1045. Translated by Schubert Ogden as "Paul," *Existence and Faith*, pp. 111-146. Rudolf Bultmann, "Die Eschatologie des Johannes-Evangeliums," *GV*, I, 134-152. Originally published in: *ZZ*, VI (1928), 4-22.

[3] Rudolf Bultmann, *Theology of the New Testament*, trans. Kendrick Grobel (2 Vols; New York: Charles Scribner's Sons, 1951-1955), I, 190-352; II, 3-94.

[4] This bibliographical data is relevant to any judgment concerning the place of demythologizing in the total scope of Bultmann's thought. First, it is clear that Bultmann's position in the history of theology, as well as in the history of biblical studies, is established independently of his demythologizing proposal. Bultmann's most important contributions as a literary-historical critic of the New Testament and as the founder of a new school of existentialist theology are made long before he introduces the concept of "entmythologisiert" in 1941. From a total perspective, the demythologizing proposal, with which his theological work has become so closely identified, appears as a postscript to the center of his work in systematic theology and historical-exegetical studies. Second, it is important to recognize that Bultmann develops an existentialist theology and historiography before he develops an existentialist formulation of myth. The direction of this existentialist theology, prior to 1934, was still open to move in several possible

The purpose of this section, however, is limited to a delineation of the meaning of objectifying as an anthropological concept in Bultmann's theology. For this purpose, I will compare and contrast this anthropological use of the concept with its original epistemological meaning. I will also consider the various uses of objectifying in the early philosophical writings of Martin Heidegger. I intend to show that Bultmann's anthropological use of objectifying is consistent with the Neo-Kantian Lutheran theology of Wilhelm Herrmann but may not be made consistent with the use of objectifying in Heidegger's ontology of *in-der-Welt-sein*.

Bultmann's 1935 essay, "Welchen Sinn hat es, von Gott zu reden?" provides the textual focus for examining the theological-anthropological meaning of 'objectifying.' Before turning to that essay, however, it may be helpful to summarize the basic points of Bultmann's 1920 essay on "Religion und Kultur." In this way, the transition from 'objectifying' as a strictly epistemological category to 'objectifying' as a theological-anthropological category should become clear.

The 1920 essay disclosed Bultmann's continuity with the Neo-Kantian account of knowledge, as objectification in accordance with law. Like the other Neo-Kantians, Bultmann understood this nature of knowledge to be definitive for not only the mathematical sciences, but for all disciplines of thought: e.g., for history. Indeed, the whole of culture, including morality and art, was considered to be of this same nature. In correspondence with this nature of knowledge was a certain sphere or spheres of reality which, however, were not given the status of the "really real" in Bultmann's postwar Neo-Kantianism. This fell to the sphere of the individual and his experience, not to the sphere of reason and its objective forms. Religion was also a phenomenon of the order of individuality and thus could be stipulated, negatively, in terms of the absence of the objectifying activity or lawful connection of reason and positively, through its presence in the realization of individuality.

Bultmann continues to employ this basic Neo-Kantian perspective and categories of thought in this first essay written from an

---

directions. It was only after 1934 that the direction of this existentialist theology became fixed in the form specified by the concept of demythologizing.

existentialist point of view.[1] To be sure, there occurs in the 1925 essay a basic change of perspective and corresponding vocabulary. The subject matter is now "God," "faith," and "our real, concrete, existential self," not the more abstract and self-detached categories of religion, *Erlebnis*, and the individual. Nevertheless, within this fundamental change of perspective and linguistic context, one may still hear the familiar Neo-Kantian themes.

For example, in the essay of 1925, God may not be considered as an object of thought, in any sense of the term or for any purpose, just as religion, in 1920, could not be confused with any objective form.[2] The notion of God as object, or as provable in some scheme of knowledge, is only a "phantom," "a way of speaking that has no meaning." [3] Like object, so the Neo-Kantian category of lawfulness is also still determinative for man's speaking of God. God may not be integrated into a sytem of "earthly objects through a structure of causal lawfulness," nor may God be identified with some compre-

---

[1] I use the phrase "existentialist point of view" because of the particular anthropological perspective central to this essay. As will appear in the later discussion of vocabulary, Bultmann did not yet have available to him the category of *"existential"* in distinction from *"existentielle."* This point may also be illustrated by referring to Bultmann's discussion of theological and exegetical methodology which appeared in the same year: "Das Problem einer theologischen Exegese des Neuen Testaments," *ZZ*, III (1925), pp. 334-357. The relevant exegetical question now is the strictly personal one: "What does it mean for me, not what did it mean in all its idiosyncracies then ? " (*ibid.*, p. 337). The relevant understanding of the exegete's relationship to the text is the familiar model of personal encounter: "Ich und Du, friend to friend, father to child" (*ibid.*, p. 348). The relevant knowledge in the work of the exegete is "the knowledge of our own insecurity . . . that it rests in our free deed of decision" (*ibid.*, p. 351). Bultmann thus insists that he is not proposing a new method, which would lapse once more into some objectifying schema, but simply a new attitude or orientation of the interpreter to the text:

> The fundamental issue is not the proclamation of a new method—for a method does not grasp real history because it always only grasps that over which we already have disposal. The results of an existential, shaken exegesis do not allow themselves to be justified and grounded like those of a methodological exegesis. For the possibilities of understanding the text . . . may be fixed just as little as the possibilities which arise out of the meeting of *Ich und Du* (*ibid.*, p. 351).

In a technically precise sense of the term, I would therefore have to speak of an existential, rather than an existentialist theology, in conjunction with these writings.

[2] Rudolf Bultmann, "Welchen Sinn hat es, von Gott zu reden ? " *GV*, I, 26 [*ThBl* (1925)].

[3] *Ibid.*

hensive "general law" or "principle," nor may the deed of God be
considered from "the point of view of happenings ordered by law." [1]
There can be no knowledge of God in 1925 just as there could be no
religious knowledge in 1920. Just as science was autonomous, and so
absolutely unable to speak of religious matters, in 1920, so is
science in 1925 to be regarded as atheistic, not if it denies God, but
if it should attempt to affirm God.[2] In brief, one meets in this 1925
essay the same absolute gulf between reason, with its objectifying
activity and principle of lawfulness, and faith or God as was earlier
characteristic of reason and religion.

In a similar manner, there is presented in both essays an understanding of a definite reality appropriate to this nature of reason:
an understanding of reality which, in turn, is understood to be the
expression of a particular Greco-modern scientific tradition of
thought:

> The reality of which we usually speak is the *Weltbild* which, since
> the time of the Renaissance and Enlightenment—under the in-
> fluence of Greek thought—has come to dominate our thinking. We
> see something as real when we are able to understand it in the
> unified context of this world, whether the context be regarded as
> determined by a causal or teleological principle, whether its elements
> be conceived of as spiritual or material. For the difference between
> the materialist and idealist *Weltanschauung* is in regards to this
> question, of no significance.[3]

This *Wirklichkeit*, however, which is the construct of the objectifying activity of reason, is of no more real concern in 1925 than it
was in 1920.[4]

A final point of continuity between these two essays is this: the
sphere of faith or religion is identified with the interior dynamics and
tensions of human existence in its concrete particularity. However,
the understanding of the nature and meaning of these dynamics and
tensions has changed so sharply as to require a new focus of exposition in order to present that new understanding of human existence which Bultmann develops here. For while Bultmann's understanding of the nature of thought and its reality remains essentially
continuous with his Neo-Kantian origins throughout the whole of

---

[1] *Ibid.*, p. 28; p. 36.
[2] *Ibid* , p. 37.
[3] *Ibid.*, p. 27.
[4] *Ibid.*, p. 31. Note this clear statement of the Enlightenment motif in this
1925 essay, though it is not yet bound up with the concept of myth.

his career, his understanding of the nature of man changes abruptly from the anthropology of individuality which we saw present in the 1920 essay.

The most obvious difference appears at the level of vocabulary. The fundamental anthropological category of 1920 was *"Individuum"*; in 1925, it is *Existenz* or *existentielle*, as modified by *"konkreten"* or a personal pronoun:

> *"der Wirklichkeit seiner konkreten Existenz ..."*[1]
> *"der Frage nach unserer eigentlichen Existenz ..."*[2]
> *"der Problematik seiner konkreten Existenz ..."*[3]
> *"der konkrete existentielle Situation des Redenden."*[4]
> *"mein existentielle Ich ..."*[5]
> *"unserer eigen konkreten Existenz ..."*[6]

In 1920, the concept of *Erlebnis* was used to designate that event which was most fundamental to the expression of, or constitutive for the being of, the individual; in 1925, it is the concept of the "free deed" in which existence is both manifest and constituted.[7] Thus, it is the free deed which "alone goes forth out of our existential being, in this alone are we ourselves and are we whole."[8] "Only in it [the free deed] and nowhere else do we really exist in the authentic sense, since it is nothing else but our existence itself."[9]

More significant than this change of terminology, however, is the different understanding of the human problem which appeared in the 1925 essay. In 1920, the fundamental problem of human existence was still understood by reference to reason and its tension

---

[1] *Ibid.*, p. 30.
[2] *Ibid.*, p. 31.
[3] *Ibid.*
[4] *Ibid.*, p. 26.
[5] *Ibid.*, p. 29.
[6] *Ibid.*, p. 28.
[7] While the existentialist concept of *"Entscheidung"* is not yet available to Bultmann, he is clearly using *"frei Tat"* with this meaning. In an essay written two years later (1927), "Zur Frage der Christologie," he brings the two together, speaking of *"frei Tat der Entscheidung"* (*GV*, I, 101). This also occurs in the same context of discussion (the meaning of obedience) and in relation to the same theme of the fulfillment of existence: "Only in the free deed of decision does the being of man fulfill itself as historical" (*ibid.*). "There thus arises the theological task of securing this deed of faith against its misunderstanding as a work" (*ibid.*). For a similar use, see the same essay, *GV*, I, 110.
[8] *Ibid.*, p. 34.
[9] *Ibid.*, p. 35.

with the irrational within (as the natural) or without (as the events of history which befall us). The problem of being human was equivalent with the problem of avoiding the tyranny of reason (through the deification of culture) on the one hand, and the chaos of nature or the meaninglessness of history, on the other hand. The problem of being human was the problem of transcending the reason-nature, reason-destiny polarities through a discovery of that individual identity which encompassed both without being determined by either. In 1925, however, the fundamental problem of human existence is understood quite differently; it is no longer reason and its limits, but *Sorge* and man's limits to dispose of that being which is his own, for which he cares and for which he is responsible.[1] As a result of the fundamental discrepancy between man's care and responsibility for his being, on the one hand, and his powers to dispose over his own future, on the other hand, insecurity comes to be the fundamental characteristic of all human existence. The basic question of existence is thus this: how shall man exist freely in that insecurity which is constituitive for the very structure of his existence.

It is this particular interpretation of the problem of human existence which becomes fundamental to Bultmann's total theological anthropology. In this 1925 essay he expresses the matter quite simply as follows:

> A certain double-sidedness of our existence has thus become clear to us: 1) that we have the care and responsibility for it; and that means: *tua res agitur*; 2) that it is absolutely insecure and we are not able to secure it; for to do that, we would have to stand outside of it and be God Himself.[2]

The same theme appears in the much later discussion of Pauline anthropology as presented in Bultmann's *Theology of the New Testament*:

> As the investigation of the term *soma* showed, man, according to Paul, is a being who has a relationship to himself, is placed at his own disposal, and is responsible for his own existence. But this existence of his, as the investigation of the terms *psyche, pneuma, zoe, nous,* and *kardia* showed, is never to be found in the present as a fulfilled reality, but always lies ahead of him. In other words, his

---

[1] *Ibid.*, p. 31.

[2] *Ibid.*, p. 33. Bultmann does not yet have the concept of future so important to the later statements of this anthropology.

existence is always an intention and a quest, and in it he may find himself or lose his grip upon himself, gain his self or fail to do so.[1]

It is also this theme which is central to the original proposal of demythologizing:

> Paul sees that the life of men is burdened with *"Sorgen"* (*merimnan*). Every man is directed with his *Sorge* to something. The natural man cares to secure his life, and, corresponding with his possibilities and achievements in the visible world, "he trusts in the flesh." The consciousness of this security finds its expression in glorying.
> This attitude of man, however, is not appropriate to his actual situation, for he is not secure. He loses his "life," his authentic existence, and falls victim to the sphere over which he thought he would dispose and out of which he thought he would win his security.[2]

To be human is to care for and be responsible for one's own existence; to be human is to be limited in one's power to dispose of that existence and hence to be insecure. After 1925, this comes to constitute for Bultmann the fundamental structure of human existence, for the natural man as well as for the man of faith.

Thus, it is in light of this ontological structure that the ontic possibilities of sin and faith are to be understood.[3] Sin is the false resolution to this situation of insecurity. For sin is man's effort to secure his being in terms of his own powers and/or in terms of the known, visible, world at his disposal.

> For the creation stands at man's disposal: hence to seek life in it means to have the presumption to seek life in the disposable; i.e., to presume to have life at one's own disposal. Hence, the ultimate sin reveals itself to be the false assumption of receiving life not as the gift of the Creator but procuring it by one's own power, of living from oneself rather than from God.[4]

By man's effort to derive his security from the tangible, known, controllable world, the world becomes the master of man and man its slave. The actual result of this false resolution to human insecurity is the *Angst* of man who lives as the slave of alien worldly powers.[5]

In contrast with this is the life of faith. Faith is the authentic

---

[1] Bultmann, *Theology of the New Testament*, I, 227.
[2] Bultmann, *KuM*, I, 28.
[3] Bultmann, *Theology of the New Testament*, I, 227.
[4] *Ibid.*, p. 232.
[5] Bultmann, *KuM*, I, 28.

resolution to the human condition of insecurity. For in faith, man
lives out of "that which is not seen, is not at his disposal, and thus
gives up all self-contrived security." [1]

> Faith is obedience because it is man's turning away from himself,
> the giving up of all security, the surrender of all trust in oneself. . . . [2]

To exist in faith, freed from an attitude of worldly dependence, is to
exist eschatologically. It is the true, dialectical meaning of "*Entweltlichung*," of being in the world "as if it were not": to be in the
world as if the known, disposable, visible, tangible world were not
determinative for the security of one's being. To exist eschatologically is to exist beyond both the anxiety and the security of the
world, trusting in our insecurity to the God who meets us in love
out of our future and whose deed in Jesus Christ makes possible
our free deed of decision.[3]

It is only in the context of this theological anthropology that one
can understand Bultmann's anthropological use of objectifying as
synonymous with inauthentic self-understanding or sin. Objectifying
here comes to express a fundamental attitude of the self toward its
own existence, or the crucial moments of its existence; it is an
attitude of escape from the real existence of *Sorge* and insecurity
as self-understanding acquires the form or pose of world-understanding. Bultmann's 1925 discussion of the existential meaning of
Weltanschauung offers a classic example of this use of objectifying:

> For it [a *Weltanschauung*] does a great service for man in that it
> disengages him from himself, it releases him from the problem of
> his concrete existence, his care and responsibility for his existence.
> The desire of man for a so-called *Weltanschauung* is thus grounded
> in this: he can withdraw himself from confrontation with the riddle
> of his destiny and death through it; he can free himself from taking
> seriously the moment—the moment in which his existence is shaken
> and doubtful –by understanding such a moment as one instance of
> a general rule, by joining it in a coherent connection, by objectifying
> it, and so leap out of his own existence.[4]

What is novel in this use of objectifying is its anthropological
focus and critical intention. In the 1920 essay, Bultmann consistently used the concept of objectifying in its traditional Neo-

[1] *Ibid.*, p. 29.
[2] *Ibid.*
[3] *Ibid.*
[4] Bultmann, "*Welchen Sinn* . . .," p. 31.

Kantian epistemological meaning and as applied only to the sphere of reality constituted by reason. Objectifying was thus never used in connection with the discussion of anthropology, but rather was set in decisive opposition with the proper anthropological categories of *Individuum* and *Erlebnis*. From 1925 on, however, objectifying, especially in its self-reflexive form, comes to mean the sinful or inauthentic form of resolution to the fundamental problem of human insecurity.

In this usage, objectifying becomes synonymous with a particular existential stance, a stance which Bultmann expresses in a variety of prepositional and verbal forms. It is a way of speaking *"über"* rather than *"von"* or *"aus"*; it is a standing *"ausserhalb"*; it is a seeing *"von aussen"* ("to see oneself from the outside as an object of self-oriented thinking: this is the *proton pseudos*"); it is an orientation to the other as *"Woraufhin."* [1] It is an existential stance which is characteristically expressed through the predominance of verbs of "seeing" (*sehen, absehen, ansehen, umsehen*) in contrast with verbs of speaking, hearing, and acting. It is an existential stance which creates a false split in the self. Through making oneself an object of his own reflection, there is created a double self:

> The I that takes up a position is the real existential I; the other I, to which I relate myself, which I regard as something given, is a phantom without existential reality. The existential I which thus examines and inquires into itself proves itself, in this examining and inquiring, to be godless. [2]

In all these ways, objectifying retains its continuity with the earlier epistemological use. In reason one relates to reality not as that which is immediately given and not out of the particularity of his own individuality, but only from the distance of the object, which is the construct of reason, and through the mediation of the principle of law, which determines the organization and response to this reality. It is this same formal mode of orientation which Bultmann has now taken up into the realm of anthropology and theology as expressive of the illegitimate resolution to the fundamental problem of human insecurity.

In light of this interpretation of the human situation and the new understanding of the pervasiveness of this self-alienating, objecti-

---

[1] *Ibid.*, p. 26; p. 27; p. 33; p. 32; p. 27; p. 29.
[2] *Ibid.*, p. 29. Cf. Natorp's description of the objectified "Ich" as a "fiction" (Above, p. 69).

fying mode of being, it is now necessary for Bultmann to be more specific and critical in his use of the older Neo-Kantian categories of thought. It is no longer sufficient to say that one really speaks of God in confession, in *Erlebnis*, and in our inner life. To be sure, this may well be the case. However, if a man makes his confession, his *Erlebnis*, his inner life into an object, into a *"Woraufhin"* to which he relates himself, why then he no longer speaks of God, but only of himself: i.e., himself as objectified and as deplete of any existential reality.

> If we would speak of God, so we are obviously not able to begin by speaking of our *Erlebnissen* and our inner life which, as we objectify it, loses its existential character.[1]

In a similar manner, it is also necessary to be more stringent in terms of the meaning of an objectifying speech about God. From a Neo-Kantian epistemological perspective, any such speech of God was false, an expression of a primitive, naïve, or uncritical mind. From Bultmann's 1925 anthropological perspective, however, any such speech of God is synonymous with sin: "To speak of God in this sense, however, is not only an error and wrong, but it is sin." [2] According to Bultmann, Luther had made this same point in his commentary on the nature of Adam's sin. This consisted not in the eating of the forbidden fruit, but in the asking of the question, "Should God have said? "[3] Bultmann regards this as the prototype of the *"disputare de deo"* in which the speaker sets himself outside of God and the claim of God. Just as the objectifying of self is the first falsehood and can only lead to self-deception, so the objectifying of God is sin which can lead only to a phantom.[4] One can understand the new association of objectifying with this strong theological, critical language, in contrast with its earlier neutral epistemological status, only as one apprehends the meaning of objectifying in an anthropology of insecurity.

While I have maintained the distinction between objectifying as an epistemological category and objectifying as an existential norm, it is clear that Bultmann does not draw such a distinction here or in his later uses of this term. Rather, the two meanings become blended into each other. The result of this merger is often somewhat

---

[1] *Ibid.*, p. 29.
[2] *Ibid.*, p. 27.
[3] *Ibid.*
[4] *Ibid.*, p. 26; p. 32.

bizarre, since there is such a wide discrepancy between objectifying as a particular existential intention and objectifying as a mode of reason appropriate to the world.[1] Thus, for example, in this essay, Bultmann can write that any such speech about God is a sin, even if it proceeds out of an honest seeking after God.[2] One can only conclude here that sin is defined, not simply by the intentionality of the heart, but by a particular form of thought regardless of intention. In a similar manner, Bultmann can describe the world as being godless, not in accordance with such an intention, but simply because of the fact of "seeing our world from the outside."[3] Here it is apparently the objectifying perspective in itself that is identified as sinful.

This same confusion of epistemological perspective and anthropological norm appears in Bultmann's 1961 discussion of demythologizing. He is here discussing the two methods for the interpretation of history and their relationship to each other: namely, an objectifying and an existentialist interpretation of history. Since he has insisted upon the legitimate role of both of these historical perspectives and methods of inquiry, he is led to inquire as to whether these two interpretations of history are "mutually contradictory . . . so that one must speak of two realms of reality or even of a double truth."[4] Bultmann rejects this conclusion, and chooses instead to ground the duality of historical methodologies in the two anthropological possibilities of authentic and inauthentic existence:

> The one reality, however, can be seen under a double aspect in accordance with man's double possibility of authentic or inauthentic existence. In inauthentic existence man understands himself in

---

[1] It is because of this conceptual confusion that it is virtually impossible for Bultmann to secure science or technology from the automatic status of sin or inauthenticity. For science is objectifying, as a mode of thought, and hence, according to the anthropological meaning of the term, expressive of man's intention to win his security in a worldly manner. While I can understand such a wholesale theological repudiation of the modern technological world as a response to the excess of the bourgeois spirit, just as I can understand the radical repudiation of sexuality by the early Church in response to the excesses of the pagan world, in neither case may I accept, as logically consistent or theologically defensible, the identification of sin with any particular expression of man's being in the world.

[2] *Ibid.*, p. 28.

[3] *Ibid.*, p. 33. Later in this same paragraph, Bultmann qualifies this interpretation of the sinfulness of our world: not only is it seen from the outside, but it is also the world which we take seriously (*ibid.*).

[4] Bultmann, "On the Problem of Demythologizing," *JR* (1962), p. 100.

> terms of the world that stands at his disposal, whereas in authen-
> tic existence he understands himself in terms of the future of
> which he cannot dispose. Correspondingly, he can regard the
> history of the past in an objectifying way, or else as personal
> address, insofar as in it he perceives the possibilities of human
> existence and is summoned to responsible choice.[1]

An objectifying historiography is thus expressive of man's inauthentic self-understanding ("in terms of the world that stands at
his disposal") while an existentialist historiography is expressive of
an authentic self-understanding ("in terms of the future of which he
cannot dispose"). In light of such passages, one must regard the
confusion between objectifying as an epistemological category and
objectifying as an existential norm as a systematic and continuing
principle of Bultmann's thought.

Having set forth the meaning of objectifying in its anthropological context and as distinguished from and fused with the meaning
of objectifying as an epistemological category, I now turn to the
examination of the sources for this theological-anthropological use
of objectifying. Since this anthropological use of the concept first
appears in conjunction with Bultmann's appropriation of Heidegger's philosophical categories, it is only appropriate to examine
first Heidegger's use of objectifying. I will thus briefly set forth: 1)
the nature of Heidegger's use of objectifying as an anthropological
concept; 2) the nature of Heidegger's use of objectifying as a
traditional Neo-Kantian epistemological category; and 3) Heidegger's use of objectifying within the ontological schema of his own
thought.

It is clear from the introduction to *Sein und Zeit* that Heidegger
is familiar with an anthropological use of objectifying. In his discussion of the personalistic philosophy of Scheler, there appears the
very clear use of this concept as synonymous with a false form of
self-understanding.

> For Scheler, the person is never to be thought of as a thing or sub-
> stance; the person is rather the *unity* of living-through (*Er-Lebens*)
> which is immediately experienced in and with our Experiences—not
> a Thing merely thought of behind and outside what is immediately
> experienced. The person is no thinglike and substantial being. Nor
> can the being of a person be entirely absorbed in being a subject
> of rational acts which follow certain laws.

---

[1] *Ibid.*

The person is not a thing, not a substance, not an object. . . . Essentially the person exists only in the performance of intentional acts, and is therefore essentially not an object. Any psychical *Objektivierung* of acts, and hence any way of taking them as something psychical, is tantamount to depersonalization.[1]

While Heidegger can thus use the concepts of object or objectification in the context of a 'thingification' of person, it is also clear that he is here presenting Scheler's position and not his own. When speaking on his own right, he never uses the concept of objectification with this anthropological meaning, except as qualified by quotation marks or context to indicate a particular limited, partial, and borrowed use of the term. After the quotation cited above, Heidegger proceeds to reject Scheler's understanding of the problem as inadequate; it is not primarily a new anthropology which is needed, an anthropology which distinguishes clearly the being of man from the being of worldly entities; rather, it is a new ontology which is needed which reinterprets the meaning of being, and thus also sets free the possibility of a new anthropology.

> But what stands in the way of the basic question of *Dasein's* Being (or leads it off the track) is an orientation thoroughly colored by the anthropology of Christianity and the ancient world, whose inadequate ontological foundations have been overlooked both by the philosophy of life and by personalism.[2]

Thus, while Heidegger is familiar with this anthropological use of *"Objektivierung"* in philosophical personalism, he will not accept the anthropological limitations determinative for this use of the concept.

In a later discussion of world-time, Heidegger can also use the concept of objectifying as equivalent with an illegitimate "reifying" (*verdinglicht*) of time.

> The time "in which" the present-at-hand is in motion or at rest is *not "Objective"* (*objektiv*), if what we mean by that is the Being-present-at-hand-in-itself of entities encountered within-the-world.

---

[1] Martin Heidegger, *Sein und Zeit* (9th edition; Tübingen: Max Niemeyer Verlag, 1960), pp. 47-48; *Being and Time*, trans. John Macquarrie & Edward Robinson (London: SCM Press Ltd., 1962), p. 73. Citations are from the Macquarrie-Robinson translation, except as indicated. Page references shall be given to both the original and translation (abbreviated as tr.) since the technical concepts involved in the discussion have been used in their original German form.

[2] *Ibid.*, p. 48; tr., p. 74.

> But *just as little* is time "subjective," if by this we understand
> Being-present-at-hand and occurring in a "subject."
> ....
> If world-time thus belongs to the temporalizing of temporality,
> then it can neither be volatilized "subjectivistically" nor "reified"
> by a vicious "Objectification" (*Objektivierung*).[1]

In both of these instances, the context of *"objektiv"* or *"Objekti-vierung"* makes it clear that they are being used in a partial and inappropriate sense: that is, they are used to express an understanding of reality in terms of the older subject-object structure of knowledge and being. Lest the reader miss the point of the inappropriateness of this usage of the concepts, Heidegger inserts into the discussion of world-time his own understanding of the proper usage of these terms:

> *World-time is "more Objective" (objektiv) than any possible Object*
> *because, with the disclosedness of the world, it already becomes "Objec-*
> *tified" (objiciert) in an ecstatico-horizontal manner as the condition for*
> *the possibility of entities within-the-world.*[2]

Thus, Heidegger only uses the concept of objectifying, in either its Neo-Kantian epistemological form or in its anthropological form, with radical qualifications. At neither point will Heidegger identify his own thought with those uses of the concept which are characteristic of Bultmann.

This difference in the use of objectifying discloses, as clearly as any other point, the gulf between Bultmann and Heidegger: the distinctive thrust of Heidegger's thought appears precisely in his radical re-interpretation of the Neo-Kantian understanding of reason and world reality, while Bultmann's thought is continuous with his Neo-Kantian sources at these points. Heidegger's 1927 review of Ernst Cassirer's *Philosophie der symbolischen Formen*, Vol. II illustrates the gulf between his position and Bultmann's Neo-Kantianism.[3]

Heidegger understands Cassirer to stand in a line of unbroken continuity with the Neo-Kantians. Indeed, this constitutes the fundamental weakness of his thought, and for two reasons. First, Heidegger objects to the attempt to transplant Kant's Copernican

---

[1] *Ibid.*, pp. 419-420; tr., pp. 471-472.
[2] *Ibid.*, p. 419; tr., p. 471
[3] Martin Heidegger, Review of *Philosophie der symbolischen Formen*, Vol. II, by Ernst Cassirer, *Deutsche Literaturzeitung*, V (1928), 1000-1012.

revolution from the sphere of nature to the sphere of culture.[1] Cassirer has not attempted to rethink this Copernican revolution in light of a new problem but has simply expanded upon the traditional Kantian formulation. As a result, Cassirer attempts to interpret the nature of myth by means of the epistemological norm constructed by Cohen on the basis of mathematical physics.[2] Cassirer thus conceives of the nature of the task of myth analysis primarily in terms of the analysis of a mode of thought or perception.[3] In contrast with this, Heidegger would insist upon an analysis of the mythical *Lebensraum* which had as its purpose the manifestation of a particular mode of being in the world disclosed in the mythical experience.

Apart from the illegitimate extension of the Neo-Kantian position into the sphere of culture and myth analysis, Heidegger is critical of Cassirer for his fidelity to a position which requires radical revision. He regards the fundamental categories of Neo-Kantian thought—*Geist, Leben, Bewusstsein, Vernunft*—as unclear and ontologically inadequate, even in their proper sphere of use.[4] He describes the fundamental ontology of Cassirer and Cohen in its traditional Neo-Kantian categories. Out of a passively given chaos of *Empfindung, Dasein* forms a cosmos.[5] In this understanding of *Dasein* objectifying a world out of the unstructured flow of immediate experience, Cassirer and Cohen are one. The reality of mythical thought, like the reality of mathematical physics, is to be understood as the product of this *"gestaltenden Bewusstsein."* [6] It is this total apprehension of the nature of the relationship of *Dasein* to his world that Heidegger finds inadequate, and it is to the task of reformulating the ontological foundations for the understanding of the world, and the nature of the knowledge of the world, that Heidegger turns in *Sein und Zeit.*

The first existentialist category which Heidegger develops, and which he regards as fundamental for all others is Being-in-the-world. For the theory of knowledge, this means that *Dasein* always already transcends himself into his world prior to the articulation of any subject-object schema of knowledge. This ontological condition

---

[1] *Ibid.*, p. 1008.
[2] *Ibid.*, p. 1001.
[3] *Ibid* , p. 1008.
[4] *Ibid.*
[5] *Ibid.*
[6] *Ibid.*

of being-in is the essential presupposition for all relationships of *Dasein* to his world. On the basis of this ontology, it is impossible to conceive of scientific knowledge as *Dasein*'s active construction of a world of objective forms independent of his own being and its structure. Rather, scientific objectifying is now understood as *Dasein*'s act of letting the entities of the world in and with which he always already finds himself "stand free." This is thus the meaning which Heidegger gives to "objectifying" when used in the context of his own fundamental ontology of *in-der-Welt-sein*: to objectify is to free the entities, which we have somehow already encountered within the world, so that they may throw themselves against a pure discovering.[1]

Heidegger gives clearest expression to his own concept of objectifying in the context of his analysis of the existentialist roots of science. His central concept here is "thematizing." [2] Thematizing includes the articulation of an understanding of being, the limitation of an area of subject matter, and the sketching-out of the method of thought appropriate to such a subject matter. The aim of thematizing is to let the worldly entities, with which *Dasein* always already is, become objects.

> Thematizing objectifies. (*Die Thematisierung objektiviert.*) It does not first posit (*setzt*) the entities, but frees them so that one can interrogate them and determine their character objectively (*sondern gibt es so frei, dass es "objektiv" befragbar und bestimmbar wird*).[3]

That which is disclosed in such thematizing or objectifying is not *Dasein*'s fallenness into his world, but rather *Dasein*'s transcendence in relation to the entities of his world. "Transcendence does not consist in objectifying, but is presupposed by it." [4] Transcendence is for Heidegger a technical concept which has nothing to do with a religious or metaphysical notion of "*Jenseits.*" Transcendence is an immanental term which designates *Dasein*'s transcendence of his own being toward the world in which he is.[5] It is this transcendence which is made manifest, though not constituted, in objectifying.

As a result of the fundamental ontological-epistemological gulf

---

[1] Heidegger, *Sein und Zeit*, p. 363; tr., p. 414.
[2] *Ibid.*
[3] *Ibid.*, p. 363; tr., p. 414.
[4] *Ibid.*, p. 363; tr., p. 415.
[5] On Heidegger's concept of transcendence, see Ott, *Denken und Sein*, pp. 57 ff.; Barthel, *Interprétation du language mythique . . .*, pp. 71 ff.

which divides the thought of Bultmann and Heidegger, it is no accident that the anthropological meaning of objectifying should be conceived of so differently in each. For Bultmann, objectifying thought is explicitly understood to be grounded in inauthentic existence; for Heidegger, the objectifying of science "has its source in authentic existence." [1] While Heidegger only notes this point in *Sein und Zeit*, and does not develop it, it is quite clearly a point that is consistent with his total ontological revolution.

It is thus obvious that Bultmann's anthropological use of objectifying as a false form of self-understanding may not be derived from, or made consistent with, Heidegger's understanding of the meaning of objectifying. While Heidegger can use objectifying in this anthropological sense, he does so only in the particular context which identifies this usage as not expressive of his own position. It is also clear that Heidegger rejects the traditional Neo-Kantian epistemology and ontology which comes to expression in the concept of objectifying. In his own understanding of the being of *Dasein* as *in-der-Welt-sein*, Heidegger attempts to provide the ontological foundation for a new interpretation of the nature of objectifying knowledge. Since *Dasein* always already is in and with the entities of his world, prior to any subject-object schema of knowledge, objectifying comes to express, not *Dasein's* construction out of a chaos of formless experience a world of objective forms in a distinct mode of being alien to his own, nor *Dasein's* false interpretation of his own existence as a mere thing, but rather the project of letting stand free for a particular purpose and in a particular way the entities with which he already is. For this reason, science as thematizing or objectifying is grounded in authentic existence. In this understanding of the nature of science or objectifying, one sees most clearly the fundamental difference between Bultmann's limited anthropological revision of Neo-Kantian thought and Heidegger's ontological revolution.

Were it not for the widespread confusion concerning Bultmann's dependence upon Heidegger, it should not have been necessary to make this brief examination of Heidegger's use of objectifying.[2]

---

[1] Heidegger, *Sein und Zeit*, p. 363; tr., p. 415.

[2] The obvious disparity between Bultmann and Heidegger in the interpretation of the being and knowledge of the world does not obliterate the equally obvious continuity between them at many points in the interpretation of man. For an analysis of the nature and specific forms of continuity

For one needs scratch very lightly the surface of this anthropological use of objectifying to let the Lutheran-Neo-Kantian theology
of Wilhelm Herrmann stand forth. The presupposition for this use of
objectifying is a theological anthropology which takes as its point
of departure the human problem of insecurity. It takes only one
further step to note that the authentic and inauthentic resolutions
to the problem of existence are identified with justification by faith
and justification by works, respectively.

I can summarize this particular form of Lutheran theology
characteristic of Bultmann and Herrmann as follows. Objectifying
thought is grounded in an inauthentic mode of self-understanding
because objectifying thought is simply the expression at a conceptual level of that fundamental orientation of man to his reality
which comes to expression at an existential level in work. In work
man attempts to win his security by his own powers and through
his disposal of the visible, tangible, familiar work-world. Work, as an
existential expression of existence, is thus understood to be continuous with the false understanding of existence designated by the
theological phrase, justification by works. In contrast, existentialist
thought is grounded in an authentic mode of self-understanding
because existentialist thought is an expression at a conceptual level
of that fundamental orientation of man to his reality which comes
to expression at an existential level in personal relations: i.e., friendship, love, and trust. In the inter-personal, man does not attempt to
secure his being but receives, only in trust and as a gift, the fulfillment of his own being in the moment of encounter. The understanding of existence appropriate to such a mode of being is anal-
agous with the theological meaning of justification by faith.

In this anthropologized version of theology, there are two points
of connection to be noted: 1) the connection between objectifying
thought and work or existentialist thought and personal relations;
2) the connection between the act of work and the meaning of justification by works or the event of personal encounter and the meaning of justification by faith.

The link between objectifying thought and work was established
before Bultmann in the thought of Herrmann. I have already noted
Bultmann's appropriation of this motif in his later discussion of

---

between Bultmann and Heidegger, made in the light of Ott's critique, see
Helmut Franz, "Das Denken Heideggers und das Theologie," *ZThK* (1961),
pp. 81 ff.

Weltbild.[1] In his essay on miracles written in 1933, Bultmann develops this same theme. He here insists that the concept of law or lawfulness is not to be understood as subjective nor as an historically limited phenomenon of modernity.[2] Rather, the idea of law is "given with our *Dasein* in the world," "belongs to *Dasein* himself, a wholly primitive idea which is radically executed and conceived in science." [3] Objectifying thought in accordance with law, which is the basic form of Neo-Kantian epistemology, is thus to be understood as the systematic explication of that far more primitive and fundamental orientation of man to his world that is expressed in the idea of work (*Arbeitsgedanken*).[4] Bultmann here acknowledges Herrmann as the one who first brought together this understanding of science with this understanding of work, and quotes him as follows:

> The simple decision to work includes in itself the notion that the thing, on which we will work, belongs in its origin and effects to a structure of law which can be mastered by our thought.[5]

Having established the link between objectifying thought and work, it is but one step further to link the idea of work with the meaning of justification by works. The following passage from Bultmann is so basic to understanding his total project of demythologizing, as well as the specific anthropologized theological form of objectifying, that I will quote it at length.

> However this is just the root of the sin of the world: to understand self and God out of accomplishment and work (*Leistung und Werk*). Therefore, insofar as one asks about God, the miracle is an object of desire; wonder, however, which lacks the character of an accomplishment proving itself, is an offense (*Anstoss*). We saw: the primitive idea of miracle corresponds to the understanding of our world as the work-world, in which we presume the regularity and lawfulness of events. The miracle is an offense (*Verstoss*) against the laws of the world; however, it is still firmly conceived within the sphere of meaning of this world since it is an accomplishment of God provable within the world. The idea of wonder, however,

---

[1] Above, Chapter IV, pp. 159-160.
[2] Rudolf Bultmann, "Zur Frage des Wunders," *GV*, I, 215.
[3] *Ibid.*
[4] *Ibid.* Bultmann's discussion of "objektivierend" and/or *Weltbild* as timeless and universal modes of being in the world must be understood in light of this connection between "objektivierend" and "the idea of work."
[5] W. Herrmann, *Offenbarung und Wunder* (1908), pp. 36 f. as quoted by Bultmann, "Zur Frage . . .," p. 215.

> radically transcends the character of the disposable work-world.
> ... However, the wonder directs to man the critical question: how
> far does he understand the world rightly when he understands it
> as the work-world disposable to him; how far does he understand
> himself rightly when he understands himself out of his work and
> will secure himself through his work. The idea of wonder transcends
> the character of the work-world radically because it transcends the
> understanding of man as securing his own self through his work.[1]

The objectifying mode of thought, expressed in the primitive idea
of miracle, corresponds with an understanding of the world as a
work-world. The work-world in turn, expresses that understanding
of man as justifying himself, securing himself, through his own
works. Ergo: objectifying thought is an expression, at a conceptual
level, of inauthentic existence or sin.

It is this pattern of connections which is crucial to the theological argument for demythologizing which Bultmann offers in his
1952 defense of that proposal. He here notes that while demythologizing first developed out of the conflict between the mythological
and scientific world views, it was now clear that demythologizing
was to be understood as a demand intrinsic to faith itself.[2] As long
as faith expressed itself in an objectifying form of thought, as long
as it conceived of God and his activity in the terms of the world
known in work and science, it had not yet found a conceptuality
appropriate to its own essence.[3] Faith, therefore, needed to find a
conceptuality that was expressive, not of the existential mode of
work and the understanding of existence as secured through works,
but of the existential mode of encounter and the understanding of
existence as justified through faith.

It is the intention of demythologizing, in offering its radical
critique of the mythological *Weltbild* of the Bible, to call faith to a
radical reflection upon its own essence.[4]

> Radical demythologizing is the parallel to the Pauline-Lutheran
> doctrine of justification without works of the law through faith
> alone. Or rather, it is the consistent execution of this doctrine for
> the sphere of knowledge. The doctrine of justification destroys every
> false security and every false demand for security by men, whether

---

[1] *Ibid.*, p. 222.
[2] Rudolf Bultmann, "Zum Problem der Entmythologisierung," *KuM*, II,
207.
[3] *Ibid.*
[4] *Ibid.*

he tries to ground this security in his good works or in his well substantiated knowledge. .... Security can be found only by letting go of security, only by being ready—in the words of Luther—to enter into the innermost darkness.[1]

Demythologizing, in the sense of the elimination of an objectifying conceptuality and the interpretation of faith in an existentialist conceptuality, is thus to be understood as a systematic extension, in the sphere of knowledge, of the doctrine of justification by faith. In the elimination of an objectifying conceptuality, there is also eliminated any notion of the provability of God, and thus also any orientation of man to God which would express only his own efforts to secure his own existence.

Thus, there are three distinct (if not distinguished) steps in Bultmann's theological argument against an objectifying conceptuality:

1) Objectifying in accordance with the principle of law is a mode of thought that comes to its logical and historical fulfillment in science;
2) However, the objectification of a world and the notion of law may not be confined to science, but must be understood as expressive of that fundamental and primitive orientation of man to his reality that comes to expression in work;
3) Since the intention of work is the establishment of a knowing-controlling relationship of man to his environment, the idea of work corresponds to the understanding of existence as justified or secured through works.

The debt of Bultmann to the Neo-Kantian Lutheranism of Herrmann at each of these points is considerable. Herrmann established the fundamental connection between an epistemology of objectification in accordance with law and the idea of work; Herrmann also bound together the idea of work with the theological meaning of justification by works. On the other side, Herrmann established the meaning of justification by faith through the paradigm of the interpersonal relationships of friendship, love, and trust. What Bultmann found in Heidegger, then, was a conceptuality appropriate to the personal mode of relation in encounter and therefore appropriate to a theology committed to the explication of the meaning of justification by faith. Bultmann thus brought to its conceptual completion the fundamental understanding of faith and theology first formulated in Herrmann's Neo-Kantian Lutheranism.

---

[1] *Ibid.*

I have described this anthropological use of objectifying as Lutheran because its meaning is determined in accordance with that particular religious either-or that finds expression in justification by faith or justification by works, an option which is regarded as decisive for the authenticity or salvation of man. It should be obvious, however, that Bultmann's anthropology is different from that particular understanding of man which came to expression in Luther's formulation of justification by faith. (I am not concerned with the question of the relationship between Luther and Paul on this point.[1]) Bultmann develops his theology in response to his own world and in the categories appropriate to the late nineteenth-century interpretation of culture. His thought must be understood within the social-existential as well as philosophical context of his own history. The Reformation theme of justification by faith may be used for the interpretation of Bultmann's theology only if understood in a limited, analogous, and indirect manner. Since Reformation theology has not always been used within these limits in the interpretation of Bultmann's thought, it will be well to note briefly the fundamental difference between Bultmann and Luther in their use of justification by faith.

For Luther, the crucial existential question was this: how may I find a gracious God? The anthropological locus for this theological question was the problem of conscience: man's knowledge of himself according to the accusing voice of the law, man's anxious and guilty understanding of his own existence before the wrath of God.[2] The sociological locus for the question was the medieval system of penance, of which the famous indulgence was only one manifestation. In this context, the problem of human security—if it could be called that—was the problem of the secure conscience, the good conscience, the new conscience freed from the tyranny of the law by the hearing of the Gospel in faith. To be justified by faith meant to be made secure in one's standing before God, in one's conscience, by the belieful hearing of the preached Word. To be justified by works was to attempt to win a right conscience by the deeds of the

---

[1] For a discussion of the relation between Luther and Paul on law, see Gerhard Ebeling, "Reflexions on the Doctrine of the Law," *Word and Faith*, especially pp. 253-270.

[2] For a discussion of Luther's theological interpretation of man as conscience, see Gerhard Ebeling, "Theological Reflexions on Conscience," *Word and Faith*; also, "The Necessity of the Doctrine of the Two Kingdoms," *ibid.*

law, by the "works of satisfaction" prescribed by the Church. The *Angst* of which Luther speaks is not the *Angst* of man before death, but the *Angst* of the tormented conscience. Faith is always faith in the Word of forgiveness, the Word which, when received in faith, frees the believer from both the system of ecclesiastical penance and the interior anguish of the annihilating conscience. Faith frees man for the insecurity of his guilty existence by justifying him before God.

In Bultmann, the total discussion has shifted grounds: the social-existential situation is no longer that of the sixteenth century, but that of the early twentieth century. The crucial question is this: how may I find that existence which is really my own? The anthropological locus for this question is not the conscience, but the ego: that rational, world-adapting, autonomous center of the personality. In the excess of the bourgeois spirit, the ego has become detached from the total self-structure of which it is a part. Self-alienation thus comes to be the distinctive phenomenon of early modernity as the correlate of the overdeveloped rational, autonomous ego. The sociological locus for this human problem lies in the institutions of technology and the rationalization of primary social modes of existence. From a theological perspective, it appears as if bourgeois, technological man had lost his own existence and become part of "*das Man*" because he had tried to win his security on a false basis. He was so desperate to secure his existence through the expansion of the powers of his rational ego and his scientific technology that he had finally lost touch with that deeper self which is his own true identity and real source of life. The focus of proclamation, in this situation, falls upon the proclamation of a God who calls man out of his false self-understanding, who calls man out of his efforts to win his security through the powers of ego in control of the world, who calls man back to a self which is insecure but real, his own—not alienated—not objectified—self, who calls man back from the spent quest for security to the promise of ever new fulfillment of his self—not his ego—in encounter. To be justified by works now means to attempt to win security by the deeds of the ego, by the works prescribed by the rational work-world. To be anxious is to be anxious in the face of death, or in the finitude which acknowledges the limits of the ego's powers: in the confrontation with the world, not as familiar, visible, tangible and controllable but the world as enigmatic, mysterious, threatening. Faith is now faith in the deed of God in Jesus Christ which constitutes the actual historical freeing of the believer from his old false self-understanding and which opens up to him the possibility of authentic existence as a real self open to his own future. Faith thus frees man from both the worldly quest for security and the anxiety of insecurity. Faith frees man for the insecurity of his threatened and death-oriented existence by justifying him before God.

The distinction between these two theological anthropologies, and the corresponding meaning of justification by faith, is clear enough. The problem of guilt at the point of conscience is not the same as the problem of self-alienation at the point of ego. The insecurity of conscience, threatened by law and judgment, is not the same as the insecurity of existence, threatened by an enigmatic world and death. Faith as trust in forgiveness, in spite of the accusations of conscience, is not the same as trust in the Word of God, in spite of the rational, ordered, godless world structure. The existential reality of which Luther speaks is theological and ethical in its center: it is man as conscience, bound to his neighbor in responsibility by God's law and freed for his neighbor in love by God's forgiveness. The decisive question of faith is therefore the right understanding of this self-God-neighbor triad in accordance with the law-Gospel distinction. The existential reality of which Bultmann speaks is self-relational in its center: it is man as *Sorge,* responsible for his own being and unable to dispose of his own future. As his discussion of Pauline anthropology makes clear, it is this primary phenomenon of self-relatedness that constitutes the fundamental structure of human existence, and it is in light of this fundamental phenomenon that the meaning of good and evil, together with the meaning of a relationship to God, must be determined.[1] The decisive question of faith is

---

[1] After summarizing his discussion of *soma* as self-relatedness and *psyche, pneuma, zoe, nous,* and *kardia* as future fulfillment, Bultmann writes: "This brings in the possibility that man can be good or bad; for just because he must first find his life (that which is "good"—meaning the existence that at heart he wants), this existence comes to have for him the character of the "good"—in the sense of that which is required of him" (Bultmann, *Theology of the New Testament,* I, 227). Later he supplements this as follows: "Paul constantly sees man as placed before God. The ontological possibility of being good or evil is simultaneously the ontic possibility of having a relationship to God; and God, for Paul, is not the mythological designation for an ontological state of affairs but the personal God, man's Creator who demands obedience of him. The ontological possibility of being good or evil is ontically the choice of either acknowledging the Creator and obeying Him, or refusing Him obedience" (*ibid.,* p. 228).

the right understanding of this self-relatedness: i.e., the sinful self-sufficiency of one who presumes to have his life at his own disposal, or the laying hold of one's true existence as a gift from God.[1] For Bultmann, justification by faith means literally a new form of self-understanding: that is, a new understanding of self-relatedness; as his discussion with Gogarten shows, it is ontologically this, however much it might also be interpreted theologically to include a new understanding of the neighbor.[2] For Luther, justification by faith means a new understanding of that existential reality of neighbor-God relationship which is my own. Justification brings a new freedom from the neighbor, and all his worldly institutions, since the right standing of man is now dependent upon his standing in and with Christ before God through faith. Justification also brings a new freedom for the neighbor, and all his worldly institutions, since man is freed through grace from the destructive self-concern of the guilty conscience to meet the neighbor's needs in love and thus to obey the law.

In proposing these distinctions, I am not judging Bultmann's fidelity to his Lutheran heritage. Hopefully, the days of this activity are over. The word of Bultmann has proven its own power in the Church of the modern era as the word of Luther did in the medieval epoch. Even more, there is the obvious analogue between Luther's use of the law, as the decisively overcome but still retained form of understanding of old conscience, and Bultmann's use of nineteenth-century reason, as the decisively overcome but still retained form of understanding of inauthentic existence. However, just as it is fruitless to judge Bultmann's theology by the norm of Luther, so it is simply an historical error and theologically confusing to interpret Bultmann's theology as an expression of the theology of Luther.[3] The effort to bypass the distinct Neo-Kantian form

---

[1] *Ibid.*, p. 232; p. 239.

[2] Rudolf Bultmann, "The Historicity of Man and Faith," *Existence and Faith*, pp. 102 ff.

[3] Gerhard Gloege's study of Bultmann, *Mythologie und Luthertum: Recht und Grenze der Entmythologisierung* (3rd ed., Göttingen: Vandenhoeck & Ruprecht, 1963) ignores both the philosophical and socio-existential contexts of Bultmann's thought. As a result, Gloege interprets demythologizing in terms of its conceptual continuity with Luther's theology and evaluates its adequacy in terms of Luther's Law-Gospel dialectic. Such an approach to the question of Bultmann's Lutheran origins only further confuses the genuine complexities of his thought. Because of the wide influence of Gloege's work, I have consistently stressed the fact that Bultmann's Lutheranism is partic-

of Lutheran theology, which provides the authentic historical matrix
for that thought which is Bultmann's, by a direct appeal to the
Reformation can only be construed as an expression of the illegitimate wish to baptize a highly novel theological formulation by
reference to an earlier mode of thought.

The quest for the origins of the theological-anthropological
meaning of objectifying has thus led, not to Heidegger's existentialist philosophy, but to Wilhelm Herrmann's Neo-Kantian
Lutheranism. After 1925, 'objectifying' designates for Bultmann,
not only an epistemological category, but also a false form of self-
understanding or sin. However, during the years 1925-1933, Bultmann does not use 'objectifying' in its anthropological meaning for
myth interpretation. As the following two sections will indicate,
'objectifying' becomes a decisive category for the interpretation of
mythology only after Hans Jonas adds a hermeneutical dimension
to this concept.

2. BULTMANN'S EARLY (1927-1933) EXISTENTIALIST DISCUSSION OF MYTH

In this section, I will examine the preliminary and partial existentialist discussion of myth which appears in Bultmann's writings
during the years 1927-1933. The task is relatively brief since the discussion of myth is not central to Bultmann's writings during these
years. He is primarily concerned to appropriate the existentialist
conceptuality in his work as a systematic and exegetical theologian.
As a result, he continues to use myth predominantly in the old *Religionsgeschichtliche* sense of the term. At the same time, however, he
does attempt to bring together his new anthropology with his older
Religionsgeschichtliche understanding of myth. However, he does not
yet have available to him the technical hermeneutical concept of
objectifying. Indeed, he does not use the concept of objectifying in
conjunction with his interpretation of myth during these years. My
concern, therefore, is to examine the way in which Bultmann relates
his new understanding of anthropology with his old understanding
of mythology prior to his appropriation of objectifying as a hermeneutical concept.

---

ularized by Neo-Kantian conceptuality, on the one hand, and the existential
crisis of the modern bourgeois work ethos and the alienated ego, on the other
hand.

One of the earliest efforts in this direction appeared in Bultmann's 1927 discussion of the Gospel of John. In this essay, he quite clearly understands myth to express a particular understanding of existence and transcendence.

> One would, however, falsely understand the Gospel if one regarded its use of myth as purely historical, accidental, a causally determined fact. In truth, the myth expresses how man understands himself in his being in the world. ... In myth there comes to expression the insight that man stands lost in the world, as a stranger, who cannot find his way, who cannot secure his being. The myth speaks of God as being "beyond" man, even when it speaks of God in a human manner. The Gospel of John can make use of myth, for myth knows the idea of revelation. Hence, the evangelist can say what he has to say of revelation in the form of myth.[1]

The continuity between this description of myth and his later writings is clear. Myth is here identified with the expression of a particular understanding of existence—man standing as a stranger in the world before the transcendent God—that understanding of existence which is so familiar from Bultmann's later essays. Yet, while noting this continuity, it is also clear that myth has not yet become a hermeneutical concept designating a particular problem of interpretation. Indeed, there would appear from this citation to be no distinctive problem of interpretation in myth. Even when myth speaks of God *"Menschliches,"* it speaks of God *"Jenseits."* Bultmann's later demythologized, analogical speech of God hopes to achieve no more than is already achieved in myth itself! There is thus present in this discussion of myth, which moves fundamentally within a *Religionsgeschichtliche* perspective, the new existentialist vocabulary and anthropology of insecurity, but there is totally absent from it the hermeneutical formulation of myth as an alien, objectifying form of expression which must first be demythologized and interpreted in an existentialist conceptuality in order to express what it intends.

The other writings of this period which discuss myth also disclose the striking absence of the hermeneutical concept of objectifying. However, the pattern of discussion is characteristically quite different from this 1927 citation. Most often, Bultmann does not identify myth with this theological anthropology. Quite the contrary. The new understanding of existence is seen to be the distinctive

---

[1] Bultmann, "Das Johannesevangelium . . .," *ChrW* (1927), col. 510.

essence of the early Christian Church as a particular historical movement. As a result, mythology is related to this new understanding by way of juxtaposition: i.e., the Christian understanding is stipulated as it comes into being over against the older mythological traditions. Or, mythology is related to the Christian understanding of faith as a confusing remnant from the past in conflict with the central intention of the text. Or again, mythology is related to the new understanding of faith as a vehicle of expression adapted by the New Testament author to serve the purposes of faith. In this latter case, however, Bultmann makes it clear that in the New Testament usage, the original mythological meaning of a given mythological motif has been stripped away so that it has become simply a notion or an image for the expression of the self-understanding of faith.

For an example of this pattern of relating the new understanding of faith with the old mythological ideas on antiquity, I refer to Bultmann's 1930 essay on Paul. The theme of juxtaposition is set forth early in the essay:

> However much his [Paul's] thought still moved within the mythological ideas of antiquity, still, on the one hand, he extricated Christian thinking from the realm of mythology and speculation and made it into an unfolding of the understanding of man, the world, and God that is given in faith itself.[1]

Paul thus freed the Christian faith from the realm of mythology, as well as from the realm of Judaism, by giving a "firm conceptual expression" to its faith.[2] While the "mythological ideas of antiquity" are still present in the thought of Paul, insofar as he is a child of his age, their role is fundamentally irrelevant and peripheral to "the firm conceptual expression" of "the self-understanding of the Christian community."[3]

> The extent to which Paul has at the same time formulated his thought in terms of mythological ideas is unimportant, if one sees what the understanding of existence is that is hereby expressed.[4]

In contrast with the earlier discussion of John, it is not mythology which is associated with a particular understanding of existence, but

---

[1] Rudolf Bultmann, "Paulus," *RGG*[1] (1930), 1019-1045; trans. Schubert Ogden, *Existence and Faith*, pp. 111-146. Page citations are to Ogden's translation: p. 120.
[2] *Ibid.*
[3] *Ibid.*
[4] *Ibid.*, p. 131.

rather the New Testament author who develops his new understanding of existence, in spite of and over against, the mythological
atmosphere in which his own thought develops. Thus, at times, the
old mythological traditions come to confuse the new understanding
of existence.

> In order to illustrate this fact of sin's sovereignty, Paul makes use
> of the myth of the primal man and interprets it in terms of the
> contrast between Adam and Christ. And from the crossing of his
> own ideas with the notions of the myth there arise confusions that
> cannot be considered here.[1]

More often, however, Paul uses these "mythological notions . . .
simply in order to express a certain understanding of existence." [2]
He thus does not use mythological notions in a mythological manner (i.e., for the purpose of speculation or explanation), but rather in
a manner consistent with the self-understanding of faith.

Bultmann makes this same point in his 1933 discussion of New
Testament Christology. Here also there is the fundamental juxtaposition of "traditional cosmological and anthropological categories" and "the thinking through of one's own new existence." [3]
Paul uses the former but is to be understood in terms of the latter.
Thus, Bousset was incorrect in failing to recognize the central
meaning of justification by faith in Paul's thought. The new understanding of existence which comes to expression here is not to be
interpreted by the mythological-cultic language of Paul, but rather
his appropriation of the language of the cult is to be seen as expressive of his new self-understanding.

> In the doctrine of justification it is made clear that Christology does
> not consist in speculation about "natures," but in the proclamation
> of the Christ event and that the appropriate mode of understanding
> of this event is not speculative but self-reflective, a thinking through
> of one's own existence.[4]

As an 'example, Bultmann shows the ways in which the old
mythological notions of *sarx* and *pneuma* have been divested by
Paul of their original mythological meaning and become expressive
of the "Christian understanding of being." [5]

---

[1] *Ibid.*, p. 134.
[2] *Ibid.*, p. 130.
[3] Rudolf Bultmann, "Die Christologie des Neuen Testaments," *GV*, I,
262.
[4] *Ibid.*
[5] *Ibid.*, pp. 262-263.

In all of these passages, mythology is identified with a pre-Christian mode of speculation which provides the intellectual atmosphere for the New Testament writers, which is occasionally present in the text as a confusing and self-contradictory element, but which, more often, is baptized by the Christian understanding of being or existence and made a vehicle for its expression. What is true for Paul is also true for Jesus.

> If men are standing in the crisis of decision, and if precisely this crisis is the essential characteristic of their humanity, then every hour is the last hour, and we can understand that for Jesus, the whole contemporary mythology is pressed into the service of this conception of human existence.[1]

From the perspective of Bultmann's later hermeneutical formulation of myth, one would have to judge these early attempts to relate anthropology and mythology as partial and inconsistent. Sometimes the new anthropology and mythology appear to coincide, as in the 1927 John citation, where mythology is identified as the form of expression appropriate to the manifestation of revelation and the understanding of existence as a stranger to the world. More often, the two are presented in a relationship of juxtaposition, contradiction, and conversion. Mythology is thus the historical antecedent of the new Christian understanding of being, which provides the background over against which the Christian understanding of being is set forth, which occasionally intrudes itself into a New Testament text as a diversion and contradiction of its real meaning, and which may be transmuted to become the vehicle for the expression of this faith.

In all these instances, it is clear that myth is still understood primarily from the historically-oriented perspective of the *Religionsgeschichtliche Schule*. The relationship between mythology and the new understanding of existence is rooted essentially in the historical dynamics of the birth of the early Christian Church in the midst of a mythologically oriented culture. Similarly, the new understanding of being or existence is specified as a phenomenon distinctive to the early Christian faith. After 1934, the hermeneutical concept of objectifying systematically connects together the new anthropology and the old mythology in the orderly dialectical movement of being in history. It is mythology that is now identified as

---

[1] Bultmann, *Jesus and the Word*, p. 52.

intending the new and particular understanding of existence while concealing this intention in its objectifying form. The enigma of mythology is henceforth to be resolved, not in the untidy transitions of history, but in the methodical unfolding of being which, in coming to expression, necessarily comes to expression in an alien mode.

3. 'OBJECTIVATION' AS A HERMENEUTICAL CONCEPT: M. HEIDEGGER, H. JONAS, AND BULTMANN

In order to apprehend the origins of "objectifying" as a technical hermeneutical concept, in contrast with the epistemological and anthropological forms of this concept, I turn now to a consideration of the early writings of Hans Jonas. For it is Jonas who first formulates the technical hermeneutical concept of "objectifying" and it is from the thought of Jonas that Bultmann borrows this concept and appropriates it into his own thought.

In this consideration of Jonas, attention shall be focused exclusively upon the meaning of this hermeneutical concept. I am not concerned with the actual results of Jonas' interpretation of Gnosticism and Augustine, but solely with his development of the methodological concept of "objectivation." [1] In explicating this concept I will pursue a method of inquiry consistent with earlier discussions of Bultmann's formulation of myth. The texts which enter into this exegesis and analysis are the followings:

1) "Über die hermeneutische Struktur des Dogmas," printed as an appendix in *Augustin und das paulinische Freiheitsproblem* ..., pp. 65-76.
2) "Zur Problem der Objektivation und ihres Formwandels," which appears as the introduction to *Gnosis und spätantiker Geist*, II, 1, pp. 1-23.[2]
3) "Zur Geschichte und Methodologie der Forschung," which appears as the introduction to *Gnosis und spätantiker Geist*, I, 1-91.

---

[1] I have chosen, through the course of this exposition, to simply transliterate Jonas' term, "*Objektivation*." "Being objective" or "the condition or mode of being objective" might serve as English equivalents, but do not lend themselves to a consistent usage within the limits of grammar. A discussion of the significance of the term "*Objektivation*" in contrast with Bultmann's "*Objektivierung*" appears later in this section.

[2] As previously noted, the methodological introduction to this volume, published in 1954, was originally published under the title *Der Begriff der Gnosis* (above, p. 176). While citations are from this 1954 edition, I have compared the 1954 text with the original edition published in 1930. While there are interesting changes which distinguish these two texts from each

In examining these texts, I will specify the meaning of objectivation by means of the following questions:

1) What is the relationship of Jonas to Bultmann and Heidegger
   at the point of his concept of objectivation? In what sense is he
   continuous with his academic mentors, in what sense does his
   understanding of this concept develop in a distinct and new
   direction?
2) What are the philosophical presuppositions for Jonas' use of
   objectivation? What presuppositions concerning the nature of
   being and history are implicit in that use of the concept distinctive to his thought?
3) What are the hermeneutical implications of Jonas' concept of
   objectivation? How is the context and subject matter of the text
   specified? How is the relation of language and meaning understood? How is the relation of the interpreter to the text apprehended? How is the task and/or problem of interpretation
   specified?

By locating the particularity of Jonas' thought in relation to
Heidegger and Bultmann and by recovering for the concept of
objectivation its original and distinctive philosophical presuppositions, I intend to disclose the hermeneutical significance of objectivation in that specific historical and conceptual nexus in which it
was first formulated.

In the beginning of his second volume on Gnosis, Jonas sets
himself the task of "clarifying what the fundamental hermeneutical
concept of objectivation means." [1] In order to do this, he develops,
at least initially, an ontology of *Dasein* which suggests his basic
continuity with Heidegger. He thus begins with the question: why
does *Dasein* mirror himself, his own proper being, upon the world,
in the mode of a worldly being?[2] However, while beginning here,
Jonas will not accept this formulation of the question as adequate
to the hermeneutical problem, since the question itself presupposes
the old subject-object schema: *Dasein* as autonomous subject using
a neutralized world which stands over against him as a foil for the
projection of his own being. Jonas finds the inadequacy of this formulation of the question exposed in the fact that the opposite

---

other, none affect my use of this 1954 text in the development of this argument. Therefore, I have used this 1954 text as an authentic expression of the
thought of Jonas available to Bultmann in the early thirties.

[1] Jonas, *Gnosis* . . ., II, 4.
[2] *Ibid.*, pp. 4-5.

question might just as well be asked: namely, why is the world anthropologized? why is the object interpreted subjectively?[1] For in myth there occurs both the objectifying of the subjective and the subjectifying of the objective. Jonas thus concludes:

> Perhaps there is disclosed in this doublesidedness the fact that we are here dealing with an original phenomenon, whose poles are not to be hypostasized over against each other.[2]

This "original phenomenon," of course, is that which Heidegger expresses in his fundamental existentialist category: *"in-der-Welt-sein."* Jonas expresses this as follows:

> The relation of *Dasein-Welt* ... is an *"existenziales"*: that is, a condition of being of *Dasein* himself as a whole. We do not use world here ontically, as the sum total of entities (therefore in the worldly sense), but ontologically, as the horizon of transcendence of *Dasein* (therefore in the existentialist sense, or to speak with Heidegger, as *Existenzial*).[3]

The ontological root for the objectivation of the being of *Dasein* in the mode of the being of the world, as this phenomenon appears in myth, would thus appear to be Heidegger's ontology of being, in which *Dasein* and world are always given only in and with each other. Myth, as objectivation, would then simply be one instance of such a primordial confusion: "the undifferentiated in-one-another of subject and object, I and thing."[4]

An examination of Heidegger's analysis of myth discloses, at several points, Jonas' continuity with Heidegger's ontology. In his 1927 review of Cassirer's volume on mythical thinking, Heidegger sketches in a preliminary manner and over against Cassirer, an interpretation of myth which would depart from a fundamental ontology of *Dasein*. Heidegger selects two phenomena expressive of mythical *Dasein* as decisive for the interpretation of myth: *mana* and wish. In the phenomenon of *mana*, Heidegger finds disclosed the "basic mode of being of mythical life ... its particular understanding of being."[5] This is that mode of *Dasein*'s being which Heidegger calls: *Geworfenheit.*

---

[1] *Ibid.,* p. 5.
[2] *Ibid.*
[3] *Ibid.,* pp. 6-7.
[4] *Ibid.,* p. 7.
[5] Heidegger, Review of Cassirer, *Die Philosophie ... II, DLZ* (1928), p. 1009.

> In his being thrown there is a fundamental being bound up with
> the world which is of such an order that his own being in the world
> is overpowered by that with which he is bound up.[1]

In this thrownness, *Dasein* becomes "confused," identifying the
power of his own being with the being of the world, and thus
transmuting his own substance into one reality with the world.[2]
The phenomenon of *mana* thus expresses both the fact of his being
thrown and the confused interpretation of his own being under the
power of the being of the world.

While *mana* discloses *Dasein*'s confused interpretation of his own
being as worldly being, the wish discloses *Dasein*'s false understanding of worldly being as his own being. Here also, however, there is
a fundamental ontological phenomenon which finds expression:
namely, the world as the transcendent horizon of *Dasein*.[1] The
ontological significance of the mythical wish is thus parallel with
the ontological meaning of objectifying thinking; in both instances
there is made manifest, but not constituted, the transcendence of
Dasein to his world (*enthüllt aber nie erst hergestellt wird*).[4] What is
thus manifest in myth, for Heidegger, is the fundamental ontological structure of *Dasein* in the particular form of understanding of
myth-making *Dasein*.

The continuity between Jonas and Heidegger, in their account of
the ontological roots of myth, is clear from a comparison of these
two passages. However, it should also be clear, from the previous
analysis of Heidegger's use of objectification, that Jonas, in selecting
the category of objectivation as central to the structure of myth,
has moved in a direction quite different from that of Heidegger. It is
axiomatic for Heidegger that objectification, as a particular form of
world or self-interpretation, is an historically limited phenomenon
which may not be imputed to mythical *Dasein*. The wish is the
expression of mythical *Dasein* which corresponds to the objectifying
thinking of science, but it is obviously not the same as this. Heidegger develops most extensively his understanding of the historical
limits of objectification in *Die Zeit des Weltbilds*. However, he has
also made this point quite clearly in the *Sein und Zeit* discussion of
the significance of sign for primitive *Dasein*.

---

[1] *Ibid.*
[2] *Ibid.*
[3] *Ibid.*
[4] *Ibid.*, p. 1010.

One might be tempted to cite the abundant use of "signs" in primitive *Dasein*, as in fetishism and magic, to illustrate the remarkable role which they play in everyday concern when it comes to our understanding of the world. Certainly the establishment of signs which underlies this way of using them is not performed with any theoretical aim or in the course of theoretical speculation. This way of using them always remains completely with a Being-in-the-world which is immediate. But on closer inspection it becomes plain that to interpret fetishism and magic by taking our clue from the idea of signs in general is not enough to enable us to grasp the kind of "Being-ready-to-hand" which belongs to entities encountered within the primitive world. With regard to the sign-phenomenon, the following interpretation may be given: for primitive man the sign coincides with that which is indicated. Not only can the sign represent this in the sense of serving as a substitute for what it indicates, but it can do so in such a way that the sign itself always is what it indicates. This remarkable coinciding does not mean, however, that the sign-thing has already undergone a certain "Objectification"—that it has been experienced as a mere Thing and misplaced into the same realm of Being of the present-at-hand as what it indicates. (*Dieses merkwürdiges Zusammenfallen des Zeichens mit dem Gezeigten liegt aber nicht daran, dass das Zeichending schon eine Gewisse "Objektivierung" erfahren hat, als pure Ding erfahren und mit dem Gezeigten in dieselbe Seinsregion des Vorhandenen versetzt wird.*) This "coinciding" is not an identification of things which have hitherto been isolated from each other: it consists rather in the fact that the sign has not as yet become free from that of which it is a sign. Such a use of signs is still absorbed completely in Being-towards what is indicated, so that a sign as such cannot detach itself at all. This coinciding is based not on a prior objectification but on the fact that such objectification is completely lacking. ... Perhaps even readiness-to-hand and equipment have nothing to contribute as ontological clues in interpreting the primitive world; and certainly the ontology of thinghood does even less.[1]

From this discussion of primitive signs, together with his discussion of myth in the Cassirer review, one may conclude that Heidegger would not interpret myth under the rubric of objectification. To be sure, there is a primordial confusion of *Dasein* with his world manifest in myth; however, this confusion is rooted in the absence of any objectification, and may not be construed as an instance of objectification. Therefore, it is not possible to use the ontology of thinghood, the understanding of being as *Vorhandensein*, and the category of objectifying in the interpretation of myth.

---

[1] Heidegger, *Sein und Zeit*, pp. 81-82; tr., pp. 112-113.

While Jonas' use of objectifying and related categories discloses his discontinuity with Heidegger, it discloses simultaneously his continuity with Bultmann. For objectivation means for Jonas at least that false form of self-understanding, in which *Dasein* apprehends his being in the mode of objectified worldly being, which is characteristic of Bultmann's anthropological use of the term. Jonas thus speaks of *Dasein* as objectifying himself (*Sich-Objektivieren*) in the apprehension of his being as *Vorhandensein*, as innerworldly *Seiendem, etwas Gegenständlichem*, a thingified, hypostasized, externalized being.

> *Dasein* thus comes up against himself only *"von aussen"* and as *"ein Äusseres"*: that is, in the mode of world-entities. Thus *Dasein* has no longer to deal with the original real relation to himself, although this remains in the background, but now deals with this in its derived, objectified mode.[1]

> The thematic I-world relation, which is constituted in the transcendence of *Dasein*, is objectified as a worldly being at hand, that is, worldlized (*in ein welthaft vorhandenes objektiviert, d.h., verweltlicht*).[2]

> This is what is ontologically specific and decisive for this type of self-objectification: the hypostasizing of strictly existentialist phenomena into quasi-thing-like and perceptible realities, making these existentialist phenomena analogous with worldly entities.[3]

In each of these examples, it is evident that Jonas is consistent with Bultmann in his basic categories and anthropological perspective. Objectivation, the false interpretation of *Dasein* as thing, *vorhandenes*, worldly *Seiendem, von aussen*, etc., is for Jonas, as for Bultmann, not an historically limited phenomenon—which is not yet a possibility for mythical *Dasein*—but an eternal possibility to which mythical and modern *Dasein* both fall victim. In Bultmann's case, a theologically informed anthropology allowed him to convert objectification into a timeless possibility for *Dasein*'s false form of self-understanding. Since one may not expect Jonas to share Bultmann's passion for the distinction between justification by faith and justification by works, the question arises as to the grounds for his movement beyond Heidegger in the extrapolation of the category of objectivation into the realm of myth.

---

[1] Jonas, *Gnosis*. . ., II, 9.
[2] *Ibid.*, p. 12.
[3] Jonas, *Augustin* . . ., p. 69.

In raising this question, I turn away from the task of comparing Jonas with Heidegger and Bultmann and turn toward the explication of the meaning of objectivation within the context of Jonas' own proposal. It is clearly necessary to give an account of Jonas' use of objectivation which is established independently of both Heidegger and Bultmann. To establish the distinctive meaning of objectivation within Jonas' thought, I begin by noting the terminological revision which divides Jonas from Bultmann and Heidegger.

For Bultmann, the verbal root of *"objektivieren"* provided the linguistic foundation for the derived adjective (*objektivierend*) and noun (*Objektivierung*). This semantic peculiarity reflected the Kantian, and especially the Neo-Kantian, epistemological revolution: the object given for thought became the objectified construct of thought. Heidegger was consistent with Bultmann in characteristically using the verbal root in its various forms, both in respect to the older epistemological meaning and also in relation to his own epistemological account of "thematizing."

In Jonas, however, the verbal root of *"objektivieren,"* while occasionally employed, has ceased to provide the linguistic foundation for the substance of the discussion. This has become, instead, the adjective, *"objektiv"* which in the form of the noun, *"Objektivation"* has come to specify the hermeneutical problem and/or central hermeneutical category. This change of terminology suggests, in a preliminary manner, the fundamentally different perspective and philosophical context that is decisive for Jonas' use of the concept. For in considering the meaning of objectivation in Jonas we have quite clearly stepped outside of the epistemologically formed problems which were of central concern to Bultmann and Heidegger. Objectivation, or the mode of being objective, is not rooted for Jonas in a particular understanding of the nature of reason and its knowing activity, but rather is rooted in a particular understanding of the condition of being. It is a concept that is thoroughly and consistently ontological, not epistemological, in its origins. It is therefore a far more comprehensive concept than is the case with objectification in either Bultmann or Heidegger.

For Bultmann, objectification is a concept limited to the subject-object structure of knowledge and the existential attitude appropriate to such a detached, seeing from the outside, rational, reflective perspective. Objectifying is thus used primarily to modify

Vorstellung or *Begrifflichkeit* but also *Verhaltung* and *Blick*. In all these uses it is clearly differentiated from the existential stance appropriate to personal encounter and the existentialist conceptuality appropriate to personal existence. Thus, in the sphere of speech, "I love you" could never be an objectifying mode of self-expression for Bultmann, but serves consistently, from the 1920's through the 1950's, as the paradigm for non-objectifying speech. On the basis of this fundamental epistemological-existentialist distinction between objectifying and non-objectifying modes of expression of *Dasein*, it is possible for Bultmann to allow for a non-mythological, non-objectifying use of mythological, objective, notions, images, or symbols. In such a case, a mythological form of expression has been taken out of its original objectifying perspective and intention and become simply the means of expressing the Christian understanding of man and/or God.[1] At both the level of direct speech, and also in conjunction with his understanding of mythological notions, it is clear that Bultmann's use of objectifying consistently reflects in its limits its epistemological origins.[2]

For Jonas, however, objectivation is not limited to a particular epistemological perspective, conceptuality, or corresponding existential attitude. For example, in his discussion of dogma, Jonas can

---

[1] When Bultmann describes Paul or John as "demythologizing," it is consistently this understanding of deobjectifying which he has in mind. Paul and John do not demythologize, in the sense that they do away with the antique *Weltbild*, nor do they demythologize in the sense that they eliminate the soteriological cultic salvation narrative, but they do demythologize in stripping away from the mythological notions they use the false claim to represent a thing-like object and/or to explain. This is what Bultmann means when he describes John as "giving up [*preisgegeben*]" the "original mythological meaning [*Sinn*]" of a given expression while continuing to use it as a mythological *Bild* or *Vorstellung* for his own theological purposes: *Das Evangelium des Johannes* (Göttingen: Vandenhoeck & Ruprecht, 1950), pp. 189-191; also *ibid.*, p. 104, p. 270, p. 285, p. 330, p. 379, p. 448. Or, for similar examples: *Theology of the New Testament*, II, pp. 9-10, pp. 12-13, p. 17.

[2] Because of its epistemological origins, Bultmann's use of objectifying in relation to an existentialist conceptuality is necessarily ambiguous. On the one hand, an existentialist conceptuality is given with existence itself, and is the antithesis of the objectifying conceptuality given with man's dealing with the world in work; on the other hand, an existentialist conceptuality is also a construct of reason differing qualitatively from the immediate encounters of personal existence. In his early writings, Bultmann emphasized almost exclusively the former usage; in the latter writings, especially in response to Heinrich Ott's theology of primal thinking, he has laid greater stress on the latter.

describe the "hypostasizing of strictly existential phenomena" as
that which is "ontologically specific and decisive for this type of
self-objectification." [1] This fundamental hypostasizing or symbolizing is not, however, to be understood as if it were equivalent with
a false use of reason or the intrusion of subject-object perspective.
Rather, rationalizing is to be understood as only one particular form
of symbolizing which accompanies such objectivation but is not at
their root:

> Along with such objectivation and transcendental hypostasizing
> comes necessarily the rationalizing: that is, the field of perceptions is
> abstracted into a body of concepts ... capable of free movement
> ... and incorporated into comprehensive theoretical constructions. [2]

In this same context, Jonas can speak of "symbolic representation
and rational fixation." Objectivation is not to be understood as a
product of reason in the tradition of Bultmann and Neo-Kantianism, but rather, the activity of reason is itself simply one instance
of objectivation as a comprehensive condition of being.

In a similar manner, Jonas also makes it clear that the meaning
of objectivation may not be identified with any particular mode of
Dasein's self-interpretation—an objectifying rather than a non-
objectifying form of self-understanding—or with any particular
existential attitude—a particular ontic "how" of *Dasein*'s being,
Dasein's "own existential self-apprehension." Indeed, objectivation
is not a category which falls essentially within the sphere of *Dasein*'s
self-interpretation at all. It is fundamentally ontological, not
anthropological. As Jonas writes, "Objectivation and the changing
levels of objectivation is the destiny of *Existenz*, not simply the
instrumental means of its interpretation, and therefore it is the
destiny of the '*Grund*' of *Existenz*." [3] Fundamentally, objectivation
is the necessary condition (*Bedingung*) for the "being able to be
real" (*Wirklichsein-könnens*) of *Existenz*. [4] Only on the basis of this
undifferentiated ontological category may one then proceed to raise
the question concerning the particular mode of *Dasein*'s existential
self-understanding in his objectivations.

To be sure, Jonas does not regard this purely ontological, not yet
anthropologically specified, form of the concept to be hermeneuti-

---

[1] Jonas, *Augustin* . . ., p. 69.
[2] *Ibid.*
[3] Jonas, *Gnosis* . . ., I, 88.
[4] *Ibid.*

cally adequate. Indeed, he insists explicitly that a complete hermeneutical concept move beyond the indifference of this ontological
concept to include the specification of the concrete mode of *Dasein*'s
being in his objectivation.

> However, the mere recognition of the fact that the same ground
> is present in the various forms of objectivation is not sufficient, but
> it must be concretely determined how *Dasein* enters into it [*Objekti-
> vation*], what happens in it to himself, with his own existential
> self-apprehension. Thus must the concept of objectivation, with
> which we are fundamentally concerned here, be defined out of its
> indifference and as a fully hermeneutical concept.[1]

Objectivation thus requires further existentialist specification of its
meaning, but this is not to be understood as the root of the concept.
For objectivation is constituted, not in *Dasein*'s self-interpretation,
but in the self-actualization of *Existenz*, or the *Grund* of *Existenz*, as
its necessary condition. Any particular existential self-apprehension,
like the activity of reason in its subject-object schema, occurs
within this more comprehensive ontological structure of objectivation.

There is, thus, a striking difference between Jonas' use of "*Objektivation*" and the use of "*Objektivierung*" in Bultmann or Heidegger.
It may be apparent that this fundamental conceptual change signals
a transition from the tradition of Kantian critical idealism to the
ontological idealism of Hegel. The theme with which Jonas is
fundamentally concerned is the objectivation of *Geist*: the fact that
Geist is realized in history only in a mode of being other than and
alien to its own mode of being; the fact that *Geist* is constituted in a
dynamic historical movement passing through various levels
(*Stufen*) and changing forms (*Formwandels*) of objectivation; the
fact that *Geist* comes to its fulfillment only through the dialectical
movement of thought which destroys the alien original objective
mode of being even while it recovers in a new level of conceptuality
that which was ontologically fundamental to the original objectivation. Objectivation is thus the ontological concept which designates
being in the mode of expression or manifestation of historical
actualization; it is distinct from being in itself or as itself.

It is because of this ontological use of the term that Jonas regards
any form of expression, any "symbolic representation," any

---

[1] *Ibid.*

"pressing of the phenomenon of *Dasein* into speech" as a mode of objectivation, without regard to epistemological and anthropological criteria.[1] To be sure, the problems of reason and existence enter into the determination of the nature and forms of objectivation. However, they quite obviously do not prescribe the root meaning for the concept. Therefore, if one would recover the meaning of objectivation in the early writings of Jonas, he may not turn to Bultmann or Heidegger, but must recover the presuppositions of the older, nineteenth-century ontological idealism which provides the philosophical context for Jonas' use of the term. In fulfilling this task, I will set forth the characteristic themes of this idealistic tradition, especially in its understanding of being and history, as they appear in the early writings of Jonas.

First, for this form of idealism, objectivation is a category of ontological necessity. It is not an epistemological or anthropological category; our concern now is with the necessity of objectivation. Being comes to historical reality only through the act of self-objectivation, of becoming something other than what it is in itself. In Jonas' vocabulary, he can speak of this necessity of self-objectivation in terms of *Dasein*, *Gesamtdasein*, *Existenz*, or *Geist*. His use of these concepts make it clear that there is a broad sense in which they are interchangeable concepts for him: what is true of *Dasein* in his historic totality is true of *Geist* or *Existenz*. Thus he can write:

> All of this corresponds to the fundamental structure of *Geist* as such: it interprets itself in objective forms and symbols. That it is thus symbolized is essential to *Geist* and dangerous at the same time.[2]

On the same page, in which he is still discussing the necessity of objectivation as grounded in the fundamental structure of being, he can speak not of the structure of *Geist*, but of the movement of *Dasein*.

> The movement of *Dasein* to self-objectification, which governs the entire self-apprehension and self-interpretation of *Dasein*, even to his immediate self-consciousness, is a necessary, not accidental or avoidable movement. It is precisely in this necessary movement of self-objectification that the primary existentialist ontological motive for dogma building is to be sought.[3]

---

[1] Jonas, *Augustin* . . ., p. 67.
[2] *Ibid.*, p. 68.
[3] *Ibid.*

In a passage cited earlier, Jonas speaks of objectivation as the *"Existenzschicksal,"* the *"Schicksal für den Grund selbst."* [1] By whatever term the subject of objectivation may be designated, it is clearly intended to designate the ontological movement of *Geist* which necessarily enters into a mode of being other than its own in becoming actualized.

As a second theme, the movement of objectivation is not only ontologically necessary, but also an ontological threat. In the mode of objectivation, there is a fundamental transposition (*Übereignung*) of the being of *Dasein* into a mode of being other than its own.[2] Objectivation is thus synonymous with "a transposition of the deepest structure of our being into another mode of being." [3] While this transmutation or transposition into a "non-*Dasein*-ontology of interpretation" is to be understood in a positive way— for only in this manner does *Dasein* become present and real for himself—it nevertheless remains a transposition which, insofar as it is a worldlizing (*Verweltlichung*), is also a mode of alienation, of *Dasein*'s falling under the rule of a power foreign to himself (*Überfremdung*).[4] It is because this objectivation is fraught with the peril of the loss of *Dasein*'s own being in a mode of being alien to himself that the objectivation of *Geist* is both essential and dangerous:

> In order to come to itself, it [*Geist*] necessarily takes this detour by way of the symbol, in whose enticing confusion of problems it tends to lose itself, by making the substitution of the symbol for its own being absolute, thus moving far from the original source of the symbol.[5]

However, while self-objectivation is ontologically necessary, self-alienation is only the perilous possibility given with the ontological structure. *Dasein* may also win back his own being through a critical reflection upon his earlier objectivations, even as he may lose his being. In theological language one may say that for Jonas, objectivation is not synonymous with the fall of being in sin, but provides the essential condition for it. Detour, alienation, constriction, losing the way, misunderstanding oneself: Jonas uses all of these terms to express the potential distortion of being present in objectivation.

---

[1] Jonas, *Gnosis* . . ., I, 88.
[2] Jonas, *Gnosis* . . ., II, 9.
[3] Jonas, *Augustin* . . ., p. 67.
[4] Jonas, *Gnosis* . . ., II, 9.
[5] Jonas, *Augustin* . . ., p. 68.

Third, the objectivation of being is not to be conceived of as a static product but as a dynamic process. For historical reality is the sphere of objectivation of being, so that history is constituted through the movement of *Geist* or *Dasein* in its changing forms of objectivations. The concept of change is thus fundamental to the category of objectivation. When Jonas writes his methodological introduction to Volume II, he does not speak simply of the problem of objectivation, but rather: "Zum Problem der Objektivation und ihres Formwandels." Furthermore, the changing forms of objectivations are not to be understood as an arbitrary phenomenon, but rather as following out in their own pattern of connection an inner form of movement or structure of development.[1] The pattern of movement in the objectivations of *Geist* in history is a development away from the most alien pole of objectivation and back toward an ever closer approximation to the being of *Dasein* or *Geist* itself. It is thus a law of movement from the outer to the inner, from the worldly thing to the inner person.

In the case of the late Hellenistic world, Jonas describes "the inner form of movement of the Gnostic principle of being" as follows:

> In the power of its own dynamic contents, the structure realizes itself as a form of movement: the thing in myth, the hypostasization of being in metaphysics, and the forms of the soul in mystical ethics.[2]

Through these changing forms, however, there is no fundamental change in the structure of objectivation itself. While the philosophy of Origin and Plotinus "demythicize" (*Entmythisiert*) Gnosticism, in that they cast the Gnostic myth in a "depersonalized, logical form," they nevertheless are still "mythical" in their hypostasizing of being.[3] In a similar manner, the external mythical objectivations are converted into concepts interior to *Dasein* and his ethical practice—they are "resubjectivized"—but "the mythical element is not really overcome."[4] For the fundamental conception of *Dasein* remains, even in these changed forms, mythical. While the forms of objectivation change in a determinate pattern within the late

---

[1] Jonas, *Gnosis* . . ., I, 258.
[2] *Ibid.*
[3] Jonas, *Gnosis* . . ., II, 3.
[4] *Ibid.*, p. 4.

Hellenistic world, the objectivation of myth remains decisive for the total movement of thought, including the philosophical forms.

However, while the historical movement of *Geist*, which began in the thingified form of myth, did not reach its fulfillment within the limits of the late Hellenistic world, there is a real sense in which the *Geist* of Hellenistic myth has come to a kind of fulfillment in the existentialist thought of the modern world. It has taken the "long detour from the dogma of original sin to Kierkegaard" to overcome the alien original form of objectivation and recover the original existential phenomenon in a form of conceptuality appropriate to it.[1] To Jonas, however, it seems clear that we now stand "on the other side of the creative traversing of that detour and so, from our later perspective, may approach . . . the original phenomenon in a conceptually direct form."[2] This hermeneutical possibility, of a conceptually direct recovery of the original existential phenomenon given initially in the objectivation of dogma, is a possibility that is ours because of the particular moment in the history of *Geist* in which we stand. I quote here, in its full form, the theme of the way of *Geist*, which has appeared in partial forms earlier in our discussion.

> All of this corresponds to the fundamental structure of *Geist* itself: it interprets itself in objective forms and symbols. That it is thus symbolized is essential to *Geist* and dangerous at the same time. In order to come to itself, it necessarily takes this detour by way of the symbol, in whose enticing confusion of problems it tends to lose itself, by making the substitution of the symbol for its own being absolute, thus moving far from the original source of the symbol. Only in a later critical reformulation, after a creative traversing of that detour, may a demythologized consciousness also approach, now in a conceptually direct manner, the original phenomenon concealed in this disguise.[3]

The objectivation which is ontologically necessary to the realization of *Dasein* in history is also necessary to be overcome. The necessity of any original objectivation is of a temporal and not an eternal order. In these early writings, Jonas wrote, as did many of the early Heideggerians, as a man living in the eschatological fulfillment of the *Geist*, with the radical new possibility of bringing

---

[1] Jonas, *Augustin* . . ., p. 68.
[2] *Ibid.*
[3] *Ibid.* For the sake of the historical record, it should be noted that this is the first use of the term, *"Entmythologisiert."*

to direct conceptual expression the original existential phenomena of the Hellenistic age. In his later writings, Jonas speaks more cautiously of the possibilities of existentialist interpretation, speaking now of "degrees of objectification," "a more or less adequate style of conceptuality," and hoping only to win "a closer proximity to the substance from which it had originated." [1] However, in his early writings, it does seem possible to cut through the alien, distorting forms of an earlier age and to re-present the original existential phenomena freed from the necessity of such a disguise in the new existentialist conceptuality.

At this stage of the argument, I turn my attention from objectivation as an ontological concept toward the explication of the meaning of objectivation as a hermeneutical concept. In making this transition, I do not lose sight of the philosophical presuppositions of the concept, but rather attempt to set forth the thought of Jonas as he brings to expression the problem of interpretation from his perspective of ontological idealism. I will proceed by raising several hermeneutical questions concerning the nature of the text, and the situation of the interpreter in relation to the text.

First, Jonas defines the problem of interpretation in accordance with a dialectical apprehension of the text. The text presents both the basal phenomenon and its objectivation. In this sense, the nature of the text corresponds with the nature of all historical reality: it is both the actualization of *Geist, Gesamtdasein,* or *Existenz* and the actualization of it in a form other than its own. This fundamental distinction between the original phenomenon and the objective form of expression may not be understood as a temporal distinction. It is not as if the intended meaning was present in some moment and in some form other than that of objectivation, "so that we might distinguish a primary phase in which the phenomena were immediately palpable in their pure form." [2] The original existential intention is constituted precisely and only in the original objective form of expression. This is the hermeneutical significance of the ontological category of necessity. It is for this reason that the interpreter may not simply dismiss the myths and dogmas of the past as examples of uncritical reason or "metaphysical excesses,"

---

[1] Hans Jonas, "Heidegger and Theology," *The Review of Metaphysics,* XLIII (1964), 231.

[2] Jonas, *Augustin . . .,* p. 66.

in the manner of the Kantians.[1] For such an approach to the text fails to understand that the particular existential phenomena involved are present precisely in and through the objectified forms given in these texts. The category of necessity, when combined with the category of objectivation, thus gives to myth a new status in the history of humanity, in that its strange, alien, and objective form now is understood to be firmly grounded in the historical self-manifestation of *Geist*.

Jonas describes the dialectical structure of the text in a variety of formulations. He speaks of "the fundamental phenomena" in antithesis with "the concepts and forms necessary for the argument." [2] Or, he contrasts "the fundamental phenomena" with "their expression in fixed rational structures." [3] Or, he distinguishes between "the existential phenomena fundamental to religious experience" and "the theoretical structure into which they were transposed and symbolized." [4] In each of these cases, the clear doublesided nature of the text is set forth. On the one hand, there is an existential phenomenon rooted in human experience; on the other hand, there is a theoretical structure rooted in the objective symbolizing and rationalizing form of expression. If it is true that the meaning of *Dasein*'s existence is constituted only in and through language, it is also true that that meaning remains always essentially other than, and separable from, the language in which it was constituted.

Finally, the dialectical relationship of basal phenomenon and its objectivation is one essentially of negation. While the objectivation is decisive for the first coming to be of the original meaning intended by the text, it is not decisive, except in a negative way, for the continuing manifestation of the original phenomenon. The original objectivation does not show, manifest or give the original meaning of the text; rather, it "conceals, confuses, and distorts the real subject matter in its logical form of interpretation." [5] The original phenomenon is not so much present in its objectivation as it is "concealed behind," or "lying at the root of it." [6] For this reason, it is necessary for the interpreter to enjoy a mode of access to the

---

[1] *Ibid.*, p. 67.
[2] *Ibid.*, p. 6.
[3] *Ibid.*
[4] *Ibid.*, p. 7.
[5] *Ibid.*, p. 6.
[6] *Ibid.*

concealed meaning of the text other than that given in the text itself: i.e., his own existential situation as it is understood to be continuous with the original existential phenomena of the text. The objectivation or form of expression thus comes to constitute, in the act of interpretation, the block to be overcome rather than the bridge between the interpreter and the fundamental meaning of the text.

One way to come to recognize this fundamental dialectical structure of the text is the way of rational criticism. While Jonas insists upon the limits of any purely logical, critical approach to the text, he does acknowledge that reason can discern the logical antinomies of dogma. However, these contradictions of reason which appear in dogma are not to be taken seriously as problems to be resolved by reason, but rather as symptoms of the fundamental confusion in the text between "the fundamental phenomena and its logical form of expression."[1]

> In the form of a thorough-going rational system of thought, there then arises the problem of compatibility and contradiction which, at the level of this undialectical objectivity, is necessarily unsolvable. This impasse, then, is only the clue that the original phenomenon of *Dasein* needs to be set free from this mixture of symbolic representations and rational rigidity and discovered independently from the formulation of the original phenomenon.[2]

In this way, Jonas, like Bultmann, can speak of the role of critical reason as pointing toward the real hermeneutical problem, by disclosing the contradictions and confusion in the text.

> Here, where we are concerned with the hermeneutical problem of dogma (and that is a methodological perspective), we insist upon this point: the objective rational structure of dogma in general, and the logical structure of compatibility in particular, point from the outset toward the ontological confusion of the subject matter. In a similar manner the fact that the logical antinomies thus discovered are essentially indissoluble points towards a genuine dialectic in the original fundamental existential primary level, which comes to an inappropriate expression in the rational conceptuality with its antinomies.[3]

The disclosure by critical reason of the logical antinomies of the text thus points, not only toward the ontological confusion of the

---

[1] *Ibid.*
[2] *Ibid.*, p. 69.
[3] *Ibid.*, p. 70.

text, but also to "a genuine dialectic in the original fundamental primary existential level."

However, critical reason points toward the fundamental dialectical structure of the text; in itself, critical reason is not able to apprehend this dialectic in its full significance. For in order to apprehend both sides of the dialectic, the interpreter must himself enter the scene of interpretation. Critical reason may expose the confused theoretical structure, but it may not apprehend the original existential phenomenon which is the other half of the dialectic. For it is only through his own existential lived history that the interpreter has access to the fundamental phenomena of the text. As Jonas writes:

> The presupposition for this entire hermeneutical enterprise is this: that the phenomena themselves, which are here under discussion and which were disputed in a rationalistic form of interpretation, are—insofar as they are fundamental phenomena of existence—also available to us and in such a manner that it is allowable for us to determine what was once said in them.[1]

It is this availability of the fundamental phenomena in our own existence which is a presupposition for the whole dialectical hermeneutical venture which Jonas proposes.

In elucidating this understanding of the relation of the interpreter to the text, as at every other point in Jonas' hermeneutic, it is necessary to recall the ontological presuppositions which make the hermeneutic a coherent whole. In this case, Jonas may presuppose a continuity between the original existential phenomena of the texts of Augustine and his own existence because of their mutual participation in a common history of *Geist*. Jonas obviously does not presuppose some objectified view of man, whose nature as a fixed essence might guarantee the continuity of his own existence with that of Augustine's. Nor is Jonas, as a philosopher, speaking from a theological perspective which apprehends man's standing before God as the point of existential continuity between past and present and which understands this continuity to be concretely mediated through the common life of a particular tradition-bearing historical community. Rather, the continuity of which Jonas speaks is more ontological than the latter and more historical than the former. It is the continuity of *Geist* or *Dasein* in his historic totality.

---

[1] *Ibid.*, p. 6.

Jonas makes this relationship between text and interpreter clear at several points in his discussion of dogma. In the case of Augustine and the doctrine of original sin, he finds that the fundamental existential phenomena are those originally formed around the problem of freedom, a series of phenomena that are intrinsically religious, practical and not ideational phenomena, and fully capable of being realized in the real existence of *Dasein*.[1] These phenomena, bound up with the problem of freedom, are not to be understood as general or universal human phenomena, but are inseparably bound up with a history which moves from Paul through the long detour of Augustine to Kierkegaard.[2] Indeed, it is only because the fundamental existential possibilities were first realized in Paul and Augustine that they have become "*Seinkönnen* for a whole epoch of history."[3] While these fundamental phenomena must thus be detached from their original dogmatic form, it would be an obvious error to detach them from the history of *Geist* in which they are constituted and make of them timeless possibilities. It is only because Jonas is himself a participant in the history of *Geist* that the existential phenomena present in the Augustine text are also available to him, together with, of course, the new conceptuality for their more adequate presentation. Because of this common, *geistlich* connection, it is possible for Jonas to "verify what is understood out of what is available to us in our own existence."[4] This "verification," this "determination of what was once said," is a possibility in interpretation not because of a psychological identification with Augustine, nor because of a participation in a fixed human nature or condition, nor because Jonas shares with Augustine a particular determination of existence mediated through a concrete historical community, but rather because of a participation in the history of *Gesamtdasein* common to both author and interpreter.

While the interpreter thus enjoys a relationship of existential continuity with the text, mediated through a common history of *Geist*, he also occupies, for this same reason, a position of superiority in relation to the author of the text. For the interpreter stands in a later, more fully developed moment of *Geist* than did the original author. In the case of Jonas, he stands "on the other side of the

---

[1] *Ibid.*, pp. 6-7.
[2] *Ibid.*, p. 67.
[3] *Ibid.*, p. 70.
[4] *Ibid.*, p. 6.

15

creative traversing of ... that long detour from the dogma of original sin to Kierkegaard." [1] There are thus available to him conceptual possibilities of expression which arise out of the history of *Geist* in a given epoch but which were unknown to the first crude, thingified form of expression of the new self-understanding. Because of this spiral-like movement of *Geist*, the interpreter ought to be able to say better what the author meant than the author himself could.

While the understanding of history as the history of *Geist* is the presupposition for the interpretation of the relation of the interpreter to the text, it is also the presupposition for the specification of the context of the text. It might initially appear as if a study of the doctrine of original sin would fall within the context of the history of dogma, the history of the church and its self-understanding, or even more specifically, the history of the Augustine-Pelagius polemic. This, however, is not the case.

> When we turn our attention to this controversy of the distant past, this does not mean that we ourselves will participate in it as a polemical partner, arguing on its level. We will not take sides with one side or the other, nor will we introduce a third position. These dogmatic elements, although they were of enormous importance to the consciousness of the conflicting parties and although they occupied the larger part of the literary expression of the controversy, we shall exclude from our discussion.[2]

Jonas thus does not intend to consider the meaning of Augustine's doctrine of original sin in the context of the history of dogma nor does he find the ecclesiastical issue of heresy to provide a significant point of departure for the interpretation of the texts.

While thus excluding an ecclesiastical-historical perspective of interpretation, Jonas also rejects any context of interpretation of a biographical order.[3] He is not concerned in understanding the text as an expression of the particular history of Augustine. Nor again, does he find the cultural *Zeitgeist* to provide the appropriate context of interpretation.[4] Jonas rejects the history of the Church, the life history of Augustine, and the history of the Hellenistic world at a particular moment of crisis as inappropriate contexts of interpre-

---

[1] *Ibid.*, p. 69.
[2] *Ibid.*, p. 7.
[3] *Ibid.*, p. 70.
[4] *Ibid.*

tation, for all fail to catch sight of the real subject of inquiry. This is not the *Heilige Geist* of the Church, the *geistlich Leben* of Augustine, or the *Zeitgeist* of the fourth century, but rather, plain old *Geist*, *Dasein* in his historic totality.

> The task of hermeneutics is concerned with the real author, namely, the *geschichtliche Gesamtdasein* who, reaching out beyond the individual and the generation, produces this interpretation of itself which is most intrinsic to itself. . . . Philosophical hermeneutics has only been directed towards this *geistesgeschichtliche Subjekt* as such.[1]

The significant question to direct to the text is to understand its meaning as an expression of the real subject of history which, in transcending both individual men and their communities, appears through both as its point of manifestation. It is this history of *Geist* which provides the context for the interpretation of the text, even as it provides the basis for the relation of the interpreter to the text.

Jonas makes this same point in his study of Gnosticism and the postulation of the unifying Gnostic principle must be understood in light of this particular understanding of the nature of history. He here differentiates his own methodology from a traditional objective historical mode of inquiry which concerns itself with history as "finished products." [2] He is concerned with these, the texts and concrete data of history, only as they point towards the productive source lying at their root (*ein dem zugrunde liegendes Produzierendes*).[3]

> Now this we understand not as some kind of empirical subject (individual or collective, ethnological, etc.)—which are themselves points of intersection of countless causal sequences—but as the fundamental principle of *Dasein* in its primitive stratum of imaginative apperception of being. Out of itself and in an historical act this brings to maturity the overarching constitution of the world and of the relation of *Dasein* to that world for a whole epoch. This original constitution is the *a priori* horizon for the understanding of self and world binding for a given epoch and the empirical subjects in it. Within its limits all kinds of explicit attempts at interpretation, differentiation, and change— which also include the worldly causalities as empirical realities—must be executed. We

---

[1] *Ibid.*
[2] Jonas, *Gnosis* . . ., I, pp. 12-13.
[3] *Ibid.*

understand this productive source as a transcendent constitutive which, however, is rooted in a factual historical apprehension of *Dasein*. In terms of this, the comprehensive meaning of the world, expressed in the crudest myths or most sublime philosophical forms, is determined for a given sphere of history, which acquires its essential unity out of this ground. ...[1]

Whether this original principle of being steps into time as an original birth, unfolds itself and after the creation of its possibilities, fades away, as Spengler suggests, Jonas will not say. But he does insist upon postulating such a principle of being as the ground of a temporally bound together complex of phenomena.

Seen in this particular context, the mythological and dogmatic texts of the late Hellenistic world suddenly acquire an historical meaning and status which the earlier rational critical approaches to these texts had missed. For the texts of the late Hellenistic age, seen from the perspective of the history of *Geist*, come to constitute a turning of the age, the beginning of a whole new epoch. In these texts, *Dasein* breaks through to a fundamental new understanding of his existence which stands in sharp contrast with the previous forms of self-understanding, both Hellenic and Hebrew. This is the new understanding of existence which Jonas describes under the rubric of *Entweltlichung*, the fundamental unified principle of Gnosticism. The syncretistic image, the concern with Gnosticism in terms of its past Iranian origins, the emphasis upon the cultic context: these themes of the earlier *Religionsgeschichtliche* interpretation of Gnosticism were obviously inadequate to apprehend the real meaning of Gnosticism as a decisive event in the history of *Dasein*'s self-interpretation. The fact that the objectivation was most crude in Gnostic myths, in the form of the thing, suggests also that the interpreter is here concerned with the first fruits of the *Geist* at a moment of fundamental historic transition.

In light of the dialectical nature of the text, the relation of the interpreter to the text, and the context of the text, the task of interpretation acquires a very specific double-sidedness: 1) to overcome or destroy the originally necessary but always alien and now surpassed form of objectivation through which *Dasein* first broke through to this new self-understanding; 2) to recover the original existential phenomenon concealed behind the objective form of expression but mediated through one's own existence in a

---

[1] *Ibid.*

common history of *Dasein* in the new existentialist conceptuality available now and appropriate to the original phenomenon. Stated more concisely the hermeneutical task may be described as follows: to demythologize—that is, to strip away the misleading disguise of an objective conceptuality which conceals even as it first expressed the new self-understanding; to develop an existentialist interpretation—that is, to allow the original existential phenomenon to find expression in a conceptuality appropriate to it.

This hermeneutical program must finally be understood, then, in terms of the familiar dialectical movement of thesis, antithesis, and synthesis. There is the original existential phenomenon; this comes to expression only through the objectivation essential to its actualization and essentially alien to its own intention; finally, there is the new formulation which occurs in the act of interpretation itself, which both destroys the original objectivation in which the original phenomenon was first constituted and grasps anew this original phenomenon in an appropriate form of expression. In this total hermeneutical program, demythologizing occurs as the essential negative moment in which the alien original objectivation is destroyed or overcome. In the dialectical movement of *Geist* there is no *Aufhebung* of the original phenomenon which does not also entail the destruction of the original form. Indeed, for Jonas there is a direct movement of thought from the rational criticism of dogmatic texts, which disclose the logical antinomies, to the dialectical critique of these texts, which destroys the false ontology at the root of the logical antinomies even as it apprehends the original phenomenon in a new formulation.

> This [the recognition of the logical antinomies] can provide a valuable methodological direction for a positive development of the problem of freedom, pointing to the execution of a retrogressive destruction of the mythologically conceived witness of the old church dogmatics and to the reformulation of the problem of freedom in a genuine phenomenological sphere.[1]
>
> The *terminus* of the "destructive" (analytical) retrogression effected upon the images of objectivation becomes immediately in relation to them a "constructive" (synthetic) principle for their understanding and ordering in a new apprehension. It comes to this discovery . . . only in this always functioning reflexive movement. Only in the destructive-constructive unity of both moments of

---

[1] Jonas, *Augustin . . .*, p. 71.

execution of the process of knowledge does the meaning of such a philosophical interpretation of history fulfill itself.[1]

The dialectical nature of the text requires a dialectical hermeneutic. For this reason there can be no existentialist interpretation without demythologizing, even as demythologizing itself exists only as the essential moment of destruction in the context of a more comprehensive existentialist hermeneutic.

Had it not been for the political situation in Germany after 1934, there is no doubt that Jonas' contribution to the hermeneutical discussion should have been recognized much earlier. Because he was a Jewish emigré, Jonas' work was not given significant attention during the later thirties and early forties when the existentialist myth hermeneutic was disseminated and appropriated by a variety of thinkers. The one exception was Bultmann, who both dared and cared to continue to refer to Jonas' writings during this period of time. Bultmann consistently acknowledged his own debt to Jonas, both for his understanding of Gnosticism and for his myth hermeneutic, and in his programmatic essay of 1941 cited the work of Jonas as a paradigm for his own project of demythologizing.[2] Beyond the writings of Bultmann, however, the work of Jonas fell out of sight, and one can look in vain for references to his contribution in the literature relevant to the period or subject.[3] This historical oversight is unfortunate, not only because it leaves

---

[1] Jonas, *Gnosis* . . ., I, 17.

[2] Bultmann, *KuM* I, 26.

[3] H. Ott's discussion of "Entmythologisierung" in the third edition of *RGG* cites Jonas' Augustine text, as the first instance of the use of the term, but offers no hint as to the substantive contribution of Jonas to the formulation of this hermeneutical project (H. Ott, "Entmythologisierung," *RGG*[3], IV, col. 497). The following should be noted as exceptions to this general pattern:

a) Carsten Colpe's discussion of Jonas in relation to the interpretation of Gnosticism and the hermeneutical concept of myth: *Die religionsgeschichtliche Schule*, esp. pp. 183-193; pp. 199 ff.

b) Hermann Diem's discussion of Jonas' study of Augustine in connection with the problem of dogma and hermeneutics (Hermann Diem, *Dogmatics*, trans. Harold Knight (Edinburgh and London: Oliver and Boyd, 1959), pp. 25 ff.

c) James Robinson's discussion of Jonas' contribution to the existentialist hermeneutic in "Hermeneutic Since Barth," *The New Hermeneutic*, p. 23; pp. 34-37. (Robinson has also written an introduction to a new edition of *Augustin und das paulinische Freiheitsproblem*.)

d) A. D. Nock's review of *Gnosis und spätantiker Geist*, I, *Gnomon*, XII (1936), pp. 605-612.

clouded the historical origins of the existentialist hermeneutic, but also because it has made the substantive discussion of that hermeneutic so much more difficult. For the philosophical presuppositions of objectivation which are present in Jonas' writings tend to fall out of sight in Bultmann. They are still operative in Bultmann's thought, but not available for scrutiny. As a result, the neglect of Jonas' thought in the discussion of demythologizing has contributed significantly to the enigma of demythologizing, as identified in Chapter I.

CHAPTER SIX

DEMYTHOLOGIZING AS A SYNTHETIC CONSTRUCT

By this point in the argument, all of the individual elements constitutive for Bultmann's project of demythologizing have been
identified. Each has been described as it appeared in the course of
development of Bultmann's thought and in its original sources. We
are now in a position to discern how Bultmann wove together these
many disparate strands of modern intellectual history to create a
new synthesis which, in turn, served as a catalyst for the redirection
of twentieth-century theology.

It is probably clear by now that only one of the motifs examined
in this exposition becomes virtually irrelevant for Bultmann's
proposal of 1941. This, of course, is the *Religionsgeschichtliche* formulation of myth as articulated by Bultmann in his exegetical and
theological writings of the nineteen-twenties. To be sure, Bultmann
continues to allude to Reitzenstein's historical hypothesis concerning the origins of New Testament mythological motifs, but he
never explicitly defines, or implicitly presupposes, the substance of
the *Religionsgeschichtliche* view of myth: namely, myth as a soteriological narrative inseparably bound to its cultic context and its
form of cosmic drama. It would be interesting to speculate concerning the possible shape of Bultmann's theological venture if this
interpretation of myth had provided the point of departure for
Bultmann's thought. But it did not. For myth as an intrinsically
corporate and cosmic phenomenon simply could not be contained
within the limits of a Neo-Kantian philosophy. While Bultmann
attributes his 1941 definition of myth to the *Religionsgeschichtliche
Schule*, this is clearly an historical anachronism.[1] The definition of
myth articulated in 1941 never once appears in Bultmann's copious
writings on the subject as a participant in the *Religionsgeschichtliche*
discussion of the nineteen-twenties.

Excluding this early formulation of myth, we are left with four
distinctive motifs that come together as demythologizing: Neo-
Kantian philosophy, with its absolute separation between rational,
objectified forms of reality on the one hand, and the immediate

---

[1] *KaM*, I, p. 10.

religious experience of the individual subject, on the other hand;
Lutheran theology, with its absolute soteriological dichotomy
between man's effort to achieve personal security through his own
powers (justification by work) and man's trust in a God of love
revealed for the decision of faith in the proclamation of the Kerygma and the only reliable ground for personal confidence and fulfillment (justification by grace through faith); the Enlightenment
definition of mythology as a pre-scientific world view characteristic
of an early stage in the development of human reason; and the
idealist-existentialist hermeneutic which defined mythology as an
objectifying form of expression alien to its original intention and
located this form of thought at the beginning of a new historical
epoch in the history of *Geist*. Each of these four elements is a necessary ingredient for the project of demythologizing; eliminate any
one of them and the total *Gestalt* is destroyed. For this reason, I
have repeatedly insisted that demythologizing must be understood
as a synthetic construct in which the role of each distinctive element
and its relative importance must be acknowledged. One cannot
reduce demythologizing to any single motif, Heideggerean or Neo-
Kantian, in its origins.

Because each of these elements has already been analyzed in some
detail, this concluding chapter will focus primarily on the process by
which they were synthesized. Two questions will occupy our
attention in the following pages. First, I am concerned to evaluate
the relative weight of each of these four elements in relation to
each other. While all of them are necessary for demythologizing,
they are not all equally important. The fusion of Lutheran and
Neo-Kantian motifs is constitutive for the core of Bultmann's
total theology, while the Enlightenment and idealist-existentialist
themes serve primarily as instruments for articulating an interpretation of New Testament mythology congruent with this theological nucleus. To support this evaluation, I will develop a detailed
analysis of Bultmann's borrowings from Hans Jonas. In discovering
what Bultmann accepts and what he rejects from Jonas, the core
of his own theological position becomes apparent. Second, I also
wish to demonstrate the principle of cohesion in this theological
construct. Considered in themselves, Neo-Kantian philosophy,
Lutheran theology, Enlightenment historiography, and a modified
Hegelian hermeneutic appear to have little in common. Indeed, it is
difficult to imagine a less congenial mix of persuasions. To shed

some light on the process by which these disparate motifs were joined together, I will trace the fate of the word 'objectifying' in the development of Bultmann's theology. For it is this word more than anything else that provides the glue that holds the whole project together. I deliberately speak of the 'word' objectifying and not the concept; for within this single word are contained a variety of disparate meanings.

1. BULTMANN'S APPROPRIATION OF IDEALIST-EXISTENTIALIST MOTIFS FROM JONAS

Bultmann first offers a systematic formulation of his legacy from Jonas in his 1941 programmatic essay, "New Testament and Mythology." In that essay, Bultmann clearly acknowledges his debt to Jonas at two crucial points of his argument. In the first instance, he refers to Jonas' 1930 study of Augustine, especially the hermeneutical appendix, "Über die hermeneutische Struktur des Dogmas." [1] As already noted, in this appendix Jonas clearly differentiates between his own dialectical form of myth criticism and interpretation and the earlier non-dialectical criticism of myth, from either the Kantian tradition of philosophy or an objective historiography. It is therefore appropriate that Bultmann should refer to this publication by Jonas in conjunction with establishing his own distinction between myth interpretation and myth elimination. In contrast with the non-dialectical elimination of myth characteristic of older liberal theology, Bultmann proposes here his own form of myth criticism as myth interpretation.[2] It is just this possibility which Jonas has first established in his own dialectical understanding of myth.

Later in this same essay, at the decisive point of his proposal to work out an existentialist interpretation of the New Testament which "will tax the time and strength of a whole theological generation," Bultmann again refers to the previous work of Jonas. This time he cites the 1934 study of Gnosticism as a model for his own proposal of New Testament interpretation.

> The meaning of these two types of mythology [Jewish Apocalyptic and Gnosticism] lies once more not in their imagery with its apparent objectivity, but in the understanding of human existence which

---

[1] Bultmann, *KuM*, I, 24.
[2] *Ibid.*

both are trying to express. In other words they need to be interpreted existentially (*existential*). A good example of such treatment
is to be found in Hans Jonas' book on Gnosticism.
Our task is to produce an existentialist interpretation of the dualistic mythology of the New Testament along similar lines.[1]

Bultmann's debt to Jonas, however, appears far more strikingly
in the substance of his argument than even these citations could
suggest. Our task now is to examine the hermeneutical themes
central to the proposal of demythologizing which Bultmann shares
in common with Jonas: the double-sided nature of the text; the
intrinsic defect in the structure of myth as the form of expression
conceals or confuses existential intention; the necessity for this
alien and concealing form, as point of historical breakthrough of a
fundamental new self-understanding of *Dasein* and as it provides the
continuing hermeneutical point of departure for the apprehension
of this self-understanding; the necessity, also, to overcome this
original and preliminary form of expression; the relationship of
existential continuity and conceptual superiority between the
interpreter and his text; the dialectical structure of the act of
interpretation which recovers the original existential phenomenon
as it destroys the alien objectifying form of conceptuality and as it
gives expression to the original intention in a conceptuality appropriate to it; the determination of the context of the text in a
particular moment in the historical unfolding of the self-understanding of *Dasein*: namely, the point of transition between the
"old age" of the Hellenic and Hebraic worlds and the "new age"
of the modern West. These are the themes which have already been
set forth in our consideration of Jonas. When I take them up again
in a discussion of Bultmann's proposal to demythologize, I do so
simply to sketch in the continuity between Jonas and Bultmann at
these points of hermeneutical reflection.

Hermeneutics, as the reflection upon the problem of interpreting
and understanding texts of the past, constitutes both the subject
matter of this section and its limits. In the previous discussion of

---

[1] Bultmann, *KaM*, I, 16; *KuM*, I, 26. While Fuller's English translation,
in this case as in others, is something less than literal, I have used his text,
rather than attempting a new translation of the German original, because
Fuller expresses so clearly the intent of the German: namely, that Jonas'
existentialist interpretation of the dualistic mythology of Gnosticism provides
the model for Bultmann's existentialist interpretation of the dualistic
mythology of the New Testament.

Jonas, I observed that it was not possible to begin directly with an exposition of his hermeneutical themes, but found it necessary first of all to explicate the ontological and historical presuppositions which informed his thought. We discovered through this that Jonas' hermeneutical proposal was grounded in a modified idealistic ontology and philosophy of history. However, in the present consideration of Bultmann's appropriation of Jonas' hermeneutic, I need to state very clearly and at the outset of the inquiry that Bultmann never accepts either Jonas' ontology or philosophy of history. Bultmann comes into intellectual maturity as an anti-Hegelian critic of the historiographical tradition of F. C. Baur and the Tübingen School, and he does not renounce this basic orientation in his later encounter with Jonas. Indeed, when Bultmann is confronted directly and explicitly with the idealistic ontological motifs of Jonas' thought, he responds with sharp criticism. [1]

[1] A later exchange between Jonas and Bultmann on the subject of immortality suggests something of the real gulf between them. In his interpretation of immortality, Jonas develops the familiar theme of the identification of the infinite with the totality of the finite process of historical development. "In the beginning, for unknowable reasons, the ground of being, or the Divine, chose to give itself over to the chance and risk and endless variety of becoming. And wholly so: in order that the world might be and be for itself, God renounced his own being, divesting himself of his deity to receive it back from the Odyssey of time weighted with the chance harvest of unforseeable temporal experience . . . Whatever variety evolution brings forth . . . every new dimension of world response . . . means another modality for God's trying out . . . With the appearance of man, transcendence awakened to itself . . ." [HTR, L (1962), 15-16]. The significance of this for man is that his own existential acts must be understood as the bearer of this divine self-unfolding. "Not the agents which must pass, but their acts enter into the becoming Godhead and indelibly form his never decided image. God's own destiny, his doing and undoing, is at stake in this universe to whose unknowing dealings he committed his substance, and man has become the eminent repository of this supreme and ever betrayable trust. In a sense he holds the fate of deity in his hands" (ibid., p. 13).
    In response to this, Bultmann is critical of both the immanentalist understanding of God and the non-existential (existentielle) understanding of the self. Bultmann acknowledges that the freedom and responsibility of Dasein extends to include, not only himself, but his world. However, man may not be responsible for God (Rudolf Bultmann, "Anhang: Aus einem Briefwechsel zwischen Rudolf Bultmann und dem Verfasser anlässlich des Aufsatzes über die Unsterblichkeit," Zwischen Nichts und Ewigkeit: drei Aufsätze zur Lehre vom Menschen by Hans Jonas [Göttingen: Vandenhoeck & Ruprecht, 1963], p. 66). Furthermore, Jonas has not faced the really significant question in any discussion of mortality that is the existentielle question of "my own dying," "je mein Sterben," "je meinen Tod" (ibid.). Jonas thus lapses into an esthetic, innerworldly perspective and loses sight of the meaning of death for authentic existence.

Bultmann may find the hermeneutical flower of historical idealism to be attractive, but he has little empathy with the soil and roots out of which it grows.

Therefore, in this discussion of Bultmann's hermeneutical borrowings, I will also need to make clear the purpose for which he uses this hermeneutic, the real content which he pours into this vessel. This means, of course, that we shall have to confront again that fundamental phenomenon of Neo-Kantianism, in both its Enlightenment and Lutheran variations, which has concerned us so often already. For in place of Jonas' historical dialectic of *Geist* and its objectivation steps Bultmann's theological dichotomy of faith and works, on the one hand, and the epistemological-ontological dichotomy of individual existence and objectifying reason, on the other hand. Bultmann thus borrows from Jonas as he has previously borrowed from Barth and Heidegger: namely, those motifs which express and are congruent with the Neo-Kantian rationalism and Lutheranism which is the core of his own thought. As a result, I will have to bring together in this discussion of the hermeneutical formulation of objectifying many of the threads of Bultmann's thought developed in separate chapters and sections.

While acknowledging these limits intrinsic to Bultmann's appropriation of Jonas' thought, it is nevertheless also clear that Bultmann does absorb, willy-nilly, a wide range of nineteenth-century idealistic motifs in his hermeneutical proposal. Their unlikely presence within Bultmann's eclectic mansion of many rooms has further confounded the task of understanding his proposal for demythologizing. In laying bare these motifs, in this section which concludes the substantive development of the argument, I thus unravel the last thread in the enigma of demythologizing.

In his delineation of *"das Wesen des Mythos"* in his 1941 essay, Bultmann sets forth the familiar double-sided structure of myth. On the one hand, there is the *"eigentlichen Absicht,"* *"eigentliche Sinn,"* or, as expressed in related essays, the *"eigentlichen Intention,"* *"bleibender Sinn."* [1] On the other hand, there is the *"objektivierende Charakter seiner Aussagen,"* or more simply and frequently, *"seine objektivierenden Vorstellungen."* [2] Bultmann can also express this latter pole of the double-sided structure by the use of *"objekti-*

---

[1] Bultmann, *KuM*, I, 22-23; *KuM*, II, 183-184; *Die christliche Hoffnung* . . p. 26.
[2] Bultmann, *KuM*, I, 23.

vierend," "mythisch," or *"mythologisch"* (used in these cases as synonyms) modifying *"Begriffe," "Begrifflichkeit," "Denken," "Denkweise,"* or *"Denkform."* [1]

From this vocabulary, it is clear that Bultmann understands the double-sided structure of myth to have an epistemological, not a primary ontological, basis. It is the epistemological categories of imagery, concepts, and modes of thought that provide his basic concepts for understanding the fundamental hermeneutical structure of myth. From a Neo-Kantian epistemological perspective, myth thus discloses a primordial confusion of reason's activity of world objectification in accordance with the unifying principle of law with the individual's immediate experience of his own destiny or the reality of insecure existence in its own historicity. As Bultmann writes in a later essay, myth fails to distinguish between empirical reality and existential reality and thus objectifies as does science.[2] From this fundamental epistemological perspective the meaning of worldly and unworldly is to be determined.

> Myth gives worldly objectivity to that which is unworldly. (In German one would say, *"Der Mythos objektiviert das Jenseitige zum Diesseitigen."* [3]

In Neo-Kantian terminology, one would say that myth casts the phenomenon of religion in the form and sphere of reason. Myth thus shares the epistemological form of science (*objektivierende*), its cause-effect categories of connection, and its purpose of explanation.[4] It is for this reason that myth is vulnerable to the criticism of the modern scientific *Weltbild* and the fact that it is so vulnerable discloses its fundamental conceptual confusion.

> Myth speaks of the powers and persons beyond this world actually as if they were this sided worldly entities—against its own intention.[5]

However, this epistemological confusion has also its anthropological-theological correlate. For the effect of its incorrect conceptuality is not simply to make myth false reason, which it is, but also to create confusion at the existential level of intentionality. For the

---

[1] Bultmann, *KuM*, II, 185; *KuM*, I, 26: *KuM*, II, 185; *ibid.*, p. 180; *ibid.*, p. 185.

[2] Bultmann, *Myth and Christianity* . . ., p. 61.

[3] Bultmann, *Jesus Christ and Mythology*, p. 19. Cf. Bultmann, *KuM*, II, 184.

[4] Bultmann, *KuM*, II, 183.

[5] *Ibid.*

intention, purpose, or meaning of myth is to express that knowledge of human existence as insecure, set in a world "threatened and dominated by mysterious and enigmatic powers." [1] The reality of which myth intends to speak is therefore not the reality of the work-world—that familiar, visible, tangible, disposable world systematically unfolded in science but existentially rooted in work—but rather, the transcendent reality, the unknown, invisible, ground, limits, or purpose of a world which is not placed at man's disposal or under his control. The intention of myth is thus to express the insecure condition of human existence in a premonition of transcendence.

It is just this intention which is confused through its mixture with an objectifying conceptuality. For the objectification of the beyond into the worldly is not simply an instance of naïve and pre-critical reason, but also an expression of a sinful or inauthentic understanding of human existence. For at the root of this epistemological confusion is man's pernicious desire to justify himself by his own powers and worldly possibilities—even to place the beyond under his disposal, to include the divine within the sphere of his work-world.

> In brief, myth objectifies the beyond as the worldly and thus also the disposable (*zum Verfügbaren*) which shows itself in this, that the cult more and more becomes an activity seeking to influence the attitude of the divine, seeking to turn away its wrath or win its favor.[2]

Bultmann thus formulates the double-sided structure of myth in terms of the categories of existential intention and objectifying conceptuality or imagery. In its essential structure, myth is the confusion of one fundamental existential *Haltung* with a conceptuality appropriate to a quite different, but equally fundamental, existential *Haltung*. The intention of myth, to express a particular understanding of human existence, thus requires a conceptuality appropriate to it, which is to be provided by an existentialist anthropology. The objectifying conceptuality of science, in turn, is allowed to be the pure expression of the intentionality of work. Since myth mixes these two fundamental existential orientations and their corresponding forms of conception, there arises necessarily confusion at both levels. At the conceptual level, the scientific

---

[1] Bultmann, *KuM*, I, 22.
[2] Bultmann, *KuM*, II, 184.

explication of the work-world must criticize and reject the false objectification of the world in myth. At an existential level, the original intention of myth must be purified from its mixture with an attitude of world-controlling, self-justifying works.

It should be obvious that in specifying the meaning and content of the double-sided nature of myth, I have simply drawn together the basic Neo-Kantian motifs of Bultmann's thought previously considered separately from each other. While Bultmann appropriates the understanding of myth as an intrinsically double-sided phenomenon from Jonas, he understands the nature of these two sides in accordance with his own position. In Bultmann, as in Jonas, these two sides are related to each other by way of negation: that is, the objectifying form of expression conceals, obstructs, veils, and confuses the intention of myth.[1] However, this antithetical relationship is not grounded in the structure of being itself, which necessarily becomes something other than itself in order to actualize itself, nor is it expressive of the dialectical movement of the *Geist* in history; rather, myth expresses two levels of confusion of an anthropological dichotomy that is eternal. For Bultmann, the understanding of the world through its objectification is a perennial demand of human existence. Every man in every age has his *Weltbild* through which he deals with his world. What is decisive here, in distinguishing between a right and wrong understanding of the world, is the principle of law as it unifies the objectifying of this world, as this is shown through the history of reason and science. Similarly, the understanding of the self in its fundamental insecurity and care for itself is a perennial demand of human existence. Every man in every age has his god in which he trusts and through which he resolves the question of his security. What is decisive here, in distinguishing between a right and wrong understanding of the self, is the revelation of God in Jesus Christ which gives in faith the possibility of trusting one's existence to the invisible, intangible, uncontrollable God of the future. For Bultmann, it is only this ultimate and timeless anthropological duality which provides the ground for the hermeneutical formulation of myth in its doublesidedness, and not the dialectical movement of *Geist*.

Having noted this basic formal continuity and material discontinuity between Bultmann and Jonas, I now consider some of the

---

[1] Bultmann, *KuM*, I, 23, 128.

related points of contact between them. After 1934, it becomes axiomatic for Bultmann that the texts of the New Testament, like those of Gnosticism and other phenomena of the Hellenistic age, are to be understood in the context of an historical transition between two historical epochs. In this period of human history there is constituted the beginning of a new epoch of *Dasein* and his self-understanding.[1] However syncretistic the phenomenon of Gnostic mythology may appear, there breaks forth in these myths a new understanding of existence which creates a fundamental point of division between the ancient world (both Hebraic and Hellenic) and the modern world.[2] The Hellenistic age thus comes to constitute what Bultmann describes, in his preface to Jonas' volume on Gnosticism, "the turn in world understanding from the ancient world to the Christianity of the West." [3] It is for this reason that Bultmann finds Jonas' work to have disclosed to him for the first time the meaning of this phenomenon in its full significance.[4] For by placing these Hellenistic texts in this specific moment of the history of *Geist*, their meaning as the first fruits of a fundamental new self-understanding was made clear.

Bultmann thus borrows from Jonas this interpretation of the meaning and significance of the Hellenistic age in the history of *Dasein*'s self-understanding, and places the New Testament texts in this specific context of interpretation. One consequence of this is that the New Testament is radically cut off from the Old Testament, for the two books fall in fundamentally different epochs of the history of *Dasein*'s self-understanding.[5] As a result of this division of history, the Old Testament is of limited hermeneutical relevance to the New Testament. The lateral movement of the *Geist*, which unifies contemporary phenomena on the basis of a single principle

---

[1] Rudolf Bultmann, "Zum Thema: Christentum und Antike," *ThR*, XVI (1944), p. 19.

[2] Rudolf Bultmann, Review of H. Lietzmann, *Geschichte der alten Kirche*, *ZKG*, LIII (1934), 629.

[3] Rudolf Bultmann, "Vorwort," *Gnosis* . . ., I, by Jonas, p. vii.

[4] *Ibid.*

[5] That which qualitatively distinguishes the New Testament from the Old Testament is not Jesus, who must be understood in continuity with the Old Testament as a prophet of the Law, but rather the mythology of the New Testament through which the Gospel is proclaimed. "This is what is specifically Christian and has been acknowledged as such by the Church through the centuries of her history" (Rudolf Bultmann, "Die Bedeuting des Alten Testaments für den christlichen Glauben," *GV*, I, p. 316).

of interpretation, overshadows the linear movement of the *Heilige Geist*, which follows the path of tradition-bearing historical communities. Another consequence of this specification of the context of New Testament interpretation is the decisive role which Gnosticism acquires in establishing the fundamental structure of New Testament self-understanding.

> It [the relationship between Gnosticism and Christianity] is no longer a concern limited to individual phenomena of the New Testament and ancient church history but concerns the total understanding of the world and salvation in Christianity.[1]

Bultmann's continuity with Jonas is also manifest in his use of *Entweltlichung* as the decisive anthropological category which expresses the new understanding of existence that appears in both Gnosticism and in Christianity. When Bultmann sets forth his little summaries of the understanding of human existence which finds expression in myth, he consistently presents the familiar Gnostic themes of world alienation and existential threat combined with the radical transcendence of the self and God. The world is thus experienced as menacing, enigmatic, and mysterious; the self and the divine are understood to be fundamentally other than—beyond, on the other side of, outside of, transcendent of—the world.[2] It is this very particular understanding of existence which Bultmann finds to be the essence of mythology. At the same time, this new understanding of *Dasein*'s relationship to the world is also the essence of the Christian understanding of being. *Entweltlichung* is the meaning of eschatological existence: to be related to the world "as if it were not."[3] To be sure, one may not confuse the formal, ontological continuity of Gnosticism and Christianity with the

---

[1] Rudolf Bultmann, "Vorwort," *Gnosis . . .*, I, by Jonas, p. vii. As an illustration of Bultmann's use of Gnosticism over against the Old Testament in New Testament interpretation, see his review of C. H. Dodd's *The Fourth Gospel*, trans. W. C. Robinson, *Harvard Divinity Bulletin*, XXVII (1963), 2. Bultmann's commitment to the hermeneutical priciple of unifying contemporary phenomena under a common principle of interpretation will not allow him to consider the Hellenistic age from the perspective of a socio-economic pluralism. A. D. Nock, in his review of Jonas' *Gnosis und spätantiker Geist*, I, contends that the Christian communities won their adherents from a social-economic milieu quite different from "the circles in which currents of thought akin to Gnosticism might start" (A. D. Nock, Review of *Gnosis und spätantiker Geist*, I, by Hans Jonas, *Gnomon*, XII (1936), 612).

[2] Bultmann, *KuM*, I, 22-23; *KuM*, II, 183-184; *JR*, 100.

[3] Bultmann, *KuM*, I, 29-30.

existential, ontic differentiation between them that so radically divides them. The eschatological existence which is realized in faith is only intended in the mythology of Gnosticism. Moreover, Gnosticism never did apprehend the dialectical nature of this new relationship of *Dasein* to its world. As a result, the *Entweltlichung* of Gnosticism, grounded in the possession of speculative knowledge or mystical experience, led to an ethic of asceticism or libertinism.[1] In contrast, the Christian detachment from the world was grounded in the believer's "being known by God," in no sense a work or possession of his own, but to be realized ever anew in decision and manifest in the way of love.[2] Nevertheless, the new understanding of self and world, actualized in Christian faith, remains consistent in its ontological structure with the new understanding of self and world which appears—albeit only in intention and then with distortion and partiality—in Gnosticism.

While Bultmann thus develops the particular understanding of existence which appears in myth and in the New Testament in the terms of Jonas' anthropological schema, he gives to this new understanding a content that could arise only out of the particularity of his own thought. For it is clear that the *Entweltlichung* of existence means nothing but a particular understanding of the problematic of human insecurity. The general apprehension of this condition of insecurity is the essential content of eschatology in its various forms.[3] What is peculiar to the biblical Word of God is its call to "abandon all human security and thus to overcome the despair which arises from the attempt to find security, an attempt which is always vain." [4] It is this which contitutes the fundamental call to decision and the real offense of New Testament mythology.

> The offense consists of this: that the Word of God calls man out of all *Angst*, all self-created security, to God and thus to his authentic existence—and thus also to freedom from the world.[5]

Eschatological existence means just this; *"die Preisgabe aller Sicherheit . . . die Haltung der Entweltlichung, der Freiheit."* [6]

---

[1] *Ibid.*
[2] Rudolf Bultmann, "Gnosis," trans. J. R. Coates (London: Adam and Charles Black, 1952), pp. 42-43.
[3] Bultmann, *Jesus Christ and Mythology*, pp. 24-25.
[4] *Ibid.*, p. 40.
[5] Bultmann, *KuM*, II, 188.
[6] Bultmann, *KuM*, I, 29.

It is expressed in Bultmann's characteristic Pauline shibboleth: to live in the world "as if it were not." It is an understanding of existence freed from the taint of self-justifying worldly deeds at the central juncture of *Dasein*'s insecurity.

The opposite of this is the *Haltung* of the flesh.

> What does flesh mean? It is not corporeality or sensuality, but it is the sphere of the visible, of entities-at-hand, the disposable, measurable, and as such the sphere of the fleeting, the transitory. ... For flesh includes not only natural things, but also all creating and accomplishing which is concerned with the winning of something worthy of recognition, as for example, the fulfillment of the law. To the flesh belongs every quality, every advantage which a man can have in the visible, disposable sphere.[1]

The *Haltung* of the flesh is thus the *Haltung* of the work-world existentially misplaced in the sphere of human insecurity. The flesh thus means man's quest for security in the world and by his powers, a quest inappropriate to his real situation.[2] The *Haltung* of *Entweltlichung* and the *Haltung* of the flesh thus constitute the fundamental theological-existential dichotomy in terms of which man apprehends his existence.

While Bultmann thus defines the meaning of *Entweltlichung* in accordance with his own theological-existential perspective, he nonetheless has integrated the New Testament texts into a more comprehensive historical schema. Since there is a basic epistemological-ontological dualism in his thought, the result is that for Bultmann there comes to be a double history of *Geist*. On the one hand, there is the history of *Vernunft*, objectifying reason, which has its foundations in the Hellenic age and comes to its conceptual maturity in the mathematical sciences of the modern era. On the other hand, there is a history of *Dasein*'s self-interpretation, his *Existenzverständnis*, which comes into existence in a decisive new form in Gnostic and Christian mythology of the Hellenistic age, which follows Jonas' long detour from Augustine through Luther (for Bultmann, not Jonas) to Kierkegaard and which, presumably, has come to its conceptual fulfillment in the existentialist anthropology of Martin Heidegger. At least, Bultmann's understanding of Heidegger appears to presuppose this schema of history, so that

---

[1] *Ibid.*, p. 28.
[2] *Ibid.*

Heidegger can now offer "only a profane philosophical presentation of the New Testament perception of human *Dasein*." [1]

> Man, historically existing in care for himself and grounded in *Angst*, chooses in the moment of decision between past and future, whether he will lose himself in the world of entities at hand, "*das man*," or whether he will win his authenticity in the giving up of all security and in the unreserved commitment of himself to the future. Is not man also understood this way in the New Testament? If one objects, contrary to this, that I interpret the New Testament with categories of Heidegger's philosophy of existence, he only blinds himself to the real problem. I think, rather, what should be startling is the fact that the philosopher can see of himself what the New Testament says. [2]

While Bultmann is not much concerned with exploring the "*geistesgeschichtliche Zusammenhang*" between modern existentialist philosophy and its historical origins, he does acknowledge that this existentialism has not been able to discover the nature of man without the New Testament, Luther, and Kierkegaard. [3]

Because there has been an historical development in the conceptualizing of this new self-understanding, Bultmann, like Jonas, will grant that myth is necessary, but only in a provisional sense. In myth there comes into historical reality certain truths which do not find expression in the objectifying speech of science; in this qualified sense, myth is indispensable. [4] Furthermore, it is also true that myth provides the hermeneutical point of departure for the recovery of a deeper understanding of existence, which has been lost in the spirit of science and the Enlightenment. [5] However, while Bultmann grants that myth is necessary, in that a particular

---

[1] Bultmann, *KuM*, I, 33.

[2] *Ibid.*

[3] *Ibid.*, p. 25. The fact that the later, and conceptually more adequate, formulation of the early New Testament self-understanding is nevertheless not sufficient for salvation or the realization of authentic existence does not affect our argument. If we remember correctly the Neo-Kantian philosophy of religion, religion is always defined as that which concerns the self-realization of the individual. The reality of religion is therefore always and only *existentielle*, never *existential*. Beyond the fundamental dichotomy of the existentialist and objectifying conceptualities there is still the elusive reality of the individual in that existential reality which is "*je Meinigkeit*." Religion is a phenomenon of this order of being, and therefore may not be identified with the historical unfolding of an existentialist conceptuality any more than it may be identified with the history of objectifying conceptuality.

[4] Bultmann, *KuM*, II, 186.

[5] Bultmann, *KuM*, I, 17.

understanding of existence has become available only through its form of thought, he will not convert this temporal necessity into an eternal necessity.

> In mythological speech there comes to preliminary expression (*vorläufigen Ausdruck*) that for which adequate speech must first be found.[1]

He therefore rejects any position which would insist that the language of mythology is essential to the expression of religion in general or Christianity in particular.[2] For while the meaning of myth may not be found in other forms of expression, the expressive form of myth has now been proven to be "inadequate," "inappropriate," and "insufficient." [3]

In Bultmann, as in Jonas, there is this same sense of living in an age with radical new possibilities for bringing to full, direct, conceptual expression that which had been locked in the opaque and ambiguous language of a past age. The question which is pressing for Bultmann is the question of the *"rechten Begrifflichkeit"* in which interpretation can bring to expression the meaning of these past texts.[4] The premise of the venture is that the long detour from the New Testament to Heidegger has been traversed, so that it is now possible to express the full meaning of the New Testament faith in a *"gemässe Ausdrucksform."* [5] The hidden and multi-dimensional nature of the language of faith in its original form discloses nothing of the essential character of that language, but only the partial and distorted form available in that particular moment of history. To be sure, Bultmann does accept the fact that certain mythological notions, in the form of symbols and images, are necessary to the language of the Christian faith.[6] Within certain contexts, such as the liturgy, he accepts the propriety of their usage.[7] However, this does not alter the demand which rests upon theology to give expression to the meaning of mythological concepts "without recourse to mythological terms." [8] Indeed, any speech of God, any confession of sin is mythological so long as it is

---

[1] Bultmann, *KuM*, II, 186.

[2] *Ibid.*, p. 185; Bultmann, *Jesus Christ and Mythology*, p. 67.

[3] Bultmann, *KuM*, II, 185; Bultmann, *Jesus Christ and Mythology*, p. 19.

[4] Bultmann, *KuM*, II, 191.

[5] *Ibid.*, p. 207.

[6] Bultmann, *Jesus Christ and Mythology*, p. 67.

[7] Bultmann, "On the Problem of Demythologizing," *JR* (1962), p. 100.

[8] Bultmann, *Jesus Christ and Mythology*, p. 68.

not interpreted and understood in an existentialist manner.[1] With this movement out of the density of the language of the past and into the clear, direct, full expression of its meaning in an existentialist conceptuality, Bultmann, like Jonas, acquires a relationship of superiority to the text, so that the interpreter has the possibility of grasping the meaning of the text more clearly than did its author.[2]

While noting this continuity between Bultmann and Jonas, in their understanding of the relation of the present interpreter to his past text, the roots for Bultmann's view of the language of faith lie, not in Jonas, but in Bultmann's own Neo-Kantian *Erlebnis* theology. The basic criterion for valid religious speech has always been its capacity to engage the individual directly and immediately in the center of his personal experience. Directness and immediacy were qualifications for authentic religious speech long before Bultmann met Heidegger or Jonas. The Word of God has always been understood as strictly and only analogous with the word of man expressed in his deep and intimate inter-personal relations: love, friendship and trust.[3] The paradigm for the Word of God has always been, *"Ich liebe dich."* [4] Since this was always the norm for right religious speech for Bultmann, it necessarily followed that the opaque, ambiguous, multi-dimensional, associational, cosmic and psychic language of biblical myth and symbol could only appear as a barrier to the hearing and understanding of the biblical Word. The hermeneutical problem, in light of this linguistic norm, was always to strip away the density and distance of biblical speech in order to let it appear in its direct presence as inter-personal address. With the advent of Heidegger's conceptuality, it appeared as if it was finally possible to reach this goal in a fundamental reformulation of the language of the household of faith. Here again is the pattern of Bultmann's continuity with Jonas, but rooted in motives of a prior tradition of thought.

Bultmann also follows Jonas in understanding both the logical and historical-objective criticism of past texts to be a preliminary

---

[1] Bultmann, *KuM*, I, 124.

[2] Pierre Barthel quotes Bultmann as describing interpretation as "understanding the ancient author better than he understood himself" (Barthel, *Interprétation du langage mythique* . . ., p. 69). Unfortunately, Barthel offers no page or volume citation for the quote.

[3] Bultmann, "Religion und Kultur," *ChrW* (1920), col. 438.

[4] Bultmann, *KuM*, II, 187.

mode of access to the dialectical criticism of demythologizing and existentialist interpretation. As Jonas cited the logical antinomies in the dogma of original sin, so Bultmann cites the contradictions which occur within the New Testament. These range from several minor contradictions—such as the incompatability of the Virgin Birth with the pre-existence of the Son, or the doctrine of the creation over against the alien "rulers of the world"—to the fundamental *Widerspruch* which runs through the New Testament as a whole:

> On the one hand, man is understood by way of cosmic determinism; on the other hand, there is the call to decision; on the one hand, sin is fate; on the other hand, sin is guilt. . . .[1]

Like Jonas, Bultmann will not take these contradictions seriously, as if they should be resolved in themselves, but rather sees them as symptoms, in which is expressed the New Testament need for criticism from within itself.[2]

In a similar manner, Bultmann also makes a close connection between the rational-objective criticism of the New Testament—under the norm of the scientific *Weltbild* as discussed in Chapter IV—and the dialectical critical interpretation which he now proposes. Thus, it is the initial discrepancy or conflict between the New Testament mythological *Weltbild* and the scientific *Weltbild* that provided the occasion and motive for demythologizing. However, that conflict itself pointed to the fact that faith had not yet found an appropriate form of expression.[3] Thus, the rational-objective criticism of the New Testament pointed toward the necessity for a more comprehensive hermeneutical criticism and reinterpretation of New Testament mythology.

Like Jonas, Bultmann understands demythologizing (in the existentialist hermeneutical sense of the term) as the essential negative moment of destruction in a more comprehensive existentialist recovery of the original existential intention. Demythologizing therefore means not only the stripping away of the antique *Weltbild*, as the term was used in Chapter IV. It also means the criticism of the fundamental ontology of mythology which its *Weltbild* presupposes.

---

[1] Bultmann, *KuM*, I, 23.
[2] *Ibid.*
[3] Bultmann, *KaM*, I, 210.

> Negatively, to demythologize, in my sense, means to destroy the old mythical meaning insofar as it was mythically objectified. What does it mean positively? My answer is: it must be asked: what understanding of existence comes here to expression ... which, after the overcoming or the destruction of the mythical imagery, is still an abiding and actual possibility.[1]

Or, in another passage which joins the criticism of the *Weltbild* to the recovery of the original intention:

> Negatively is demythologizing the criticism of the *Weltbild* of myth insofar as this conceals the authentic intention of myth. Positively demythologizing is existentialist interpretation as this will make clear the content of myth, its purpose, to speak of the existence of men.[2]

In either case, demythologizing is the essential negative moment in a total dialectical movement of thought which recovers the original existential intention in a new conceptuality appropriate to it only by simultaneously destroying the original false and alien form of expression.

I can summarize the relation of Bultmann to Jonas at the point of the hermeneutical meaning of objectifying by reference to the two themes developed in the course of this exposition. First, Bultmann quite obviously formulates his hermeneutical project of demythologizing only on the grounds of Jonas' prior hermeneutical writings. A study of Bultmann's discussion of myth prior to 1934 makes this amply clear. This means, however, that demythologizing may not be considered apart from the philosophical context in which it was originally formulated: namely, Jonas' fusion of nineteenth-century historical idealism with Heidegger's existentialism. To demythologize, in the manner of Bultmann's proposal, necessarily means to accept responsibility for the idealistic schema of history which is covertly, but essentially, present.

Second, while establishing the role of these older idealistic motifs in the hermeneutical proposals of Jonas and Bultmann, one may not overestimate their significance. Demythologizing, like a myriad of other twentieth-century intellectual phenomena, benefits bountifully from its nineteenth-century philosophical ancestry. Even in the case of Jonas' early writings, it is clear that these older idealistic motifs are never given an explicit and systematic form of develop-

---

[1] Bultmann, *Die christliche Hoffnung* . . ., pp. 50-51.
[2] Bultmann, *KuM*, II, 184.

ment. Rather, they are present in Jonas' thought almost as a given of the *Zeitgeist*.[1] In Bultmann's case, these motifs are even less central to his thought. As was seen repeatedly, his own position is firmly grounded in the critical idealism of Neo-Kantianism and he is consistently suspicious of any form of historical idealism, especially as a philosophical handmaiden to theology.

2. 'Objectifying' as the Semantic Point of Synthesis

The structure of Bultmann's theology in its final form of development resembles in some ways the architectural unity of a medieval cathedral. One knows as a matter of fact that the cathedral has evolved through a series of stylistic and architectural changes involving several generations and that some of these innovations should seem incongruous with the original plan. Yet the final form of the building gives the impression of an esthetic whole of which all later developments are an integral part. Considered in themselves, the Enlightenment and historical-idealist motifs appropriated by Bultmann in the nineteen-thirties seem foreign to the philosophical-theological foundations of his thought articulated in the early twenties. Yet, when these same motifs are viewed within the body of Bultmann's thought, they blend so well into the basic structure that the reader hardly recognizes them as a new addition. Indeed, the prevalent interpretation of Bultmann's theology—as an appropriation of Heidegger's philosophy which remains constant from the mid-twenties through the late sixties—confirms this impression. In this section, I hope to illumine the process by which Bultmann

---

[1] In conversation with Dr. Jonas, he has acknowledged the role of these older idealistic motifs in his early writings of the thirties. However, he had himself come to recognize their presence in his thought only recently. In no sense was he aware at the time of his work of a direct borrowing from the earlier tradition of German Idealism. Indeed, he had not even pursued any special philosophical studies in this area, other than the normal exposure to this subject matter in the course of winning a graduate degree in philosophy. He now attributes his own innocence concerning the idealistic shape of his thought at that time to the enthusiasm with which he, and other early followers of Heidegger, appropriated this new philosophical schema. Heidegger's philosophy did not appear to belong to a continuing philosophical tradition, but rather was understood as a radical new breakthrough in the history of thought, and as such was discontinuous with the past. It was in this intellectual *Sitz-im-Leben* that Jonas developed his own hermeneutic. It is for this reason that his own idealism must be recognized as a phenomenon of the *Zeitgeist*, rather than as a deliberately espoused and critically formulated positon.

blended his eclectic sources into a unified schema of thought. For this purpose, I will trace the evolution of the term 'objectifying' as the semantic point of synthesis. Whether by accident or design, this term, weighted so heavily with the philosophical legacy of Neo-Kantians, came to include a rich variety of new meanings fashioned out of the materials of Lutheran theology, existentialist philosophy, Enlightenment historiography, and historical idealism.

For Bultmann, the root meaning of objectified is derived from the Neo-Kantian use of the term to designate both the characteristic activity of reason and the multiple dimensions of reality—natural, historical, moral, and socio-institutional—open to human inquiry and management. Within a Neo-Kantian perspective, only God and/or religious experience transcend the confines of objectified reality; and, conversely, objectified reality by definition is closed to religious experience and/or transcendence. Throughout his long theological career, Bultmann continued to use objectifying as both an epistemological and ontological concept consistent with its Neo-Kantian meaning. As an expression of reason, objectifying was identified with a certain mode of conceptuality; as an attribute of reality, objectified reality and transcendent reality were consistently set in opposition with each other. To conceive of God in an objectified mode of thought was, in the first instance, simply a philosophical error. When ancient man portrayed God in terms of Kantian categories of space, time or causality, he was simply guilty of a naïve, pre-Kantian mode of reflection. Such confusion was not necessarily a theological or religious offense, but only evidence of sloppy thinking.

From the time of his earliest appropriation of this Neo-Kantian category, Bultmann gave it a particular theological twist. He never ascribed to objectified reality the ontological status of genuine reality, as was characteristic of classical Neo-Kantianism. On the contrary, objectified reality was ontologically denigrated as an inferior kind of reality, or a substitute for the "really real." More to the point, the seemingly all inclusive objectification of reality so dominant in early modern culture became the occasion for religious tempation. Men were enticed into investing their hope for personal fulfillment into something that was merely a complex extension of their work-world. In this transition, objectifying lost its theological neutrality as a philosophical concept and became identified with sin: e.g., man's effort to justify himself by his work.

What was implicit in Bultmann's writings of the nineteen-twenties became explicit in his existentialist anthropology developed after 1925. The fundamental human problem was now defined in terms of existential insecurity. Two responses to this human condition were postulated. On the one hand, man could let the desire for security become the determinative motivating power of his life, believing that his own scientific-technological powers were adequate to win a secure existence collectively and/or individually. On the other hand, man could give up this false desire to win security through his work as an unrealistic possibility and entrust his life to a God of love manifest for faith in the proclamation of the Kerygma. Between these two self-understandings, there was no middle ground: justification by work or justification by faith; *tertium non datur*.

Within the framework of this anthropological-theological dichotomy, objectifying became synonymous with the specific theological symbol of sin. The connection between objectifying reason and sin depends upon Bultmann's interpretation of work. On the one hand, Bultmann consistently views objectifying reason as an essential expression of man's work life. Primitive man, as well as modern man, objectified reality in terms of some causally integrated schema in order to perform the tasks necessary for his survival. Scientific thought is simply a radical extension of this work life. On the other hand, the whole of man's work life is informed by a specific motive and belief: namely, the desire for security and man's confidence in his own self-sufficiency. The combination of these two assertions leads to an obvious conclusion: objectifying thought is inseparably bound up with man's existence as sinner. In light of this theological judgment, primitive man's objectification of God becomes somewhat less innocent. It is not simply the result of philosophical naïveté, but also an expression of *hubris*. By making the divine into a definite object, men seek to extend their knowing-controlling relationship to reality to the sphere of the ultimate. Objectifying thought thus becomes man's ultimate weapon of self-assertion and denial of God.

This synthesis of Neo-Kantian epistemology with a Lutheran interpretation of sin came to constitute the nuclear meaning of objectifying for Bultmann. And throughout the late nineteen-twenties, he used the term with this double meaning. However, it was not yet a hermeneutical concept; it did not provide a means for bridging the gap between mythological expressions of the past and existential concerns of the present. Bultmann's discussion of mythology in the late nineteen-twenties makes it apparent that he has not yet developed a systematic principle of myth interpretation. To meet this task, he appropriates the Enlightenment concept of mythology and Jonas' modified version of historical idealism. And in both these instances, it is the term objectifying that provides the means for incorporating these two distinct traditions of thought within his own theology.

The Enlightenment hypothesis was intrinsically congenial to a Neo-Kantian epistemology. For this reason, I consistently described the Enlightenment view of mythology as an historico-epistemological formulation. Like Bultmann, the Enlightenment thinkers presupposed man's objectification of reality as a universal human activity. All men in all times and places construct their own *Weltbild* as a means for coping with the practical necessities of daily life. Objectifying thus came to function as a genus-term which could be distinguished according to two distinct species: objectification in accordance with a principle of law as manifest in the unified causal nexus of the scientific world view; objectification in a random, arbitrary pattern, determined by inner subjective needs and not by the structure of reason. Defining mythology as a pre-scientific form of objectifying thought, Bultmann was able to dismiss New Testament mythology on two grounds. First, since a mythological objectification of the world was not consistent with an inner principle of law, it was an instance of false reason: *mythos* as *pseudo-logos*. Or, to make the same point in historical terms, the scientific objectification of the world was the legitimate successor of its mythological antecedent. Second, all objectifications of reality belonged to man's work life in meeting practical tasks of his world. Therefore, neither a mythological nor a scientific mode of world objectification was ultimately relevant to man's spiritual life before God. New Testament mythological claims concerning objectified reality could thus be dismissed as both historically obsolete and theologically superfluous.

Neither as a biblical scholar nor as a theologian was Bultmann able to accept the Enlightenment hypothesis as an adequate resolution to the problem of mythology. For the solution prescribed by the Enlightenment critique of myth was simply one of elimination: identify the particular motifs and narratives of the New Testament which are mythological and then dismiss them as relics of the ancient world. While biblical critics of the nineteenth century attempted to deal with the problem of mythology in this manner, Bultmann clearly saw the impossibility of such a procedure. For mythology permeated the whole of New Testament literature; it provided the structure for the Gospel narratives of Jesus' life and the presupposition for all the basic Christian beliefs about Jesus, the church, sacraments, and the expected end of history. It could not be confined to certain isolated segments of the New Testament. Furthermore, as a Christian theologian, Bultmann confessed the Church's proclamation as decisive for the life of faith. To reduce the specific eschatological message of the Gospel to a general set of religious attitudes or ethical values would undermine the basic strength of the Christian faith in its communal and individual forms. Mythology, therefore, could not simply be dismissed in deference to non-mythological form of spirituality or morality deemed more appropriate to the age; rather, the inner meaning of New Testament mythology had to be preserved even while its external form was overcome.

Such a dialectical understanding of mythology became available to Bultmann only through Jonas' studies of Hellenistic mythology, and once again objectifying provided the semantic link. To be sure, the meaning of 'objectivation' for Jonas was quite different from any of the meanings that had already become congealed together in Bultmann's notion of objectifying. Jonas was not especially concerned with either God, the world, or sin. Therefore he did not use objectifying to signify a pre-critical conception of transcendence, a pre-scientific mode of worldly knowledge, or a particular existential attitude. Instead, Jonas was concerned with the tension between the being of man and the expression of that being in some objective linguistic form. Man actualizes his being only as it finds expression through some symbolic form; but every symbolic form of expression involves the transposition of man's being into a form other than its own; therefore, every symbolic expression of human existence is fraught with the danger of becoming alienated from its source.

When Bultmann appropriated Jonas' hermeneutic, he also acquired still another meaning for objectifying. In addition to all its previous functions, the term now came to designate that historically necessary but presently alien form through which the existential attitude of faith was first actualized. Equipped with this new acquisition, Bultmann then articulated his familiar hermeneutic of myth interpretation whose development was described in the preceding section.

Throughout this exposition, I have described objectifying as a word or notion which provides the decisive semantic link for Bultmann's integration of a variety of intellectual perspectives. I have not considered objectifying as a concept, except in relation to any one of its several uses. One generally assumes that concepts can be expressed in a univocal definition; objectifying cannot be expressed in this way. It is not as if the word has one 'true meaning' which occasionally becomes vague or cloudy. For any single use of the term may express several of its different meanings. Indeed, I expect that it would be more accurate to treat objectifying as a symbol rather than a concept, and for two reasons. First, symbols are in their essence a loose association of meanings which accumulate and change through the course of historical development. One does not try to define a symbol in a single definition nor are symbols accountable to the norms of logical discourse. The evolution of objectifying in Bultmann's thought would correspond with this pattern. Second, symbols depend for their power not upon their conceptual clarity, but on their ability to evoke a multi-dimensional existential response. The prevalent appropriation of objectifying in theological literature after Bultmann suggests this kind of appeal. Surely the popularity of the term is not due to its clarity; rather, it serves as a vehicle for expressing the diverse kinds of alienation which beset contemporary man: alienation from the dehumanizing scientific-technological structures of existence; alienation from a rationalistic, imperialistic ego which would manipulate the self and others in the name of a "value-free" objective ideology; alienation from an intellectually dishonest and psychologically repressive form of God-talk; and alienation from both secular and religious symbolizations of existence which have lost their capacity to restore a sense of purpose, wholeness, and integrity. In this sense, objectifying functions as a kind of code word to identify a host of different obstacles to man's quest for fulfillment.

To understand the power of demythologizing as a catalytic force in recent theology, it would be necessary to adopt a perspective quite different from the one articulated in this book. I have consistently focused on Bultmann's role as an intellectual—a historian, philosopher, or theologian. I would be the first to acknowledge that such a focus fails to do justice to the creative impact of his theology.

To fully appreciate Bultmann, one would have to consider him also as a prophet who passionately denounced the debilitating effects of a purely scientific culture, who protested against the dominance of the bourgoise work ethos and its reduction of human life to a sum of achievements, and who persistently struggled to reclaim for his own generation those religious resources which nourish a genuine human life of trust and love.

To consider Bultmann in this perspective, however, I would have to step far beyond the limits which I have set for this project. My sole purpose has been to explicate the enigma of demythologizing by means of an historical analysis of its diverse origins. While this limited task will not resolve the pressing problems of our present religious situation, it may enable present theologians, still indebted to Bultmann's creative legacy, to fulfill their own task with greater clarity.

BIBLIOGRAPHY

I. PUBLICATIONS OF RUDOLF BULTMANN

A complete bibliography of Bultmann's writings from 1908-1953 appears in *Theologische Rundschau*, XXII (1954), 3-20. This same bibliography, extended from 1953 through 1965 by Professor Bultmann, is also available in *The Theology of Rudolf Bultmann*, Charles Kegley, ed. (New York: Harper & Row, 1966), 289-310. The following titles have been cited because of their relevance to the subject matter of myth and/or their discussion in the book. All titles are listed in chronological order; however, republications and translations are printed in brackets below the original.

Volumes of Bultmann's collected essays are abbreviated as follows:

GV = *Glauben und Verstehen.* 4 Vols. Tübingen: J. C. B. Mohr, 1933-1965.

Essays = *Essays: Philosophical and Theological* (trans. J. C. Grieg). London: SCM Press, 1955.

EF = *Existence and Faith* (trans. Schubert Ogden). New York: Meridian Books, 1960.

FaU = *Faith and Understanding* (trans. Louise Pettibone Smith). New York: Harper & Row, 1969.

Other abbreviations follow the list of abbreviations, p. iv, or *RGG*², I, x-xi.

"Die Schriften des Neuen Testaments und der Hellenismus," *ChrW*, XXV (1911), 589-593.

"Biblische Theologie," *ThR*, XIX (1916), 113-126.

"Die Bedeutung der Eschatologie für die Religion des Neuen Testaments," *ZThK*, XXVII (1917), 76-87.

"Vom geheimnisvollen und offenbaren Gott," *ChrW*, XXXI (1917), 572-579.
["Concerning the Hidden and Revealed God," *EF*, 23-34.]

Review of M. Dibelius, *Die Formgeschichte des Evangeliums*, *ThLZ*, XLIV (1919), 173 f.

"Religion und Kultur," *ChrW*, XXXIV (1920), 417-421; 435-439; 450-453.
[*Anfänge der dialektischen Theologie*, Jürgen Moltmann, ed. München: Chr. Kaiser Verlag, 1963, II, 11-29.]
["Religion and Culture," *The Beginnings of Dialectic Theology*, James Robinson, ed. Richmond: John Knox Press, 1968, 205-220.]

"Ethische und mystische Religion im Urchristentum," *ChrW*, XXXIV (1920), 725-731: 738-743.
Anfänge der dialektischen Theologie, II, 29-47.
"Ethical and Mystical Religion in Primitive Christianity," *The Beginnings of Dialectic Theology*, 221-235.

Die Geschichte der synoptischen Tradition. Göttingen: Vandenhoeck & Ruprecht, 1921.
[*The History of the Synoptic Tradition* (trans. John Marsh). New York: Harper & Row, 1963.]

"Karl Barths Römerbrief in zweiter Auflage," *ChrW*, XXXVI (1922), 320-323; 330-334; 358-361; 369-373.

"Der religionsgeschichtliche Hintergrund des Prologs zum Johannes-Evangelium," *Eucharisterion; Festschrift für H. Gunkel.* Göttingen: Vandenhoeck & Ruprecht, 1923.

"Die Bedeutung der neuerschlossenen mandäischen und manichäischen Quellen für das Verständnis des Johannesevangeliums," *ZNW*, XXIV (1925), 100-146.

"Das Problem einer theologischen Exegese des Neuen Testaments," *ZZ*, III (1925), 334-357.
    [*Anfänge der dialektischen Theologie*, II, 47-72.]
    ["The Problem of a Theological Exegesis of the New Testament," *The Beginnings of Dialectic Theology*, 236-256.]

"Welchen Sinn hat es, von Gott zu reden?" *ThBl*, IV (1925), 129-135.
    [*GV*, I, 26-37.]
    ["What Sense is there to speak of God?" (trans. F. H. Littell), *Christian Scholar*, XLIII (1960), 213-222.]
    ["What Does it Mean to Speak of God?" *FaU*, 53-65.]

Jesus. Berlin: Deutsche Bibliothek, 1926.
    [*Jesus and the Word* (trans. Louise Pettibone Smith and Erminie Huntress Lantero). New York: Charles Scribner's Sons, 1934.]

"Geschichtliche und übergeschichtliche Religion im Christentum," *ZZ*, IV (1926), 385-403.
    [*GV*, I, 65-84.]
    ["Historical and Supra-historical Religion in Christianity," *FaU*, 66-95.]

"Wilhelm Heitmüller," *ChrW*, XL (1926), 209-213.

"Karl Barth: 'Die Auferstehung der Toten'," *ThBl*, V (1926), 1-14.
    [*GV*, I, 38-64.]
    ["Karl Barth, *The Resurrection of the Dead*," *FaU*, 66-94.]

"Urchristliche Religion (1915-1925)," *AR*, XXIV (1926), 83-164.

Review of W. Bauer, *Das Johannesevangelium* (2nd ed.), *ThLZ*, LI (1926), 246 f.

"Das Johannesevangelium in der neuesten Forschung," *ChrW*, XLI (1927), 502-511.

"Zur Frage der Christologie," *ZZ*, V (1927), 41-69.
    [*GV*, I, 85-113.]
    ["On the Question of Christology," *FaU*, 116-144.]

"Die Eschatologie des Johannesevangeliums," *ZZ*, VI (1928), 4-22.
    [*GV*, I, 134-152.]
    ["The Eschatology of the Gospel of John," *FaU*, 165-183.]

Der Begriff der Offenbarung im Neuen Testament. Tübingen: J. C B. Mohr, 1929.
    [*GV*, III, 1-34.]
    ["The Concept of Revelation in the New Testament," *EF*, 58-91.]

"Zur Geschichte der Paulus-Forschung," *ThR* (1929), I, 26-59.

"Die Geschichtlichkeit des Daseins und der Glaube," *ZThK*, N. F. XI (1930), 329-364.
    ["The Historicity of Man and Faith," *EF*, 92-110.]

"Mythus und Mythologie im Neuen Testament," *RGG*[2], IV (1930), 390-394.

"Paulus," *RGG*[2], IV (1930), 1019-1045.
    ["Paul," *EF*, 111-146.]

Review of H. Lietzmann, *Ein Beitrag zur Mandäerfrage*, *ThLZ*, LVI (1931), 577-580.

"Urchristentum und Religionsgeschichte," *ThR*, IV (1932), 1-21.

Review of R. Reitzenstein, *Die Hellenistischen Mysterienreligionen* . . ., (3rd ed.) and *Die Vorgeschichte der christliche Taufe*, *HZ*, CVL (1932), 372-376.

"Ginosko," *ThWB*, I (1933), 688-719.

[*Gnosis* (trans. J. R. Coates). New York: Harper, 1958.]
"Zur Frage des Wunders" (1933), *GV*, I, 214-228.
  ["The Question of Wonder," *FaU*, 247-262,]
"Die Christologie des Neuen Testaments" (1933), *GV*, I, 245-267.
  ["The Christology of the New Testament," *FaU*, 313-331]
"Das Problem der 'Natürlichen Theologie', " (1933), *GV*, I, 294-312.
  ["The Problem of 'Natural Theology', " *FaU*, 313-331.]
"Vorwort," *Gnosis und spätantiker Geist* by Hans Jonas. Göttingen: Vanden-
  hoeck & Ruprecht, 1934.
"Neueste Paulusforschung," *ThR*, VI (1934), 229-246.
Review of E. Stauffer, *Grundbegriffe einer Morphologie des neutestament-
  liche Denkens, ThLZ*, LIX (1934), 211-215.
Review of H. Lietzmann, *Geschichte der alten Kirche*, I, *ZKG*, LIII (1934),
  624-630.
"Neueste Paulusforschung," *ThR*, VIII (1936), 1-22.
"Reich Gottes und Menschensohn," *ThR*, IX (1937), 1-35.
Review of H. Lietzmann, *Geschichte der alten Kirche*, II, *ZKG*, LVIII (1939),
  260-266.
Review of E. Hirsch, *Die Auferstehungsgeschichten und der christliche Glaube,
  ThLZ*, LXV (1940), 224-246.
Das Evangelium des Johannes. Göttingen: Vandenhoeck & Ruprecht, 1941.
Offenbarung und Heilsgeschehen. München: Lempp, 1941.
  ["Neues Testament und Mythologie," *KuM*, I, 15-48.]
  ["New Testament and Mythology," *KaM*, I, 1-44.]
  ["Die Frage der natürlichen Offenbarung," *GV*, II, 79-104.]
  ["The Question of Natural Revelation," *Essays*, 90-118.]
Review of W. Nestle, *Vom Mythos zum Logos, ThLZ*, LXVII (1942), 146-148.
"Antwort an H. Thielicke," *Deutsches Pfarrerblatt*, XLVII (1942), 1-5.
  [*KuM*, I (3rd ed. only), 221-226.]
"Zum Thema: Christentum und Antike," *ThR* XVI (1944), 1-20.
Theologie des Neuen Testaments, I. Tübingen: J. C. B Mohr, 1948.
  [*Theology of the New Testament*, I (trans. Kendrick Grobel). New York:
  Charles Scribner's Sons, 1951.]
"Zu Schniewinds Thesen," *KuM*, I (1948), 122-138.
  ["A Reply to the Theses of J. Schniewind," *KaM*, I, 102-123.]
"Heilsgeschichte und Geschichte," *ThLZ*, LXXIII (1948), 659-666.
  ["History of Salvation and History," *EF*, 226-240.]
Das Urchristentum im Rahmen der antiken Religionen. Zürich: Artemis-Verlag,
  1949.
  [*Primitive Christianity in its Contemporary Setting* (trans. R. H. Fuller).
  New York: Meridian Books, 1957.]
"Das Problem der Hermeneutik," *ZThK*, XLVII (1950), 47-69.
  [*GV*, II, 211-235.]
  ["The Problem of Hermeneutics," *Essays*, 234-261.]
"Ursprung und Sinn der Typologie als hermeneutischer Methode," *ThLZ*,
  LXXV (1950), 205-212.
"Geleitwort," *Das Wesen des Christentums*, A. Harnack. Stuttgart: Ehern-
  fried Klotz Verlag, 1950.
Theologie des Neuen Testaments, II, Tübingen: J. C. B. Mohr, 1951.
  [*Theology of the New Testament*, II (trans. Kendrick Grobel). New York:
  Charles Scribner's Sons, 1955.]
"Das christologische Bekenntnis des Ökumenischen Rates," *Schweizerische
  Theol. Umschau*, XXI (1951), 25-36.

["The Christological Confession of the World Council of Churches,"
   Essays, pp. 273-304.]
"Zum Problem der Entmythologisierung" (1952), *KuM*, II, 177-208.
   ["Bultmann Replies to his Critics" (omitting first section of original),
   KaM, I, 191-211.]
   [*GV*, IV, 128-137.]
"Die christliche Hoffnung und das Problem der Entmythologisierung,"
   Unterwegs, VII (1953), 257-264.
   [*GV*, III, 81-90.]
   [*Die christliche Hoffnung und das Problem der Entmythologisierung*.
   Stuttgart: Evangelisches Verlagswerk, 1954.]
"Antwort an Karl Jaspers," *Schweizerische Theologische Rundschau*, III-IV
   (1953), 74-106.
   [*KuM*, III, 49-60.]
   [*Myth and Christianity: An Inquiry into the Possibility of Religion
   without Myth* by Karl Jaspers and R. Bultmann. New York: The
   Noonday Press, 1958.]
   [*KaM*, II, 181-194.]
Review of C. H. Dodd, *The Interpretation of the Fourth Gospel*, New Testament
   Studies, I (1954-1955), 77-91.
   ["Rudolf Bultmann's Review of C. H. Dodd's *The Interpretation of the
   Fourth Gospel*," (trans. W. G. Robinson). *Harvard Divinity Bulletin*,
   XXVII (1963), 9-22.]
"Ist voraussetzungslose Exegese möglich?" *Theologische Zeitschrift*, XIII
   (1957), 409-417.
   [*GV*, III, 142-150.]
"Allgemeine Wahrheiten und christliche Verkündigung," *ZThK*, LIV
   (1957), 244-254.
   [*GV*, III, 166-177.]
History and Eschatology. Edinburgh: The University Press, 1957.
"Das Befremdliche des christlichen Glaubens," *ZThK*, LV (1958), 185-200.
   [*GV*, III, 197-212.]
Jesus Christ and Mythology. New York: Charles Scribner's Sons, 1958.
"Erziehung und christlicher Glaube," *Martin Heidegger zum siebzigsten
   Geburtstag*. Tübingen: H. Laupp, 1959.
   [*GV*, IV, 52-55.]
"Zum Problem der Entmythologisierung," *Il problema della demitizzazione*,
   (ed. Enrico Castelli). Padova: A. Milani 1961.
   [*KuM*, VI-l, 20-27.]
   ["On the Problem of Demythologizing," trans. S. Ogden, *JR*, XLII
   (1962), 96-102.]
   [*GV*, IV, 128-137.]
Das Verhältnis der urchristlichen Christusbotschaft zum historischen Jesus.
   Heidelberg: Carl Winter, Universitätsverlag, 1962.
   ["The Primitive Christian Kerygma and the Historical Jesus," trans.
   Carl E. Braaten and Roy A. Harrisville, *The Historical Jesus and the
   Kerygmatic Christ*. New York: Abingdon Press, 1964.]
"Anhang: Aus einem Briefwechsel zwischen Rudolf Bultmann und dem
   Verfasser anlässlich des Aufsatzes über die Unsterblichkeit," *Zwischen
   Nichts und Ewigkeit*, Hans Jonas. Göttingen: Vandenhoeck & Ru-
   precht, 1963.
"Der Gottesgedanke und der moderne Mensch," *ZThK*, LX (1963), 335-348.
   ["The Idea of God and Modern Man," *Translating Theology into the*

Modern Age (ed. Robert W. Funk). New York: Harper & Row, 1965.]
[*GV*, IV, 113-127.]

II. GENERAL BOOKS, ESSAYS, AND ARTICLES

A comprehensive bibliography of publications relevant to Bultmann's theology appears in *Theologische Rundschau,* XXIX (1963-1964), 33-46. The selected bibliography which follows reflects the particular areas of concern developed in this book.

Backhaus, Gunther. *Kerygma und Mythos bei David Strauss und Rudolf Bultmann.* Hamburg: Herbert Reich, 1956.

Barrett, C. K. "Myth and the New Testament; how far does myth enter into the New Testament," *ExposT,* LXVIII (1957), 345-348; 359-362.

——————. "Myth and the New Testament; the Greek Word Myth," *ExposT,* LXVIII (1957), 345-348.

Barth, Karl. "Rudolf Bultmann: An Attempt to Understand Him," *KaM,* II, 83-132.

Barthel, Pierre. *Interprétation du langage mythique et théologie biblique.* Leiden: E. J. Brill, 1963.

Bartsch, H. W. (ed.). *Kerygma und Mythos.* 6 Vols. Hamburg: Herbert Reich, 1948-1964.

Bornkamm, Günther. "Die Theologie Rudolf Bultmanns in der neueren Diskussion," *ThR,* XXIX (1963-1964), 33-141.

Bornkamm, Günther, Rudolf Bultmann and Friedrich Schumann. *Die christliche Hoffnung und das Problem der Entmythologisierung.* Stuttgart: Evangelisches Verlagswerk, 1954.

Cassirer, Ernst. *The Philosophy of Symbolic Forms.* Vol. II: *Mythical Thought* (trans. Ralph Manheim). New Haven, Conn.: Yale University Press, 1955.

——————. *Language and Myth* (trans. S. Langer). New York: Harper and Bros., 1946.

——————. *The Myth of the State.* New Haven, Conn.: Yale University Press, 1946.

Castelli, Enrico (ed.). *Il problema della demitizzazione.* Padova: Cedam-Casa Editrice Dott. Antonio Milani, 1961.

——————. *Demitizzazione e immagine.* Padova: Cedam-Casa Editrice Dott. Antonio Milani, 1962.

——————. *Herméneutique et tradition.* Roma: Istituto di Studi Filosofici, 1963.

Childs, Brevard S. *Myth and Reality in the Old Testament.* Naperville, Ill.: Alec R. Alecson Inc., 1960.

Cohen, Hermann. *Logik der reinen Erkenntniss.* Berlin: Bruno Cassirer, 1902.

Colpe, Carsten. *Die religionsgeschichtliche Schule: Darstellung und Kritik ihres Bildes vom gnostischen Erlösermythus.* Göttingen: Vandenhoeck & Ruprecht, 1961.

Davis, G. W. *Existentialism and Theology.* New York: Philosophical Library, 1957.

Deegan, Daniel. "Wilhelm Herrmann; a reassessment," *Scottish Journal of Theology,* 19 (1966), 188-203.

Eichorn, Johann Gottfried. *Introduction to the Study of the Old Testament* (trans. G. T. Gallop). London: Spottiswoode and Co., 1888.

Farrer, Austin. "An English Appreciation," *KaM,* I, 212-223.

Fontenelle, Bernard. *De l'origine des fables* Critical edition and introduction by J. R. Carré. Paris: Libraire Felix Alcan, 1932.

Franz, Helmut. "Das Denken Heideggers und die Theologie," *ZThK*, LVIII (1961), 81-118.

Frye, Richard Nelson. "Reitzenstein and Qumran Revisited by an Iranian," *HTR*, LV (1962), 262-268.

Fuller, R. H. (ed. and trans.). *Kerygma and Myth*. 2 Vols. London: S.P.C.K., 1957-1962.

Gloege, Gerhard *Mythologie und Luthertum*. Berlin: Lutherisches Verlagshaus, 1953.

Gogarten, F. *Demythologizing and History*. London: SCM Press Ltd., 1955.

Hartlich, Christian und Walter Sachs. *Der Ursprung des Mythosbegriffes in der modernen Bibelwissenschaft*. Tübingen: J. C. B Mohr, 1952.

Heidegger, Martin. Review of Ernst Cassirer's *Philosophie der symbolischen Formen, DLZ*, V (1928), 1000-1012.

——————. *Sein und Zeit*. 9th ed. Tübingen: Max Niemeyer Verlag, 1960.

——————. *Being and Time* (trans. John Macquarrie and Edward Robinson). London: SCM Press Ltd., 1962.

Henderson, Ian *Myth in the New Testament*. Chicago: Henry Regnery Company, 1952.

Hepburn, Ronald W. "Demythologizing and the Problem of Validity," *New Essays in Philosophical Theology* (ed. Antony Flew and Alisdair Mac-Intyre). London: SCM Press, 1955.

Herrmann, Wilhelm. *Die Religion im Verhältnis zum Welterkennen und zur Sittlichkeit*. Halle: Max Niemeyer, 1879.

——————. *Systematic Theology* (trans. N. Mickelm and K. Saunders). London: George Allen and Unwin, Ltd., 1927.

Jaspers, Karl and Rudolf Bultmann. *Myth and Christianity: An Inquiry into the Possibility of Religion without Myth*. New York: The Noonday Press, 1958.

Jonas, Hans. *Gnosis und spätantiker Geist*. 2 Vols. Göttingen: Vandenhoeck & Ruprecht, 1934-1954.

——————. *Der Begriff der Gnosis*. Göttingen: Hubert & Co., 1930.

——————. *Augustin und das paulinische Freiheitsproblem; ein philosophrischer Beitrag zur Genesis der christlich-abendländischen Freiheitsidee*. Göttingen: Vandenhoeck & Ruprecht, 1930.

——————. "Heidegger and Theology," *The Review of Metaphysics*, XLIII (1964).

——————. *Zwischen Nichts und Ewigkeit: drei Aufsätze zur Lehre vom Menschen*. Göttingen: Vandenhoeck & Ruprecht, 1963.

——————. *The Gnostic Religion*. 2nd ed. Boston: Beacon Press, 1963.

——————. "Myth and Mysticism; A Study of Objectification and Interiorization in Religious Thought," *Journal of Religion* 49 (1969), 315-329.

Jones, G. V. *Christology and Myth in the New Testament*. London: Allen & Unwin, 1956.

Jung, Carl Gustaf. *Psyche and Symbol* (ed. Violet de Lazlo). Garden City, New York: Doubleday and Co., 1958.

Jung, Carl Gustaf and C. Kerényi. *Essays on a Science of Mythology*. New York: Pantheon Books, 1949.

Kaufmann, Fritz. "Cassirer, Neo-Kantianism, and Phenomenology," *The Philosophy of Ernst Cassirer* (ed. Paul Schillp). Evanston, Ill.: The Library of Living Philosophers, Inc., 1949.

Knevels, Wilhelm. *Die Wirklichkeit Gottes: ein Weg zur Überwindung der Orthodoxie und des Existentialismus*. Stuttgart: Calwer Verlag, 1964.

Macquarrie, John. *An Existentialist Theology: a Comparison of Heidegger and Bultmann*. New York: Macmillan, 1955.

——————. *The Scope of Demythologizing*. London: SCM Press Ltd. 1960.
Malevez, L. *The Christian Message and Myth: The Theology of Rudolf Bultmann*. London: SCM Press, 1958.
Malet, André. *Mythos et Logos: la pensée de Rudolf Bultmann*. Genève: Libraire Protestante, 1962.
Malinowski, Bronislaw. *Magic, Science, and Religion*. Garden City, New York: Doubleday and Co., 1954.
Manuel, Frank E. *The Eighteenth Century Confronts the Gods*. Cambridge, Mass.: Harvard University Press, 1959.
Marlé, René. *Bultmann et l'interprétation du Nouveau Testament*. Aubier: Editions Montaigne, 1956.
Miegge, Giovanni. *Gospel and Myth in the Thought of Rudolf Bultmann*. Richmond, Va.: John Knox Press, 1960.
Natorp, Paul. *Religion innerhalb der Grenzen der Humanität*. Leipzig: J. C. B. Mohr, 1894.
——————. *Allgemeine Psychologie nach kritischer Methode*. Tübingen: J.C.B. Mohr, 1912.
——————. *Philosophische Systematik*. Hamburg: Felix Meiner, 1958.
——————. "Paul Natorp," *Philosophie der Gegenwart in Selbstdarstellungen* (ed. Raymond Schmidt). Leipzig: Felix Meiner, 1921.
Ogden, Schubert M. *Christ Without Myth. A Study Based on the Theology of Rudolf Bultmann*. New York: Harper and Brothers, 1961.
O'Neill, J. C. "Bultmann and Hegel," *Journal of Theological Studies*, 21 (1970), 388-400.
——————. "Theology and Objectivity," *JR*, XLV (1965), 175-195.
Ott, Heinrich. *Denken und Sein: der Weg Martin Heideggers und der Weg der Theologie*. Zurich: EVZ Verlag, 1959.
——————. *Geschichte und Heilsgeschichte in der Theologie Rudolf Bultmanns*. Tübingen: J. C. B. Mohr, 1955.
Owen, H. P. *Revelation and Existence; a Study in the Theology of Rudolf Bultmann*. Cardiff: University of Wales Press, 1957.
Pepin, Jean. *Mythe et allégorie*. Paris: Editions Montaigne, 1958.
Prenter, Regin. "Myth and Gospel," *Kerygma and History* (ed. and trans. Carl Braaten and Roy H. Harrisville). New York: Abingdon Press, 1962.
Ricœur, Paul. "The Hermeneutics of Symbols and Philosophical Reflection," *IPQ*, II (1962), 191-218.
——————. *Philosophie de la volonté*. 3 Vols. *Le volontaire et l'involontaire*, Vol. I. *Finitude et culpabilité*, Vol. II: Part 1: L'homme faillible; Part 2: La symbolique du mal. Aubier: Editions Montaigne, n.d. - 1960.
Robinson, James M. "The German Discussion of the Later Heidegger," *The Later Heidegger and Theology* (ed. James M. Robinson and John B. Cobb, Jr.). New York: Harper & Row, 1963.
——————. "Hermeneutic since Barth," *The New Hermeneutic* (ed. James M. Robinson and John B. Cobb, Jr.). New York: Harper & Row, 1964.
——————. "Pre-history of Demythologization," *Interpretation*, 20 (1966), 65-77,.
Schumann, Friedrich K. "Can the Event of Jesus Christ be Demythologized?" *KaM*, I.
Strauss, David Friedrich. *The Life of Jesus Critically Examined* (trans. Marion Evans). New York: Calvin Blanchard, 1955.
Werkmeister, William H. "Cassirer's Advance beyond Neo-Kantianism," *The Philosophy of Ernst Cassirer* (ed. Paul Schillp). Evanston, Ill.: The Library of Living Philosophers, Inc., 1949.
Vornhausen, Karl. "Der Religionsphilosophie Paul Natorps," *ZThK*, VI (1925), 403-417.

NAME INDEX

SUBJECT INDEX

Kerygma 15-18, 101, 252 *see also*:
Bible, New Testament, Word of
God
Kyrios cult 89, 92, 99-102, 105

Law,
  as principle of reason (*Gesetz,
Gesetzlichkeit*) 48-68, 71, 74,
79, 145, 165-167, 179, 240, 253
  as implicit in work 157-160, 194-
197
  of nature in science 135, 140-141,
151
  theological function 85, 198-201
  see also: Reason, Science, Work
Liberal theology 13, 58, 63, 104-
107, 109, 112
Logik der reinen Erkenntniss (Cohen)
42n, 66, 261
Logos 48, 83, 97-98, 117, 152-153
  see also: Primal Man, Reason,
Word of God
Lutheran Theology 4, 25, 31, 33-36,
84-86, 172, 194-202 *see also*:
Dualism, Justification

Mandeanism 95-97, 115
Manicheanism 95-97
Miracle 8, 11, 99-101, 135, 138-139,
143, 146, 195-196
Modernity 53-54, 151, 158-159, 166,
199
Myth
  definition of 7-9, 10n, 11, 11n,
14, 89, 127, 172-173, 232
  intention of 30, 94, 106-107,
146-147, 154, 206-207, 239-240,
245
  interpretation of 13, 104, 108,
118-119, 139n, 153, 156, 203-
206, 209
  origins of 95-97, 132n, 146n
  universality of 133-139, 139n,
140
*Myth and Christianity: An Inquiry
into the Possibility of Religion
without Myth* (Jaspers and Bultmann) 12n, 260
Myth in the New Testament (Henderson) 10n, 262

Neo-Kantianism (Baden) 32, 38

Neo-Kantianism (Marburg) 31-34,
38-42, 51
  epistemology 34-36, 39n, 42-50,
78, 83, 164-168, 178, 213, 237-
238
  in Bultmann 50-65, 68-69, 72-86,
164-168
  ontology 46-50, 79-83, 190-191
  philosophy of religion 40, 65-78
  see also: Object
New Testament 25, 27n, 91, 93,
241, 241n, 248
  Bultmann studies 6, 36, 62, 96
  Gospel of John 96, 98-99, 111-
112, 203
  Prologue of John 96-97
  Gospel of Mark 99-101
  Paul 91-92, 95, 100, 102, 111-112,
182-183, 196-197, 204-205
  Q 99-100
  Synoptic Gospels 99-101, 105

Object (*Objekt*) 42-50, 52, 57
  objectification (*Objektivierung*)
39n, 47, 52-58, 68-69, 73-74, 76,
82-85, 189-190, 207n, 212-216,
239, 253
  objectify (*objektivieren*) 47, 52,
71, 73-74, 213
  objectifying (*objektivierend*) 15,
22, 30-31, 34, 47-48, 50, 52, 54n,
58, 85, 163, 166-167, 173-203, 206-
207, 212-215, 237-240, 251-255
  'objectivation' (*objektivation*)
207-223, 228-229, 254
  objective (*objektiv*) 52, 189-190,
213
  see also: *der Gegenstand*, Neo-
Kantianism
Old Testament 26, 27n, 135-140,
241, 241n *see also*: Judaism

Primal Man (myth of) 89-103
  Heavenly Ambassador 30, 89,
109, 114-115, 125

Reason (*Vernunft*) 40, 42, 45, 48-
49, 51-56, 58-62, 65, 68, 71-73,
76-86, 137-138, 150, 165-167, 178,
180, 185, 191, 213, 215, 238, 244
  primitive 12-13, 126, 131-141,
146n, 209-211, 239 *see also*:
Dualism, Law, Science